高等职业教育示范专业系列教材
浙江省重点教材建设项目

外贸单证实务

主　编　左显兰
副主编　符建利　刘文霞
参　编　吴琼芳　庄宇琪
　　　　訾　颖

机械工业出版社

本书包括十个项目，分别是落实信用证、租船订舱单据的制作与审核、投保单据的制作与审核、报检单据的制作与审核、报关单据的制作与审核、装运单据的制作与审核、结汇单据的制作与审核、收汇核销与退税单据的制作与审核、信用证支付方式下出口单证的综合训练，T/T 结汇单据的制作与审核。

本书各项目的设计以外贸实际操作流程为主线，每一项目具体任务设计都依据“列单、理单、制单、审单”这一真实的工作过程进行，注重工作过程领域向学习过程领域的转化，突出“教学做一体化”。本书任务明确，过程清晰，方便教师导学，也方便学生自学。

本书包含三笔完整的信用证支付方式下的业务单据和一笔完整的 T/T 结汇单据，通过教师的分步引导示范，学生独立分步骤作训练和综合操作训练，能较好地掌握单据的操作流程和填写规范，提高实践操作能力。

本书可作为大中专院校国际贸易、国际经济、国际商务、报关与国际货运等专业的教材，也可作为外贸行业单证岗位培训教材，以及有志从事外贸单证工作的人士自学之用。

图书在版编目（CIP）数据

外贸单证实务/左显兰主编. —北京：机械工业出版社，2011.8（2025.1 重印）
高等职业教育示范专业系列教材
ISBN 978-7-111-34657-9

Ⅰ. ①外…　Ⅱ. ①左…　Ⅲ. ①进出口贸易—原始凭证—高等职业教育—教材　Ⅳ. ①F740.44

中国版本图书馆 CIP 数据核字（2011）第 168071 号

机械工业出版社（北京市百万庄大街 22 号　邮政编码 100037）
策划编辑：孔文梅　　责任编辑：张　亮
封面设计：马精明　　责任印制：邓　博
北京盛通数码印刷有限公司印刷
2025 年 1 月第 1 版第 8 次印刷
184mm×260mm · 13 印张 · 320 千字
标准书号：ISBN 978-7-111-34657-9
定价：35.00 元

电话服务
客服电话：010-88361066
010-88379833
010-68326294

网络服务
机　工　官　网：www.cmpbook.com
机　工　官　博：weibo.com/cmp1952
金　　书　　网：www.golden-book.com
机工教育服务网：www.cmpedu.com

前　言

教育部教高[2006]16 号文件：关于全面提高高等职业教育教学质量的若干意见，明确提出加大课程建设与改革的力度，改革教学方法和手段，融“教、学、做”为一体，强化学生能力的培养；大力推行工学结合、项目导向、任务驱动等有利于增强学生能力的教学模式；加强教材建设，与行业企业共同开发紧密结合生产实际的实训教材，并确保优质教材进课堂等精神。根据这一文件精神，我们编写了本书。

“外贸单证实务”是高职高专国际贸易、国际商务、国际物流、报关与国际货运等专业的主干课程之一。能根据业务流程需要，制作并提交相关单据，办理相关业务，是外贸单证员、报关员、报检员、货代员、外销员等相关工作的基础和起点，是他们应具备的核心能力。编者结合当前高职院校“基于工作过程的，项目导向、任务驱动、工学结合”的教学改革理念，以及编者在企业实践的经验和在教学第一线长期工作的心得体会，对本书进行了全新设计，并邀请银行结算专家、企业资深单证员、业务员、同行教授等对本书的框架、编写思路进行了充分论证，最终形成本书。

本书与传统教材不同的地方体现在以下几个方面：

1．教材内容的选择与组织来自工作岗位真实的需要和企业真实的案例

通过到企业调研，编者了解到企业最常用的支付方式是信用证和电汇，教材的编写就以这两种支付方式下的单据操作流程来设计项目。鉴于不同支付方式下有些单据的填制方式是相同的，为避免重复，本书主要以信用证支付方式下一笔完整的业务流程为主线，设计具体操作项目。电汇支付方式下，只设计了 T/T 结汇单据的制作与审核一个训练项目。

教材中使用的合同、信用证等单证都是银行国际结算部和外贸公司提供的。书中用到的信用证是银行当前普遍使用的 SWIFT 格式。这些来自行业界新颖的、真实的素材有助于缩短学生与企业的“磨合期”。

2．项目设计以外贸实际操作流程为主线，以与不同部门交往，办理不同业务为依据进行

本书共设计了十个项目，前九个项目以信用证支付方式下的外贸业务流程为主线设计，具体包括落实信用证、租船订舱单据的制作与审核、投保单据的制作与审核、报检单据的制作与审核、报关单据的制作与审核、装运单据的制作与审核、结汇单据的制作与审核、出口收汇核销与退税单据的制作与审核、信用证方式下出口单证的综合训练，第十个项目是 T/T 结汇单据的制作与审核。

3．每一项目具体任务设计都依据“列单、理单、制单、审单”这一真实的工作过程进行，克服“只见树木不见森林”的现象

每一项目具体的任务设计都采用先整体后分步：首先弄清办事的流程，列单，列出办理这项业务所需单据清单；其次，理单，理出这项任务所需而完成前面的工作任务已制作过的单据；再次，制单，缮制完成这项工作任务所需而前面工作任务中又不曾涉及过的单据；最后，审单，综合审核办理该项业务所需单据是否齐全，内容是否正确、完整等。

每一项目这样设计任务，可以克服学生只会按要求填制一份份孤零零的单据，不知道办理具体的工作任务需要提交哪些全套单据，甚至不知道有些单据该向什么部门申领，这种“只见树木，不见森林”，不会独立办事的现象。

4．注重工作过程领域向学习过程领域的转化，突出“教学做一体化”

该书前九个项目是按信用证支付方式下操作流程设计的，这九个项目以三笔完整的外贸业务贯穿始终。其中第一笔业务的单据操作，要求学生在教师的引导示范下分项完成；第二笔业务的单据操作，作为巩固训练项目，要求学生独立分项完成，即学完一个项目，就要及时巩固训练，独立完成一个项目；第三笔业务的单据操作作为综合训练项目，要求学生在分项训练的基础上，独立完成一笔完整的业务单据。

完成每一任务的过程、步骤十分清楚。先给出一个具体的任务导入，然后给出完成这一任务的步骤，这样不仅让学生知道怎么学，教师知道怎样教，还让师生在教和学的过程中掌握办事的程序和方法，完成了工作过程领域的任务向学习过程领域任务的转化。

本书专门针对外贸单证学习者和教师教学设计，可作为大中专院校国际贸易、国际经济、国际商务、报关与国际货运等专业的教材，也可作为外贸行业单证岗位培训教材，以及有志从事外贸单证工作的人士自学之用。

本书由宁波城市职业技术学院左显兰副教授主编，符建利老师和刘文霞副教授任副主编，吴琼芳、庄宇琪、訾颖老师参与了本书的编写。具体编写分工如下：项目一至项目七由左显兰编写；项目八由刘文霞编写；项目九由吴琼芳、庄宇琪、訾颖编写，项目十由符建利编写。

本书为浙江省重点教材建设项目，在编写的过程中得到了宁波康大进出口公司资深业务员何玲秀女士、宁波舒普机电科技公司外贸部经理毛科杰先生、宁波银行国际结算部邬凑岭女士的大力支持，他们提供了大量真实的素材和案例，在此一并表示衷心感谢。

本书在编写的过程中，参考了国内许多重要的外贸单证实务文献，在此向相关专家、同仁表示衷心的感谢。由于编者时间和水平有限，本书难免有不当之处，真诚欢迎各界人士及时批评指正。

为方便教学，本书配备电子课件等教学资源。凡选用本书作为教材的教师均可索取，请发送邮件至 cmpgaozhi@sina.com，咨询电话：010-88379375。

编　者

目　　录

项目一

落实信用证

知识目标

了解信用证支付下的一般结算程序及信用证支付条件下的国际贸易流程及单据流转程序；掌握开证申请书的填写规范及申请开证应注意的问题；掌握信用证的审核要点；了解信用证的主要内容及 SWIFT 的开证格式，信用证的作用和类型。

能力目标

能画出信用证单证操作流程图；能根据外销合同填写开证申请书；能根据外销合同审核信用证；能准确分析信用证，填写信用证分析表。

任务分析

为达到上述知识和能力目标需完成下列任务：

- 任务一：画出信用证条件下的单证操作流程图
- 任务二：填写开证申请书
- 任务三：审核信用证
- 任务四：填写信用证修改申请书
- 任务五：填写信用证分析单

任务一　画出信用证支付条件下的单证操作流程图

任务导入

作为一名能熟练进行信用证操作的单证员，首先必须熟练掌握信用证支付条件下的单证流程，以便做好制单工作的各种前期准备工作。

完成该任务的步骤如下

第一步：复习跟单信用证操作流程图

任务要求：在复习下列流程图（图 1-1）后，能独立画出跟单信用证操作流程图。

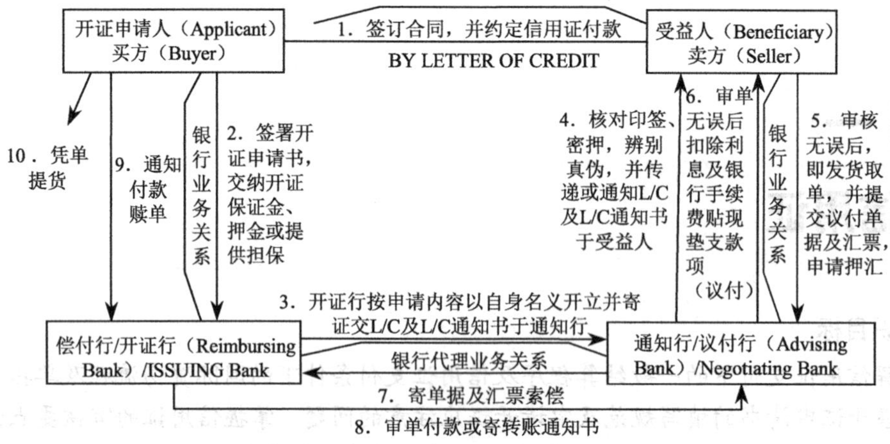

图 1-1

第二步：复习信用证支付条件下的国际贸易流程图

任务要求：在复习下列流程图（图 1-2）后，能独立画出信用证支付条件下的国际贸易流程图

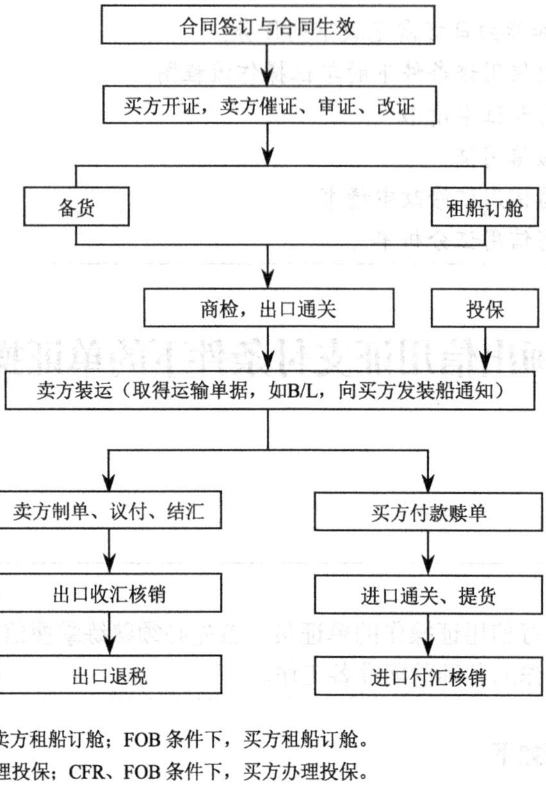

注：CIF、CFR 条件下，卖方租船订舱；FOB 条件下，买方租船订舱。
CIF 条件下，卖方办理投保；CFR、FOB 条件下，买方办理投保。

图 1-2

第三步：根据前两步的流程图，独立画出信用证支付条件下的单证操作流程图

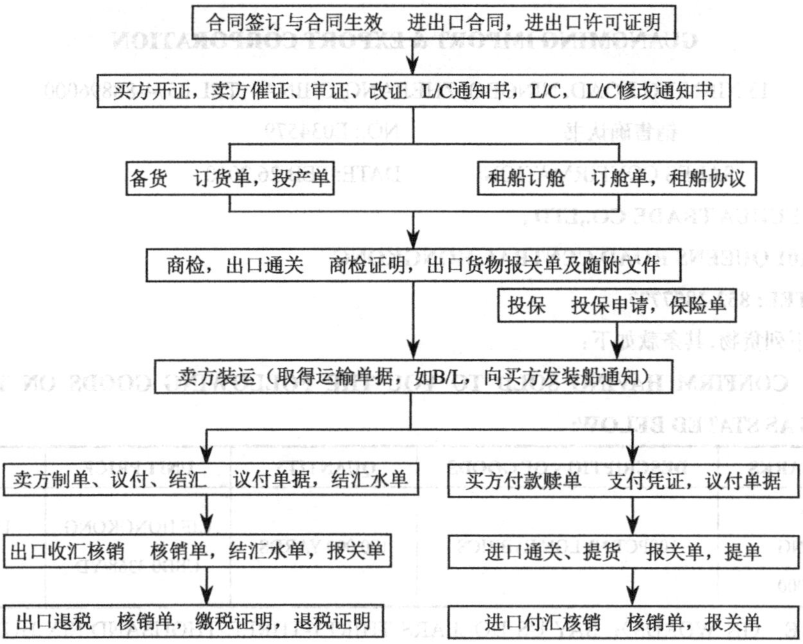

图　1-3

自我能力测评

能力形成性评价表

评价指标	分　值	实际得分
能独立完成步骤一	30 分（10 个程序，一个 3 分）	
能独立完成步骤二	30 分（13 个程序，一个 2.5 分）	
能独立完成步骤三	40 分（13 个程序，一个 3 分）	

任务二　填写开证申请书

任务导入

宁波光明进出口公司与中国香港富华贸易有限公司签订了一份出口外销合同，合同规定用即期信用证支付，小芳作为中国香港富华贸易公司的单证员，向华夏银行申请开立信用证一份。下面是两家公司的外销合同：

单证 1-1

GUANGMING IMPORT & EXPORT CORPORATION

13 XINNING ROAD, NINGBO, ZHEJIANG, CHINA TEL.0574-88896000

销售确认书 NO.: E034579

SALES CONFIRMATION DATE: FEB 26,2010

THE BUYER: FUHUA TRADE CO.,LTD.,

101 QUEENS ROAD CENTRAL,HONGKONG

TEL: 852-2857777

确认售予你方下列货物,其条款如下:

WE HEREBY CONFIRM HAVING SOLD TO YOU THE FOLLOWING GOODS ON TERMS AND CONDITIONS AS STATED BELOW:

SHIPPING MARKS	DESCRIPTION OF GOODS	QUANTITY	UNIT PRICE	AMOUNT
FUHUA HONGKONG R/NO.:1-1000	100PCT NYLON FABRICS	100,000 YARDS	CIF HONGKONG USD0.3368/YD	USD33,680.00

TOTAL VALUE （IN WORDS）：SAY US DOLLARS THIRTY-THREE THOUSAND SIX HUNDRED AND EIGHTY ONLY.

DATE OF SHIPMENT: LATEST APRIL 11, 2010

PORT OF SHIPMENT: NINGBO **PORT OF DESTINATION**: HONGKONG

PARTIAL SHIPMENT: ALLOWED **TRANSHIPMENT:** NOT ALLOWED

PACKAGE: 100 YARDS TO A ROLL **TOTAL:** 1000 ROLLS

INSURANCE: TO BE EFFECTED BY THE SELLERS FOR 110% OF INVOICE VALUE COVERING ALL RISKS AND WAR RISK AS PER CCIC. 1981.1.1.

PAYMENT: BY IRREVOCABLE AND CONFIRMED L/C AT SIGHT

MANUFACTURE AND COUNTRY OF ORIGIN: CHUNYAZI TEXTILE WORKS, CHINA

REMARKS: PLEASE SIGN AND RETURN ONE FOR OUR FILE

BUYERS: **SELLERS:**

FUHUA TRADE CO.,LTD. GUANGMING IMPORT &EXPORT CORPORATION

完成上述任务的步骤如下

第一步：分析合同条款，看懂外销合同

（1）合同的性质：SALES CONFIRMATION

（2）合同编号：E034579 合同签订的日期：**DATE**：FEB 26, 2010

（3）买卖双方地址：**THE BUYER**：FUHUA TRADE CO.,LTD.,

101 QUEENS ROAD CENTRAL, HONGKONG

TEL: 852-2857777

THE SELLER：GUANGMING IMPORT & EXPORT CORPORATION

13 XINNING ROAD, NINGBO, ZHEJIANG, CHINA

TEL：0574-88896000

（4）品名、数量、单价、总价：**DESCRIPTION OF GOODS**：100PCT NYLON FABRICS；QUANTITY：100,000YARDS；**UNIT PRICE**：USD0.3368/YD；**AMOUNT**：USD33,680.00

（5）装运期：**DATE OF SHIPMENT**：THE LATEEST APRIL 11, 2010

（6）装运港和目的港：**PORT OF SHIPMENT**：**NINGBO**；

PORT OF DESTINATION：HONGKONG

（7）包装：**PACKAGE** 100 YARDS TO A ROLL　**TOTAL**：1000 ROLLS（100 码一卷，总共 1000 卷。）

（8）是否分批装运和转运：**PARTIAL SHIPMENT**：ALLOWED

TRANSHIPMENT：NOT ALLOWED

（9）制造商与生产国：**MANUFACTURER AND COUNTRY OF ORIGIN**：CHUNYAZI TEXTILE WORKS，CHINA

（10）保险：**INSURANCE**：TO BE EFFECTED BY THE SELLERS FOR 110% OF INVOICE VALUE COVERING ALL RISKS AND WAR RISK AS PER C.C.I.C. 1981.1.1.（买方按发票金额的 110%，按 1981/1/1 中国人民保险公司保险条款，投保一切险和战争险。）

（11）付款方式：**PAYMENT**：L/C AT SIGHT（即期信用证）

（12）备注：**REMARKS**：PLEASE SIGN AND RETURN ONE FOR OUR FILE（请签署并回寄一份以便我们存档。）

（13）买卖双方签署：BUYERS:　　　　　　　　　　　　SELLERS:

第二步：导学，教师引导学生填写信用证开证申请书，并用多媒体进行演示填写过程

建议用专业机房或多媒体教室，老师引导学生根据上述外销合同，一起逐项填写信用证开证申请书各栏目，用极域电子教室广播教学或 PPT 展示全部填写过程。

单证　1-2

信用证开证申请书范本

IRREVOCABLE DOCUMENTARY CREDIT APPLICATION

TO：HUA XIA BANK CO. LTD.　　　L/C No.　　　　Date: MARCH 1，2010

<table>
<tr><td colspan="2">Applicant
FUHUA TRADE CO.,LTD.,
101 QUEENS ROAD CENTRAL,HONGKONG
TEL: 852-2857777</td><td>Beneficiary(full name, address and tel. etc.)
GUANGMING IMPORT & EXPORT CORPORATION
13 XINNING ROAD, NINGBO, ZHEJIANG, CHINA
TEL.0574-88896000</td></tr>
<tr><td>Partial shipments
(×) allowed
(　) not allowed</td><td>Transshipment
(　) allowed
(×) not allowed</td><td>issued by
(　) telex/ SWIFT
(　) express delivery　(　) air mail
(　) with brief advice by teletransmission</td></tr>
</table>

（续）

Loading on board/dispatch/ taking in charge at/from NINGBO PORT **Not later than** APRIL 11, 2010 **For transportation to** HONGKONG	**Contract No.:** E034579 **Credit Amount (both in figures and words):** USD33,680.00 SAY US DOLLARS THIRTY-THREE THOUSAND SIX HUNDRED AND EIGHTY ONLY. **Trade Term:** ( ) FOB ( ) CFR (×) CIF ( ) 0thers:
Description of goods: 100PCT NYLON FABRICS QUANTITY：100,000YARDS UNIT PRICE：USD0.3368/YD AMOUNT：USD33,680.00 Marks: FUHUA HONGKONG R/NO.:1-3298	**Date and place of expiry: APRIL 25, 2010 CHINA** Credit available with______ (×) by sight payment ( ) by acceptance ( ) by negotiation ( ) by deferred payment at against the documents detailed herein (×) and beneficiary's draft for 100% of invoice value at ××× sight draft on issuing bank

Documents required: (marked with X)

1. (×) Signed commercial invoice in 3 originals indicating L/ C No. and Contract No..

2. (×) Full set of clean on board Bills of Lading made out [×] to order/ [ ] to the order of ______and blank endorsed, marked " freight [×] prepaid/ [ ] to collect showing freight amount" notifying [×]the applicant/ [ ]____

3. ( ) Air Way bills showing "freight [ ]prepaid/ [ ] to collect indicating freight amount" and consigned to____

4. (×) Insurance Policy/Certificate for 110 % of the invoice value showing claims payable in HONGKONG in currency of the draft, blank endorsed, covering [ ] Ocean Marine Transportation / [ ] Air Transportation / [ ] Over Land Transportation, [×] All Risks, [×] War Risks as per [×] CCIC/[ ]ICC,1981/1/1.

5. (×) Packing list / Weight Memo in 2 originals indicating TOTAL NUMBER OF CARTONS, GROSS WEIGHT/ NET WEIGHT AND MEAMUREMENTS OF EXPORT CARTONS.

6. ( ) Certificate of Quantity/ Weight in 1 originals issued by [×] manufacturer / [ ] Seller / [ ] independent surveyor at the loading port, indicating the actual surveyed quantity / weight of shipped goods as well as the packing condition.

7. (×) Certificate of Quality in 2 originals issued by [×] manufacturer / [ ] public recognized surveyor / [ ]____

8. (×) Beneficiary's Certified copy of fax dispatched to the applicant within 2 days after shipment advising the contract number, name of commodity, quantity, invoice value, bill of lading no., bill of lading date, the ETA date and shipping Co.

9. ( ) Beneficiary's Certificate certifying that extra copies of the documents have been dispatched to the [ ] applicant/ [ ]____

10. (×) Certificate of Origin in 2 originals certifying that the goods are of Chinese origin.

11. ( ) Other documents, if any:________

Additional instruction: (marked with×)

1. (×) All banking charges outside the opening bank are for beneficiary's account.

2. (×) Documents must be presented within 21 days after the date of issuance of the transport documents but within the validity of this credit.

3. ( ) Third party as shipper is not acceptable, Short Form / Blank B/L is not acceptable.

4. ( ) Both quantity and amount____% more or less are allowed.

5. ( ) All documents to be forwarded in one lot by express unless otherwise stated above.

6. ( ) Other terms, if any:

Seal and / or Signature checked by ( ) L/C Margin____% checked by ( ) Credit Facility checked by ( ) Ent. ( ) Ver. ( ) App. ( ) Date:	我公司承担本申请书背面所列责任及承诺，并保证按照办理。 （申请人名称及印鉴章） RMB A/C No. USD or ( ) A/C No. 联系人：小芳 电话：852-2857777

This L/C is subject to the Uniform Customs and Practice for Documentary Credit (2007 Revision) ICC Publication No. 600.

第三步：巩固训练，引导学生自学开证申请书的填写规范和申请开立信用证的注意事项，并根据给出的外销合同独立填写一份信用证开证申请书

4．根据下列外销合同，参照上述模本，独立填写一份开证申请书

训练任务

孟加拉 SOUTH EAST EXIM LTD.公司的单证员 SMITH 先生收到宁波舒普机电科技公司的销售合同，随即向孟加拉进出口银行（IMPORT& EXPORT BANK OF BANGLADESH LTD，SHARIF MANSION，56-57 MOTUHEEL COMMERCAIL AREA，1000DHAKA）申请开证。

单证　1-3

宁波舒普机电科技公司

NINGBO SUPPER ELECTRONIC MACHINERY CO. LTD.

528,JINYUAN,ROAD,INVESTMENT AND ENTERPRISE CENTRAL ZONE,YINZHOU DISTRICT, NINGBO, CHINA

销售确认书

SALES　CONFIRMATION

DATE: 25TH,NOVEMBER, 2008

S/C NO.:SP8021

BUYERS：SOUTH EAST EXIM LTD.
476/C.D.I. ROAD MALIBAGH
DHAKA-1219, BANGLADESH

THE UNDERSIGNED SELLERS AND BUYERS HAVE AGREED TO CLOSE THE FOLLOWING TRANSACTION ACCORDING TO THE TERMS AND CONDITIONS STIPULATED BELOW:

ITEM NO.	DESCRIPTION OF GOODS	QUANTITY	UNIT PRICE(USD)	AMOUNT(USD)
01	**Supreme Brand Sewing Machine Model CSM -430D** Direct drive High Speed Electronic lock Bartack machine progam panel 89 programmed designs X & Y bartaks complete head table Z Stand Servo motor with caster wheels and standard accessories.	10 SETS	CIF CHITTAGONG 8850	88 500.00
02	**Supreme Brand Sewing Machine Model CSM -438D** Direct drive High Speed Electronic lock Button stitch machine progam panel 49 programmed designs complete head table Z Stand Servo motor with caster wheels and stand and standard accessories	15 SETS	2200	33 000.00
TOTAL		25 SETS		121 500.00

TOTAL VALUE: SAY US DOLLARS ONE HUNDRED AND TWENTY-ONE THOUSAND FIVE HUNDRED ONLY

TERMS & CONDITIONS

Payment terms: BY IRREVOCABLE AND CONFIRMED L/C AT SIGHT

Port of Shipment: ANY PORT IN CHINA

Port of destination: CHITTAGONG

Partial shipment: ALLOWED

Packing: ONE SET TO A SEA WORTHY CARTON, TOTAL 25 CARTONS

Delivery: 45 DAY FROM RECEIPT OF L/C

Certificate of Origin: LOCAL CHAMBER OF COMMERCE

Insurance: TO BE EFFECTED BY SELLERS COVERING W.P.A. AND WAR RISKS FOR 10% OVER THE INVOICE VALUE

THE SELLER:	**THE BUYER :**
NINGBO SUPPER ELECTRONIC MACHINERY CO. LTD.	SOUTH EAST EXIM LTD.
×××	×××

单证 1-4

IRREVOCABLE DOCUMENTARY CREDIT APPLICATION

TO: **Date:**

<table>
<tr><td colspan="2" rowspan="2">Beneficiary (Full name and address)</td><td>L/C No.
Ex-Card No.
Contract No.</td></tr>
<tr><td>Date and place of expiry of the credit</td></tr>
<tr><td>Partial shipments</td><td>Transhipment</td><td rowspan="2">□Issue by airmail □With brief advice by teletransmission
□Issue by express delivery
□Issue by teletransmission (which shall be the operative instrument)</td></tr>
<tr><td>□allowed □not allowed</td><td>□allowed □not allowed</td></tr>
<tr><td colspan="2" rowspan="2">Loading on board/dispatch/taking in charge at/from

not later than
For transportation to:</td><td>Amount</td></tr>
<tr><td rowspan="2">Credit available with
□by sight payment □by acceptance □by negotiation
□by deferred payment at</td></tr>
<tr><td colspan="2">Description of goods:</td></tr>
<tr><td colspan="2"></td><td>against the documents detailed herein
□and beneficiary's draft(s) for % of invoice value
at
on</td></tr>
<tr><td colspan="2">Packing:</td><td>□FOB □CFR □CIF
□or other terms</td></tr>
</table>

（续）

Documents required: (marked with ×)

1. ( ) Signed commercial invoice in ____ originals indicating L/C No. and Contract No.

2. ( ) Full set of clean on board Bills of Lading made out ____ and [ ] blank endorsed, marked "freight [ ] to collect / [ ] prepaid".

3. ( ) Airway bills showing "freight [ ] to collect/[ ] prepaid [ ] indicating freight amount" and consigned to____

4. ( ) Insurance Policy/Certificate in ____ originals for ____ % of the invoice value showing claims payable in China in currency of the draft, blank endorsed, covering [ ] Ocean Marine Transportation / [ ] Air Transportation / [ ]Over Land Transportation [ ] All Risks, [ ] War Risks, [ ] WPA, [ ] ____.

5. ( ) Packing List/Weight Memo in ____ originals indicating quantity, gross and net weights of each package and packing conditions as called for by the L/C.

6. ( ) Certificate of Quantity / Weight in ____ originals issued by an independent surveyor at the loading port, indicating the actual surveyed quantity / weight of shipped goods as well as the packing condition.

7. ( ) Certificate of Quality in ____ originals issued by [ ] manufacturer/ [ ] public recognized surveyor/ [ ].____

8. ( ) Beneficiary's Certified copy of cable / telex dispatched to the accountees within ____ hours after shipment advising [ ] name of vessel / [ ] fight No. / [ ] voyage No., date, quantity, weight and value of shipment.

9. ( ) Beneficiary's Certificate Certifying that extra copies of the documents have been dispatched according to the contract terms.

10. ( ) Shipping Co's certificate attesting that the carrying vessel is chartered or booked by accountee or their shipping agents.

11. ( ) Certificate of origin in 2 originals certifying that the goods are of Chinese Origin.

12. ( ) Other documents, if any:____

Additional instructions:

1. ( ) All banking charges outside the opening bank are for beneficiary's account.

2. ( ) Documents must be presented within ____ days after date of issuance of the transport documents but within the validity of this credit.

3. ( ) Third party as shipper is not acceptable, Short Form/Blank back B/L is not acceptable.

4. ( ) Both quantity and credit amount ____ % more or less are allowed.

5. ( ) Prepaid freight drawn in excess of L/C amount is acceptable against presentation of original charges voucher issued by shipping Co / Air Line / or it's agent.

6. ( ) All documents to be forwarded in one cover, unless otherwise stated above.

7. ( ) Other terms, if any:____

Account No. with ________________ (name of bank)

Transacted by:

Telephone No.: (Applicant: name signature of authorized person)

(with seal)

第四步：教师点评，核对答案

填写完毕，教师随机选择一个或多个小组某一同学的作业进行集中点评，核对答案。

知识链接

1．开证申请书的填写规范

开证申请书为一式三份，一份留业务部门，一份留财会部门，一份交银行，作为其开立信用证的依据。

（1）申请开证的时间（Date）：按实际日期填写，一般在交货期前一个月。

（2）开证（传递）方式（by）：已经印好，在相应的方式前划"√"或"×"即可。当前银行一般采用 SWIFT 开证，其次采用 TELEX 开证。

（3）信用证性质、号码："不可撤销"的字样一般已印好，如果是保兑或可转让信用证，则必须写明：号码由开证行填写。

（4）申请人（Applicant）、受益人（Beneficiary）：须按合同分别填写买方和卖方详细名称和地址（包括电话、传真、E-MAIL）。

（5）通知行（Advising Bank）：由开证行确定。

（6）金额（Amount）：填写合同规定的总值，小写和大写分别用数字和文字两种形式表示，并且要标明币种。如果有一定比例的上下浮动幅度，也要在信用证中表示出来，如“USD 145,000 WITH 5% MORE OR LESS”。

（7）运输条款（Shipment from…to…）：填写装运港（Loading on board/dispatch/ taking in charge at/from）、目的港（For transportation to）、装运期（Not later than），并按合同选择是否允许分批（Partial shipments）及或转运（Transshipment）。

（8）货物条款（Evidencing shipment of 或 Description of goods…）：填写货物名称、规格，同时按提示分别填写货物的包装、价格、运输标志等。

（9）信用证有效期（Date of Expiry）、到期地点（Place of Expiry）：有效期一般在装运期后 15 日或者 21 日，到期地点一般为议付行所在地，以便做到及时交单。

（10）信用证的付款方式和汇票条款：“Credit available with”这个栏目由开证行填写议付或付款银行。下面是四种具体的付款方式，根据合同规定的付款方式，在该项括号中打“×”。如果合同中标明“L/C AT SIGHT”，即期信用证通常是凭即期汇票向指定银行提示请求付款的信用证。所以选择如下：

（×）by sight payment 即期支付（　）by acceptance 承兑支付

（　）by negotiation 议付

（　）by deferred payment at____against the documents detailed herein 延期多少天后支付

汇票要求主要有三方面的内容：①汇票金额，按照合同规定填写，信用证方式下如果合同规定所有货款都用信用证支付，则应填写发票金额的100%；如果合同规定该笔货款电汇30%，信用证支付 70%，则信用证下汇票为发票金额的 70%。注意：这里汇票金额不能超过发票金额，即不能大于 100%。②支付期限，主要有即期、远期。如是即期在横线上标“×××”，如为远期，在横线上标明具体的天数，如“30 days”。③付款人，信用证支付下汇票的付款人不能填写开证申请人。根据《UCP 600》的规定，信用证下的汇票的付款人必须是开证行或指定付款行，如：

（×）and beneficiary's draft for 100 % of invoice value at×××sight draft on issuing bank

（11）单据条款（accompanied by …）：根据需要选择需随汇票提供的单据，并在选项前划“√”或“×”，在其后空白栏中填写或选择所需单据份数、出具单位及/或单据内容。如：“[×] Signed commercial invoice in 3 copies indicating Contract No. 12345”。如需提供上述单据以外的单据，可选“[×]Other documents”选项，并在空白处填写所需的其他单据名称、份数及其他要求。注意：申请人必须根据合同规定填写单据条款，不能随意提出超出合同规定的要求，也不能降低或减少合同规定的要求。

（12）附加条款（Special instructions）：需要时选填。

（13）交单期限（Documents should be presented within____）：一般填写 15 天或 21 天。注意：交单期限和前面信用证的装船日期和有效期的关系。如前面最迟装运期为 4 月 11 日，信用证有效期为 4 月 26 日，交单期限就应为装船日期后 15 日内，这里就填写“15 days”.

（14）其他：开户银行及账号（Account No…. with…）、执行人、联系电话、申请人（法人代表）签字等内容，按实际填写。

2．申请开立信用证应注意的问题

向银行申请开立信用证，是一件技术性和专业性都很强的工作，做得不恰当就有可能引起多次改证和支付不必要的费用，从而使进口方增加进口成本，因此在申请开立信用证时，应注意：

（1）信用证条款要与买卖合同一致。按照《UCP600》的规定，不要把过多的细节在信用证中列明，如品名、规格、数量、单价及装运期限等，只要简单地列明即可，若货物描述过长，也可以注明“参照××合同”的字样。

（2）汇票期限要与买卖合同的付款期限相吻合。

（3）单据条款要明确。信用证中必须列明所需单据的名称及份数，若有特别要求，还必须要详细列明。

（4）特别条款的利用。若开证人有一些特别的指示，而该指示又不能以单据方式表现出来，则可利用特别条款来说明，如技术规格、质量的说明、包装的搭配及迟期提单可以接受等。

（5）对于信用证的修改，最好先通过 FAX 或 E-MAIL 等方式与受益人事先进行沟通，待双方达成一致以后，一次性地进行，从而节省费用。

（6）开证时间一般应在装运期之前 1 个月至 45 天左右，若合同另有规定者除外。

（7）申请开证，最少应向银行提供三份文件，即合同、进口付汇核销单和购汇用汇申请书。必要时应有进口许可证、配额证及某些部门的批文等。

（8）开证行收到进口商的开证申请后，应立即对开证申请书、合同、开证申请人的资信状况等进行审核，在确信可以接受申请并收到押金及开证手续费后，即依申请开出信用证，副本交开证申请人确认后，通过其在受益人所在地的分行或代理行（统称通知行），将正本信用证通知受益人。

3．申请开立信用证的程序

申请开立信用证的程序为：

（1）递交有关合同的副本及附件。进口商在向银行申请开立信用证时，应向银行递交有关的进口合同副本及附件，如进口许可证、进口配额证（进口许可证及配额商品时）、某些部门的批文等。

（2）填写信用证开证申请书。进口商填写银行统一印制的信用证开证申请书，是进口商申请开立信用证过程中最重要的工作。它是开证银行对外开立信用证的基础和依据。进口商填写开证申请书时，必须按合同条款规定，写明对信用证的各项要求，内容须明确、完整，无词意不清的记载。

（3）交纳押金和开证手续费。按国际惯例，进口人向银行申请开立信用证，应向银行交付一定比例的押金或其他担保金。押金一般为信用证金额的百分之几到百分之几十，根据进口人的资信情况而定。我国开证行根据不同企业和交易情况，要求开证申请人缴付一定比例的人民币保证金，然后开证。此外，银行为进口商开证时，开证申请人（进口商）还必须按规定支付一定金额的开证手续费。

（4）银行开立信用证。开证行收到进口商的开证申请，立即对开证申请书的内容及其与合同的关系、开证申请人的资信状况等进行审核，在确信可以接受开证申请人的申请并收到开证申请人提交的押金及开证手续费后，即向信用证受益人开出信用证，副本交开证申请人确认后，通知行将信用证通知受益人并将信用证正本寄交（有时使用电传开证）受益人所在地分行或代理行（统称通知行）。

申请开立信用证的时间须按合同规定。合同没有规定时，一般掌握在合同规定的装运期前一个月到一个半月左右。

自我能力测评

能力形成性评价表

评价指标	分值		实际得分
能看懂外销合同	快速准确看懂	40 分	
	花很长时间看懂	30 分	
	基本看不懂	0～20 分	
能根据外销合同填写开证申请书	60 分（根据需填写栏目算出各栏目均分）		

任务三　审核信用证

任务导入

宁波光明进出口公司与香港富华贸易有限公司签订了出口外销合同，合同规定用即期信用证支付（见任务二，单证 1-1），香港富华贸易公司的单证员小芳向香港华夏银行申请开立信用证后不久，华夏银行即开立了以宁波光明进出口公司为受益人的信用证。宁波光明进出口公司收到中国光大银行宁波分行作为通知行转交的信用证之后，其单证员小兰随即对照合同审核下列信用证。

中国光大银行宁波分行的通知书及随附的华夏银行开立的信用证如下所示。

单证　1-5

中国光大银行

CHINA EVERBRIGHT BANK

CHINA EVERBRIGHT BANK，NINGBO BRANCH

ADDRESS: 148 JIEFANG　SOUTH ROAD NINGBO

CABLE CHUNGKUO

TELEX: 34116/34127 BOCJS CN

信 用 证 通 知 书

NOTIFICATION OF DOCUMENTARY CREDIT

SWIFT:EVERCNBJNBI 7688 148842

FAX: 4208843

2010/04/09

TO 致：GUANGMING IMPORT & EXPORT CORPORATION 13 XINNING ROAD, NINGBO, ZHEJIANG, CHINA TEL. 0574-88896000	WHEN CORRESPONDING PLEASE QUOTE OUT REF NO.	AD94001A40576

（续）

ISSUING BANK 开证行 HUA XIA BANK CO., LTD. HONGKONG HK		TRANSMITTED TO US THROUGH 转递行 REF NO.	
L/C NO.信用证号 006CIM000489SBRT	DATED 开证日期 2010/03/05	AMOUNT 金额 USD3368 00	EXPIRY PLACE 有效地 FOREIGN
EXPIRY DATE 效期 2010/05/09	TENOR 期限 SIGHT	CHARGE 未付费用 RMB0.00	CHARGE BY 费用承担人 BENE
RECEIVED VIA 来证方式 SWIFT	AVAILABLE 是否生效 VALID	TEST/SIGN 印押是否相符 YES	CONFIRM 我行是否保兑 YES

DEAR SIRS 敬启者：

WE HAVE PLEASURE IN ADVISING YOU THAT WE HAVE RECEIVED FROM THE A/M BANK A(N) **LETTER OF CREDIT**, CONTENTS OF WHICH ARE AS PER ATTACHED SHEET(S).

THIS ADVICE AND THE ATTACHED SHEET(S) MUST ACCOMPANY THE RELATIVE DOCUMENTS WHEN PRESENTED FOR NEGOTIATION.

兹通知贵公司，我行收自上述银行信用证一份，现随附通知。贵公司交单时，请将本通知书及信用证一并提示。

REMARK 备注：______

THIS L/C CONSISTS OF TWO SHEET(S), INCLUDING THE COVERING LETTER AND ATTACHMENT(S). 本信用证连同附信及附件共 2 页。

IF YOU FIND ANY TERMS AND CONDITIONS IN THE L/C WHICH YOU ARE UNABLE TO COMPLY WITH AND OR ANY ERROR(S), IT IS SUGGESTED THAT YOU CONTACT APPLICANT DIRECTLY FOR NECESSARY AMENDMENT(S) SO AS TO AVOID AND DIFFICULTIES WHICH MAY ARISE WHEN DOCUMENTS ARE PRESENED.

如本信用证中有无法办到的条款及/或错误，请与开证申请人联系，进行必要的修改，以排除交单时可能发生的问题。

THIS L/C IS ADVISED SUBJECT TO ICC UCP PUBLICATION NO.600.

本信用证之通知系遵循《国际商会跟单信用证统一惯例》第 600 号出版物办理。

此证如有任何问题及疑虑，请与结算业务部审证科联络，电话：0574-5129696，5129595。

YOURS FAITHFULLY

FOR CHINA EVERBRIGHT BANK

单证　1-6

MT700 格式信用证

ISSUE OF A DOCUMENTARY CREDIT

05/03/10-09:30:34　　LocalSwiftAcks-8414-136437

……………………………… Instance Type and Transmission……………………………..

Notification (Transmission) of Original Sent to SWIFT(ACK)

Network Delivery Status:	Network Ack
Priority/Delivery:	Normal
Message Input Reference:	2025 100305BKHYHK JA92A 1496 555995

…………………………… Header………………………………………………

Swift Input:	FIN 700 Issue of a Documentary Credit
Sender:	BKHYHK JA92A 1496 555995 HUA XIA BANK CO. LTD HONGKONG HK
Receiver:	EVERCNBJNBI 7688 148842

（续）

CHINA EVERBRIGHT BANK
NINGBO CN
MUR: 2010030502001540

………………………………… Message Text …………………………………

SEQUENCE OF TOTAL *27：1 / 1
FORM OF DOC，CREDIT *40A：IRREVOCABLE
SENDER'S REF. *20：HX0190123
DOC. CREDIT NUMBER *21：006CIM000489SBRT
DATE OF ISSUE 31C：100305
APPLICABLE RULES *40E：UCP LATEST VERSION
DATE AND PLACE OF EXPIRY *31D：DATE 100509 AT HUA XIA BANK'S COUNTER
APPLICANT *50：FUHU TRADE CO.,LTD.,
105 QUEENS ROAD CENTRAL,HONGKONG
TEL：852-2857777
BENEFICIARY *59：GUANGMING IMPORT & EXPORT CORPORATION
13 XINNING ROAD, NINGBO, ZHEJAING, CHINA TEL.0574-88896123
CURRENCY CODE,AMOUNT *32B：USD3368, 00
MAXIMUM CREDIT AMOUNT 39B：NOT EXCEEDING L/C AMOUT
AVAILABLE WITH / BY *41D：ANY BANK IN CHINA BY NEGOTIATION
DRAFTS AT 42C：DRAFTS AT SIGHT FOR FULL INVOICE COST
DRAWEE 52A：BKHYHK JA92A 1496 555995
HUA XIA BANK CO. LTD
HONGKONG. HK
PARTIAL SHIPMENTS 43P：PROHIBITED
TRANSSHIPMENT 43T：ALLOWED
LOADING ON BOARD 44A：ANY PORT IN CHINA
FOR TRANSPORTATION TO …44B：HONGKONG
LATEST DATE OF SHIPMENT 44C：100405
DESCRIPTION OF GOODS 45A：100PCT NYLON. FABRICS
OTHER DETAILS AS PER S/C NO. E034579
INCOTERM：CIF HONGKONG
DOCUMENTS REQUIRED 46A：

1．SIGNED COMMERCIAL INVOICE IN TRIPLICATE AND MUST CERTIFIED BY CHINA'S CHAMBER OF COMMERCE.THE GOODS ARE OF CHINESE ORIGIN ONLY.

2．FULL SET OF CLEAN ON BOARD OCEAN BILLS OF LADING, MADE OUT TO ORDER OF SHIPPER AND BLANK ENDORSED AND MARKED " FREIGHT COLLECT "AND NOTIFY APPLICANT.

3．PACKING LIST IN DUPLICATE.

4．FULL SET OF NEGOTIABLE INSURANCE POLICY OR CERTIFICATE BLANK ENDORSED FOR 140 PERCENT OF THE INVOICE VALUE COVERING ALL RISKS.

5．CERTIFICATE OF QUALITY IN 2 ORIGINALS ISSUED BY MANUFACTURER.

6．CERTIFICATE OF ORIGIN ISSUED BY THE CHINA'S CHAMBER OF COMMERCE ORIGINALS. IN ADDITON，THE CERTIFICATE OF ORIGIN MUST STATE THAT THE COUNTRY OF ORIGIN OF GOODS SHIPPED HAS BEEN MENTIONED ON EACH CARTON OF THE CONSIGNMENT.

7．SHIP'S CLASSIFICATION ISSUED BY LIOYDS' IN LONDON.

8．BENEFICIARY'S CERTIFIED COPY OF FAX DISPATCHED TO THE APPLICANT WITHIN 2 DAYS AFTER SHIPMENT ADVISING THE CONTRACT NUMBER, NAME OF COMMODITY, QUANTITY, INVOICE VALUE, BILL OF LADING NO., BILL OF LOADING DATE, THE ETA DATE AND SHIPPING CO.

ADDITIONAL CONDITIONS 47A：

1．SHIPMENT MUST NOT BE MADE EARLIER THAN THE CREDIT ISSUING DATE.

2．ONE SET OF NON-NEGOTIABLE SHIPPING DOCUMENTS TO BE SENT TO THE APPLICANT THROUGTH COURIER SERVICE WITHIN 7 WORKING DAY AFTER SHIPMENT AND A COURIER RECEIPT OF WHICH MUST ACCOMPANY THE

（续）

ORIGINAL DOCUMENTS SATATED ABOVE.

3. DISCREPANCY FEE OF USD35.00 WILL BE DEDUCTED FROM THE PROCEEDS OF EACH PRESENTATION OF DISCREPANT DOCUMENTS.

4. ALL DOCUMENTS MUST BE FORWARDED IN ONE LOT BY EXPRESS.

5. ALL DOCUMENTS MUST INDICATE L/C NO. CONTRACT NO. AND NAME OF ISSUING BANK.

CHARGES 71B:

All BANKING CHARGES INSIDE THE OPENING BANK ARE FOR BENEFICIARY'S ACCOUNT.

PERIOD FOR PRESENTATION 48:

21 DAYS FROM THE DATE OF SHIPMENT,

BUT NOT LATER THAN THE CREDIT VALIDITY.

CONFIRMATION INSTRUCTION 49: CONFIRM

INSTR TO THE PAY/ACCE/NEG BANK 78:

+ DISCREPPANT DOCUMENTS MUST NOT BE NEGOTIATED WITHOUT OUR PRIOR APPOVAL.

+DOCUMENTS SHOULD BE MAILED BY COURIER IN ONE LOT TO HUA XIA BANK CO.,LTD.

HONGKONG HKSHARIF MANSION,56-57 MOTUHEEL COMMERCIAL AREA ,HK.

+AS PER THE INSTRUCTION OF THE NEGOTIATING BANK REIMBURSEMENT WILL BE PROVIDED BY US UPON RECEIPT OF ORIGINAL DOCUMENTS BY HUA XIA BANK CO., LTD. HONGKONG ,COMPLIED WITH L/C TERMS AND CONDITIONS.

+ADVISE THROUGH BANK 57A: EVERCNBJNBI 7688 148842

CHINA EVERBRIGHT BANK

NINGBO CN

SENDER TO RECEIVER INFORMATION 72: .

PLS ADVISE US WHEN ADVISING THIS L/C TO BENEFICIARY

…………………………………….. MESSAGE TRAILER…………………………………………………………………

TRAILER ORDER IS《MAC:》《PAC:》《ENC:》《CHK:》《TNG:》《PDE:》

MAC: CF6F97BC

CHK: F04138D93C1B

DLM: BKHYHKJAXXX 1003032233

完成上述任务的步骤如下

第一步： 快速看懂外销合同，弄清合同条款（如同任务二的第一步）

第二步： 引导学生小组分工合作，逐条翻译信用证条款

第三步： 导学，教师引导学生一起对照合同条款逐条审核信用证条款，并用多媒体进行演示

导学步骤如下： 首先教师引导学生一起对照合同条款逐条审核信用证条款，并用多媒体进行展示整个审核的过程，把信用证条款与合同条款不符的内容和我方不能接受的内容标示出来。建议用专业机房或多媒体教室上课，教师易于引导和演示。

单证　1-7

ISSUE OF A DOCUMENTARY CREDIT

05/03/10-09:30:34　　LocalSwiftAcks-8414-136437

…………………………………………………**Instance Type and Transmission**…………………………………

Notification (Transmission) of Original Sent to SWIFT(ACK)

Network Delivery Status : Network Ack

Priority/Delivery : Normal

Message Input Reference : 2025 100305BKHYHK JA92A 1496 555995

………………………………………………**Message Header**……………………………………………………

Swift Input : FIN 701 Issue of a Documentary Credit

（续）

Sender : BKHYHK JA92A 1496 555995
HUA XIA BANK CO.,LTD.
HONGKONG. HK
Receiver : EVERCNBJNBI 7688 148842
CHINA EVERBRIGHT BANK
NINGBO.CN
MUR : 2010030502001540

…………Message Text……………………………………

SEQUENCE OF TOTAL *27：1 / 1
FORM OF DOC，CREDIT *40A：IRREVOCABLE
SENDER'S REF. *20：HX0190123
DOC. CREDIT NUMBER *21：006CIM000489SBRT
DATE OF ISSUE 31 C：100305
APPLICABLE RULES *40E：UCP LATEST VERSION
DATE AND PLACE OF EXPIRY *31D：DATE100509~~AT HUA XIA BANK'S COUNTER~~（应为 *IN CHINA*）
APPLICAN *50： ~~FUHU~~（应为 *FUHUA* ） TRADE CO.,LTD.,
~~105~~（应为 *101*）QUEENS
ROAD CENTRAL,HONGKONG
TEL: 852-2857777
BENEFICIARY *59：GUANGMING IMPORT & EXPORT CORPORATION
13 XINNING ROAD, NINGBO, ZHEJAING, CHINA
TEL.0574-8889~~6123~~（应为 *0574-88896000* ）
CURRENCY CODE,AMOUNT *32B：~~USD3368, 00~~（应为 *USD33 680，00*）
MAXIMUM CREDIT AMOUNT 39B：NOT EXCEEDING L/C AMOUT
AVAILABLE WITH / BY *41D：ANY BANK IN CHINA
BY NEGOTIATION
DRAFTS AT 42C：DRAFTS AT SIGHT
FOR FULL INVOICE COST
DRAWEE 52A：BKHYHK JA92A 1496 555995
HUA XIA BANK CO. LTD
HONGKONG. HK
PARTIAL SHIPMENTS 43P：~~PROHIBITED~~ （应为 *ALLOWED*）
TRANSSHIPMENT 43T：~~ALLOWED~~ （应为 *PROHIBITED*）
LOADING ON BOARD 44E：ANY PORT IN CHINA
FOR TRANSPORTATION TO …44F：HONGKONG
LATEST DATE OF SHIPMENT 44C：100405
DESCRIPT OF GOODS 45A：100PCT NYLON FABRICS
OTHER DETAILS AS PER S/C NO E034579
INCOTERM：CIF HONGKONG
DOCUMENTS REQUIRED 46A：

1．SIGNED COMMERCIAL INVOICE IN TRIPLICATE AND MUST CERTIFIED BY CHINA'S CHAMBER OF COMMERCE THE GOODS ARE OF CHINESE ORIGIN ONLY.

2．FULL SET OF CLEAN ON BOARD OCEAN BILLS OF LADING, MADE OUT TO ORDER OF SHIPPER AND BLANK ENDORSED AND MARKED " ~~FREIGHT PREPAID~~ "AND NOTIFY APPLICANT.

3．PACKING LIST IN DUPLICATE.

4．FULL SET OF NEGOTIABLE INSURANCE POLICY OR CERTIFICATE BLANK ENDORSED FOR ~~140~~ （应为 *110%*） PERCENT OF THE INVOICE VALUE COVERING ~~ALL RISKS~~（应为 *ALL RISKS AND WAR RISKS AS PER CCIC. 1981.1.1*）.

5．CERTIFICATE OF QUALITY IN 2 ORIGINALS ISSUED BY MANUFACTURER.

（续）

6. CERTIFICATE OF ORIGIN GSP IN FORM A ISSUED BY THE AUTHORITY IN TWO ORIGINALS . IN ADDITON, THE CERTIFICATE OF ORIGIN MUST STATE THAT THE COUNTRY OF ORIGIN OF GOODS SHIPPED HAS BEEN MENTIONED ON EACH CATON OF THE CONSIGNMENT. 7. SHIP'S CLASSIFICATION ISSUED BY LIOYDS' IN LONDON. 8. BENEFICIARY'S CERTIFIED COPY OF FAX DISPATCHED TO THE APPLICANT WITHIN 2 DAYS AFTER SHIPMENT ADVISING THE CONTRACT NUMBER, NAME OF COMMODITY, QUANTITY, INVOICE VALUE, BILL OF LADING NO., BILL OF LADING DATE, THE ETA DATE AND SHIPPING CO. ADDITIONAL CONDITIONS 47A： 1. SHIPMENT MUST NOT BE MADE EARLIER THAN THE CREDIT ISSUING DATE. 2. ONE SET OF NON-NEGOTIABLE SHIPPING DOCUMENTS TO BE SENT TO THE APPLICANT THROUGH COURIER SERVICE WITHIN 7 DAY AFTER SHIPMENT AND A COURIER RECEIPT OF WHICH MUST ACCOMPANY THE ORIGINAL DOCUMENTS STATED ABOVE. 3. DISCREPANCY FEE OF USD35.00 WILL BE DEDUCTED FROM THE PROCEEDS OF EACH PRESENTATION OF DISCREPANT DOCUMENTS. 4. ALL DOCUMENTS MUST BE FORWARDED IN ONE LOT BY EXPRESS. 5. ALL DOCUMENTS MUST INDICATE L/C NO. CONTRACT NO.AND NAME OF ISSUING BANK. CHARGES 71B： All BANKING CHARGES ~~INSIDE~~ （应为 *OUTSIDE*）THE OPENING BANK ARE FOR BENEFICIARY'S ACCOUNT. PERIOD FOR PRESENTATION 48： 21 DAYS FROM THE DATE OF SHIPMENT, BUT NOT LATER THAN THE CREDIT VALIDITY. CONFIRMATION INSTRUCTION 49：CONFIRM ADVISE THROUGH BANK 57A：EVERCNBJNBI 7688 148842 CHINA EVERBRIGHT BANK NINGBO CN SENDER TO RECEIVER INFORMATION 72： PLS ADVISE US WHEN ADVISING THIS L/C TO BENEFICIARY ………………………………….. ……………..MESSAGE TRAILER……………………………………………… TRAILER ORDER IS MAC: PAC: ENC: CHK: TNG: PDE: MAC: CF6F97BC CHK: F04138D93C1B DLM：BKHYHKJAXXX 1003032233

其次，整理审核结果，填写信用证审核结果单如下。

单证 1-8

信用证审核结果单

信 用 证 号	006CIM000489SBRT
合 同 号	E034579
审证结果	1. 到期地点不能接受，应改为 IN CHINA，否则易造成交单逾期。 2. 开证申请人名称和地址错误，名称应改为 FUHUA 贸易公司，地址应该是 QUEENS ROAD 101 号，因为与合同不符。 3. 受益人的名称和地址栏电话号码错误，应改为 0574-88896000，因为与合同不符。 4. 信用证金额错误，应为 USD33 680，00，因为与合同不符。 5. 运输条款错误，分批应该是允许“ALLOWED”，转运应该是禁止“PROHIBITED”，因为与合同不符。 6. 保险条款错误，金额应为发票金额的 110%，险别应为 ALL RISKS AND WAR RISKS AS PER CCIC. 1981.1.1，因为与合同不符。 7. 费用条款不能接受，应该将 INSIDE 改为“OUTSIDE…”包括开证行在内的所有银行费用由受益人承担不符合惯例，不能接受。

信用证审核结果单填写说明：首先指出信用证存在的问题，然后提出应该怎样修改，并指出修改的理由。

第四步：巩固训练，学生独自对照外销合同审核信用证

第五步：教师点评，核对答案

填写完毕，教师随机选择一个或多个小组某一同学作业进行集中点评，核对答案。

训练任务

孟加拉进出口银行（IMPORT& EXPORT BANK OF BANGLADESH LTD, SHARIF MANSION, 56-57MOTUHEE COMMERCAIL AREA, 1000DHAKA）受理 SOUTH EAST EXIM LTD 公司开证申请后，立即开立了以宁波舒普机电科技公司为受益人的信用证。宁波舒普机电科技公司收到中国银行宁波分行作为通知行转交的信用证之后，单证员马林随即对照相关外销合同（单证 1-3，详见任务 2 中 3.4 根据下列外销合同填写开证申请书）审核下列信用证，填写信用证审核结果单。

单证 1-9

MT701 格式信用证

Our Reference:00333-11-1725025-1 ISS 000

Sender exbkbddh001
IMPORT& EXPORT BANK OF BANGLADESH LTD.
SHARIF MANSION
56-57MOTUHEE
COMMERCIAL AREA
1000DHAKA

Message Type: MT 700
27: SEQUENCE OF TOTAL
1/1
40A: FORM OF DOC, CREDIT
IRREVOCABLE
20: DOC. CREDIT NUMBER
194508011405MALL
31C: DATE OF ISSUE
081203
40E: APPLICABLE RULES
UCP LATEST VERSION
31D: DATE AND PLACE OF EXPIRY
090130 AT NEGOT BANK'S COUNTER
50: APPLICANT
SOUTH EAST EXIM LTD.
476/C.D.I. ROAD MALIBAGH
DHAKA-1219, BANGLADESH
59: BENEFICIARY
NINGBO SUPPER ELECTRONIC MACHINERY CO.,LTD.
528, JINYUAN, ROAD
INVESTMENT AND ENTERPRISE CENTRAL ZONE
YINZHOU DISTRICT, NINGBO, CHINA

（续）

32B: CURRENCY CODE, AMOUNT
HKD121,500.00
41D: AVAILABLE WITH / BY
ANY BANK IN BENEFICIARY COUNTRY
BY NEGOTIATION
42C: DRAFTS AT
90 DAYS FROM B/L DATE DRAWN ON US
52A: DRAWEE
EXPORT & IMPORT BANK OF BANGLADESH LTD.
EXBKBDDH001
43 P: PARTIAL SHIPMENTS
PROHIBITED
43T: TRANSSHIPMENT
ALLOWED
44E: LOADING ON BOARD
ANY PORT IN CHINA
44F: FOR TRANSPORTATION TO
CHITTANGONG
44C: LATEST DATE OF SHIPMENT
090119
45A: DESCRIPT OF GOODS
SUPREME BRAND SEWING MACHINE, OTHER DETAILS AS PER S/C NO.8021 DTD25-NOV-2008
INCOTREMS: CIF CASABLANKA
46A: DOCUMENTS REQUIRED
A) SIGNED COMMERCIAL INVOICE IN EIGHT FOLD IN ENGLISH CERTIFYING MERCHANDISE TO BE OF CHINA ORIGIN QUOTING L/C NO. 194508011405MALL, ALL DULY SIGNED AND COUNTER-SIGNED BY L/C APPLICANT WHOSE SIGNATURES MUST BE IN CONFORMITY WITH THE SPECIMEN SIGNATURES HELD IN EXBKBDDH001 BANK.
B) SET OF CLEAN ON BOARD OCEAN BILLS OF LADING, ISSUED TO ORDER OF L/C ISSUING BANK SHOULD BE MARKED " FREIGHT PREPAID "AND NOTIFY APPLICANT.
C) PACKING SHOULD BE EXPORT STANDARD SEA WORTHY AND FIVE COPIES OF PACKING LIST MUST ACCOMPANY THE ORIGINAL DOCUMENTS.
D) FULL SET OF NEGOTIABLE INSURANCE POLICY OR CERTIFICATE BLANK ENDORSED FOR 130 PERCENT OF THE INVOICE VALUE COVERING WPA.
E) NO SOLID WOOD PACKING CERTIFICATE ISSUED BY MANUFACTURER.
F) CERTIFICATE OF QUALITY ISSUED BY APPLICANT.
G) CERTIFICATE OF ORIGIN ISSUED BY THE LOCAL CHAMBER OF COMERCE.
H) BENEFICIARY'S CERTIFIED COPY OF FAX DISPATCHED TO THE APPLICANT WITHIN 2 WORKING DAYS AFTER SHIPMENT ADVISING PARTICULAR OF SHIPMENT.
47A: ADDITIONAL CONDITIONS
A) TELEGRAPHIC TRANSFER REIMBURSEMENT CLAIMS ARE SPECIFICALLY PROHIBITED UNDER THIS CREDIT.
B) ONE SET OF NEGOTIABLE SHIPPING DOCUMENTS TO BE SENT TO THE APPLICANT THROUGH COURIER SERVICE WITHIN 2 DAYS AFTER SHIPMENT AND A COURIER RECEIPT OF WHICH MUST ACCOMPANY THE ORIGINAL DOCUMENTS.
C) EACH DRAFT ACCOMPANYING DOCUMENTS MUST STATE "DRAWN UNDER CREDIT NUMBER 194508011405MALL OF EXBKBDDH001, IMPORT& EXPORT BANK OF BANGLADESH LTD SHARIF MANSION, 56-57MOTUHEE, COMMERCIAL AREA, 1000DHAKA".
D) SHIPMENT/TRANSHIPMENT BY ISRAEL ARE STICTLY PRIHIBITED AND A CERTIFICATE TO THIS EFFECT

（续）

SHOULD ACCOMPANY EACH SET OF DOCUMENTS. 71B：CHARGES All BANKING CHARGES OUTSIDE THE OPENING BANK ARE FOR BENEFICIARY'S ACCOUNT. 48：PERIOD FOR PRESENTATION 15 DAYS FROM THE DATE OF SHIPMENT, BUT NOT LATER THAN THE CREDIT VALIDITY. 49：CONFIRMATION INSTRUCTION WITHOUT 78：INSTR TO THE PAY/ACCE/NEG BANK A) DISCREPANT DOCUMENTS MUST NOT BE NEGOTIATED WITHOUT OUR PRIOR APPROVAL. B) DOCUMENT SHOULD BE MAILED BY COURIER IN ONE LOTS TO EXBKBDDH001, SHARIF MANSION, 56-57MOTUHEE, COMMERCAIL AREA,1000 DHAKA. C) WE SHALL ARRANGE REIMBURSEMENT /PAYMENT OF THE BILL AS PER THE INSTRUCTION OF THE NEGOTIATING BANK WILL UPON RECEIPT OF CREDIT CONFORM DOCUMENTS AT OUR COUNTER. 57A：ADVISE THROUGH BANK BKNBCN2NXXX BANK OF NINGBO NINGBO CN 72：SENDER TO RECEIVER INFORMATION THIS CREDIT IS SUBJECT TO UCP DC (2007 RIVISION) ICC PULICATION NO.600. ……………………………………END OF MESSAGE……………………………………………………

单证 1-10

信用证审核结果

信用证号	
合同号	
审证结果	

知识链接

作用证审核要点

许多不符点单据的产生及单据提交后被银行退回，大多是对收到的信用证审核不当造成的，使原本可以纠正的错误由于审核不及时未加以及时地修改。因此，一般应在收到信用证的当天对照有关的合同认真地按下列各条仔细检查，这样可以及早发现错误并采取相应的补救措施。收到信用证后对照买卖合同条款，检查和审核的要点如下。

1．出口企业的审核要点

（1）审核信用证的性质。根据《跟单信用证统一惯例》第600号出版物（以下简称UCP600）的规定，信用证无论是即期、远期、保兑、可转让、循环或备用信用证，都是不可撤销的，都应有“IRREVOCABLE”字样。如合同规定是保兑信用证，在SWIFT信用证“CONFIRMATION

INSTRUCTION 49”栏目应有“WITH”或“CONFIRMED”字样，如为可转让信用证，在“FORM OF DOC，CREDIT *40 A”栏目应有“IRREVOCABLE，TRANSFERABLE”字样。

（2）审核信用证有效期、到期地、装运期、交单期。根据 UCP600 的规定，若信用证没有规定有效期（Expiry date），视为无效信用证。注意信用证的有效期、最迟装运日期（latest date for shipment）和信用证交单日期（Date for presentation of document）之间的关系。原则上信用证的到期日与最迟装运期应有一定的间隔，以便出口商有时间办理制单、交单、议付等工作。但如果出现“双到期”情况，即信用证规定的最迟装运期和议付到期日为同一天，或未规定装运期限，实践中称之为“双到期”，出口商应注意在信用证到期日前提早几天（一般在有效期前 10 天）将货物装上运输工具或交给承运人，以便有足够的时间制备各种单据、交单和办理议付等手续。交单期即运输单据出单日期后必须向信用证指定的银行提交单据要求付款、承兑或议付的特定期限。信用证中如有规定，必须在规定的期限内交单；如没有规定，一般为 15 天，最迟于运输单据日期 21 天内交单。综上所述，有关信用证的这几个日期的关系可以这样表述：信用证的有效期/到期日 ≥ 交单期+最迟装船期；理想的有效期/到期日=最迟装船期+交单期。

信用证的到期地点一般在出口商所在地，以便做到及时交单。如规定信用证国外到期，有关单据必须寄送国外，由于我们无法掌握单据到达国外银行所需的时间且容易延误或丢失，有一定的风险，因此要求修改成在国内交单、付款。在来不及修改的情况下，必须应提前一个邮程（邮程的长短应根据地区远近而定），以最快方式寄送。

（3）审核开证申请人、受益人名称、地址是否与合同一致。开证申请人、受益人名称、地址，包括电话、传真、电传号码等是否与合同完全一致。

（4）审核信用证的金额、币制是否符合合同规定。检查币制是否正确，如合同中规定的币制是“英镑”，而信用证中使用的是“美元”，则要求修改。金额不能出现错误。注意：如合同中货物数量上可以有一定幅度的伸缩，那么，信用证也应相应规定在支付金额时允许有一定幅度增减；如果在金额前使用了“大约”一词，其意思是允许金额有 10%的伸缩。

（5）审核信用证的汇票条款是否与合同一致。如合同规定凭即期汇票议付，SWIFT（“环球同业银行金融电讯协会”）信用证“DRAFT AT 42C”栏目应有“SIGHT”字样，如为远期汇票，远期多少天应与合同一致。

（6）分批装运和转运。是否允许分批装运和转运要与合同一致。如合同中没有明确规定，信用证也没有特别规定，则视作允许分批和转运。

如果合同中没有明确规定，来证不准分批的，又没有数量溢短装条款，则实际装运数量不得少装。但 UCP 600 第 32 条 b 款规定，在付款金额不超过信用证金额的情况下，如是大宗散装货物，除非信用证规定数量不得有增减，那么，在付款金额不超过信用证金额的情况下，货物数量可以容许有 5%的增减。注意 5%增减的规定一般适用于大宗货物，对于以包装单位或以个体为计算单位的货物不适用。如：5000PCS 100% COTTON SHIRTS（5000 件全棉衬衫）由于数量单位是“件”，实际交货时只能是 5000 件，而不能有 5%的增减。

如果合同中没有明确规定，来证不准转运的，要确定能否取得直达提单，否则必须改证。

（7）装运港和目的港。来证规定海运的起运港为 CHINESE PORT，或当地港口，甚至是亚洲口岸（ASIA PORT）都可以接受。

来证的目的港应与合同一致，除非是分几个港口，否则目的港只能列一个。来证笼统规定目的港为欧洲主要港口（EMP EUROPEAN MAIN PORT），只需按合同或买方通知的港口发货即可，不必改证。

（8）货物描述。来证的品名、货号、规格、包装和合同号码与合同一致。

来证所列单价、价格术语要与合同一致。

（9）单据要求。审核信用证所要求单据的种类、份数及填制要求是否与合同规定一致，合同没有明确规定的，看我方是否能够办到，否则要求对方修改。

特别注意：

1）商业发票（COMMERCIAL INVOICE）：要求出具两份不同买主名称的商业发票时，应要求改证。

2）提单（BILL OF LADING），如 FOB 成交，提单应标明“FREIGHT COLLECT”，如 CIF、CFR 成交，提单应标明“FREIGHT PREPAID”，否则应要求改证。

3）保险单（INSURANCE）：保险险别、保险加成、保险依据、保险人和理赔人等方面的内容应与合同一致。

4）产地证（CERTIFICATE OF ORIGIN）：一般原产地证（C/O）可以由出入境检验检疫局出具，也可由贸促会出具，来证要求上述任何一个机构出具都可以接受；普惠制产地证（GSP FORM A）只能由出入境检验检疫局出具，来证指定其他机构出具都不能接受。

5）品质证、数量证、重量证（CERTIFICATE OF QALITY，QUANTITY，WEIGHT）和检验证（INSPECTION CERTIFICATE）：可由出口公司、生产商或出入境检验检疫局出具，来证要求由贸促会出具则要求改证。

6）受益人证明（BENEFICIARY'S CERTIFICATE）：主要有寄单证明、履约证明等。来证要求的受益人证明书应是受益人已经完成或受益人力所能及的任务的证明，否则要求改证。比如，来证要求受益人证明“受益人已将三份正本提单中的一份于装船后 48 小时寄给开证申请人”，这个要求无法办到，因为正本提单直接寄给开证申请人风险很大，所以要求改证。

7）装运通知（ADVISE OF SHIPMENT）：来证要求装运前若干天发装运通知并且要列明装运日期，应要求改证，应该为装运后发通知。因为装运日期易受天气的影响，在装运前无法明确，要装运前发装运通知并且要列明装运日期有风险，容易造成通知上列明的日期与提单日期不一致。

8）海关发票（CUSTOMS INVOICE）：来证要求某种格式或编号的海关发票，应检查能否提供，否则应改证。

9）领事发票（CONSULAR INVOICE）：来证要求提供领事发票，应要求改证。

（10）注意信用证中的软条款。软条款是指置出口商于不利地位的条款，即信用证中所有无法由受益人自主控制的条款。软条款举例和详解如下：

1）货物检验证明或货运收据由进口商或开证人授权的人出具和签署，其印鉴应由开证行证实方可议付的条款等。

此类条款对受益人不利，因为进口商或进口商授权人如果不来履行就不能出具检验证书或货运收据，这必然影响货物出运。但是，即使进口商检验并出具了证书或货运收据，如果未经开证行证实，也会造成单证不符。

2）检验证由进口商出具和签署并由受益人会签。同时，其印鉴应与通知行持有的记录相符。

该条款对受益人很不利，因为主动权已掌握在对方手里。同时，不仅影响了议付时间，造成了单证不符，而且还影响了银行与企业间的关系。因此，受益人应和进口商通过开证行来函或来电修改或删除该条款，以便受益人操作和安全及时地收汇。

3）检验证由某某出具并签署，其印鉴必须由通知行证实。

开证行并没有将其印鉴资料寄给通知行，致使通知行无法证实，因此对受益人不利。另外根据 UCP600 规定，通知行应遵守合理谨慎的原则，检查其所通知信用证的表面真实性，以保护受益人的权益，因而没有义务审核某某进口商的印鉴。

4）票据应出具在有受益人名称的信笺上，注明全称和地址。

对于这一条款，有不同的理解。有人认为，发票出具在有受益人名称的信笺上，打上其地址就可以。但也有人认为，是在受益人的信笺上出具发票，其发票上也要打上受益人名称的全称和地址，不能只打上地址。曾有一家企业按照第一种意见制作单据，即只打上地址，结果国外开证行提出不符。因此，这个条款仍不明确，应向国外开证行询问澄清以便正确制作单据。

5）货运收据由进口商或进口商授权的人出具并签署，其印鉴必须与开证行的档案记录相符。

对于这些条款，受益人不能把握其印鉴是否相符，因此，出口商应和开证人通过开证行来函或来电报修改或删除，以便安全及时收汇。

6）由进口商授权人出具并手签的货运收据。其印鉴必须符合信用证开证行票据中心的记录。

对于这个条款，受益人不能把握其印鉴是否符合，因此，应提出修改。

7）由进口商授权人出具并签署的货运收据，其印鉴必须符合开证行持有的记录。

对于这个条款，受益人同样不能把握货运收据上的签字和图章与开证行持有的记录是否相符。

CASE ONE

2009 年 1 月，某三资企业将制好的一套单据交来交通银行汕头分行议付，经银行审核，发现其检验证书未按信用证条款要求的经开证行证实。企业得知后，希望把证书再寄给国外进口商，请其要求向开证行证实，但由于往返时间长，如果寄去后再寄回来又会影响交单时间，所以，只好以单证不符寄往国外开证行。由于该客户是老客户，又是资信较好的客商，所以，最后还是把货款收回来了，但是开证行已扣除了 150 美元的单证不符费和 30 元的电报费。

（11）银行费用。银行费用一般应由开证申请人承担，但目前大多信用证都规定开证行之外的费用由受益人承担。虽可以接受，但若来证要求包括开证行在内的所有费用都由受益人承担，则要求改证。

（12）注意信用证中的软条款。

（13）审核空白、边缘处加注的文字。这些字句往往是对信用证内容的重要补充或新的修改，必须要认真对待。

2．银行的审核要点

银行着重审核的内容包括信用证的真实性及开证行的政治背景、资信能力、付款责任和索汇路线等。此种审核中，对于审核后已确定真实性的信用证，应做出“印签相符”之类的字样；而对于无法鉴别表面真实性的信用证，根据 2007 年版 UCP600 第 7 条 b 款的规定，通知行需毫不延迟地通知开证行，说明信用证无法鉴别，如其决定通知受益人，则必须告知受益人信用证的真实性未能得到有效鉴定。具体如下：

（1）从政策上审核。包括开证行所在国是否与我国有往来关系，对我国政治态度如何，开证行的政治背景，该行对我国是否持友好态度，信用证中是否有歧视性内容等。

（2）对开证行的经营作风和资信情况进行审查。主要是审核信用证的金额是否与开证行的资信状况相称，一般地，银行开立信用证的最高金额是其总资产的 15/10000。

（3）索汇路线是否合理。如果索汇路线和索汇方法迂回曲折，就会影响到收汇时间甚至不能安全收汇。

（4）对信用证性质和开证行付款责任的审查。信用证的付款责任取决于信用证的种类。

（5）审核信用证的印鉴、密押是否相符。凡是信开信用证都须审核印鉴是否相符。电开信用证要审核其密押是否相符，SWIFT 信用证主要是“Message Header”和“MESSAGE TRAILER”部分。

自我能力测评

能力形成性评价表

评价指标	分值		实际得分
能看懂外销合同	快速准确看懂	20 分	
	花很长时间看懂	10 分	
	基本看不懂	0～10 分	
能翻译信用证	能快速看懂信用证各栏目并准确理解各条款	40 分	
	花很长时间看懂信用证各栏目并准确理解各条款	20～30 分	
	基本看不懂	0～19 分	
能根据外销合同审核信用证	40 分（根据实际需审核的问题算出平均分）		

任务四 填写信用证修改申请书

任务导入

宁波光明进出口公司的单证员小兰将信用证审核结果单（单证 1-8）交给本公司的业务员王华，王华给香港富华贸易有限公司，写了一份改证函，改证函如下，见单证 1-11。香港富华贸易有限公司的单证员小芳对照改证要求重新审核了信用证，确认对方改证要求合理随即填写改证申请书（单证 1-12），向原开证行提出改证申请。

单证 1-11

要求改证函

LETTER OF ASKING FOR AMENDMNENT OF THE L/C

Dear sirs,

We have received your L/C NO. 006CIM000489SBRT under S/C NO. XP79. On perusal，we find there are some discrepancies between them and some "soft clauses " we can't accept. Please amend the L/C as follows:

1．The expiry place of the L/C should be "IN CHINA".

2．The applicant's name should read "FUHUA" instead of "FUHU", the address "101QUEENS ROAD CENTRAL" instead of "105 QUEENS ROAD CENTRAL".

3．The beneficiary telephone should be " 0574-88896000" instead of "0574-88896123".

4．The amount should read "USD336 800,00"not "USD33 680,00".

5．Partial shipment should be "ALLOWED" and transshipment "PROHIBITED" not on the contrary.

6．The insurance policy or certificate should read " FOR 110 PERCENT OF THE INVOICE VALUE COVERING ALL RISKS AND WAR RISKS "not "140 PERCENT OF THE INVOICE VALUE COVERING ALL RISKS".

7．The charges clause should be "ALL BANKING CHARGES OUTSIDE THE OPENING BANK" not "INSIDE THE OPENING BANK".

We would like you to make the above mentioned amendments immediately. We would then ship the goods in time.

We are waiting for your quick reply.

Sincerely yours，

Wang Hua

完成上述任务的步骤如下

第一步：在收到对方的改证函后，要仔细阅读，读懂修改的要求和理由，把应修改的地方用彩色笔做上标注。

第二步：把信中提到的合同和信用证副本找出来，再次仔细审核一遍，以便确认对方的改证要求是否合理。

第三步：香港富华贸易有限公司的单证员小芳对信用证审核完毕，确认对方的改证要求是合理的，遂向原开证行提出改证申请并填写下列改证申请书。

建议用专业机房或多媒体教室，老师引导学生一起填写改证申请书各栏目，用极域电子教室广播教学或PPT展示整个填写的过程。

单证 1-12

改证申请书

APPLICATION FOR AMENDMENT TO LETTER OF CREDIT

To: HUA XIA BANK CO.,LTD.，HK **Date of APPLICATION:** MARCH 5，2010	**Amendment to L/C NO.** 006CIM000489SBRT **No. of Amendment** :01
Applicant: FUHU TRADE CO.,LTD., 105 QUEENS ROAD CENTRAL,HONGKONG TEL: 852-2857777	**Advising Bank:** CHINA EVERBRIGHT BANK NINGBO CN
Beneficiary: GUANGMING IMPORT & EXPORT CORPORATION 13 XINNING ROAD, NINGBO, ZHEJAING, CHINA TEL.0574-88896000	**Amount:** USD336 800,00 (SAY U S DOLLARS THREE HUNDRED AND SIXTY-SIX THOUDAND EIGHT HUNDRED ONLY)

（续）

Please amend the above L/C by Swift/Telex as follows <marked with (X) >: 1. The expiry place is "IN CHINA". 2. The applicant's name is "FUHUA" instead of "FUHU",the address "101QUEENS ROAD CENTRAL" instead of"105 QUEENS ROAD CENTRAL". 3. The beneficiary telephone should be "0574-88896000" instead of "0574-88896123" 4. The amount is "USD366 800,00" instead of USD33 680,00. 5. Partial shipment is "ALLOWED" instead of "PROHIBITED" and transshipment "PROHIBITED" instead of "ALLOWED". 6. The insurance policy or certificate is " FOR 110 PERCENT OF THE INVOICE VALUE COVERING ALL RISKS AND WAR RISKS". 7. The charges clause should be " ALL BANKING CHARGES OUTSIDE THE OPENING BANK"instead of"INSIDE". **ALL other terms and conditions remain unchanged.** **Stamp and signature(s) of the applicant:** **Xiaofang** **The above-mentioned Documentary Credit is subject to the Uniform and Practice for documentary Credits(2007revision, ICC., Paris, France. publication 600)**

第四步：巩固训练，根据下面给出的改证信息，填写改证申请书一份

训练任务

宁波舒普机电科技公司单证员马林审核了孟加拉进出口银行开来的信用证后，发现有些条款与两家公司先前达成的销售合同不符，还有一些软条款不能接受，随即填写了下列信用证审核结果单（单证 1-13），并写信要求孟加拉 SOUTH EAST EXIM LTD 公司修改信用证，孟加拉 SOUTH EAST EXIM LTD 公司的单证员 Mr. Smith 对照改证要求重新审核了信用证，确认对方改证要求是合理的，随即填写改证申请书，向原开证行提出改证申请。

单证 1-13

信用证审核结果单

信用证号	194508011405MALL
合同号	SP8021
审证结果	1. 币制错误，应该改为"USD"，因为与合同不符。 2. 汇票条款错误，应该改为"SIGHT"，因为与合同不符。 3. 货物描述中，合同号码错误，应该改为"SP8021"，贸易术语错误，应该改为 CIFCHITTAGONG, 因为与合同不符。 4. 分批装运条款错误，应该改为"ALLOWED"，因为与合同不符。 5. 目的港错误，应该改为 CHITTAGONG，因为与合同不符。 6. 商业发票要求不能接受，删除"ALL DULY SIGNED AND COUNTER-SIGNED BY L/C APPLICANT WHOSE SIGNATURES MUST BE IN CONFORMITY WITH THE SPECIMEN SIGNATURES HELD IN EXBKBDDH001 BANK."，无法办到的软条款。. 7. 保险加成率错误，应该改为"110"；险别错误，应该为"WPA AND WAR RISKS"，因为与合同不符。 8. 品质证由开证申请人签署不能接受，应该为"BY BENEFICARY/MANUFACTURE/PUBLIC SURVEYOR"，风险很大的软条款。 9. 补充条款 B 款不能接受，应该将单据改为"NON-NEGOTIABLE"，因为是风险很大的软条款。 10. 保兑要求错误，应该改为"CONFIRM"，因为与合同不符。

请根据上述信用证审核结果单，以孟加拉 SOUTH EAST EXIM LTD 公司的单证员 Mr Smith 的身份，填写下列改证申请书单证 1-14。

单证　1-14

改证申请书

APPLICATION FOR AMENDMENT TO LETTER OF CREDIT

To:________________ **L/C NO.**________________

Date________________ **Amendment No.**________________

Applicant: **Advising Bank:**

Beneficiary: **Amount:**

Please amend the above L/C by Swift/Telex as follows <marked with (X)>:

ALL other terms and conditions remain unchanged.

Stamp and signature(s) of the applicant:

The above-mentioned Documentary Credit is subject to the Uniform and Practice for documentary Credits(2007revision, ICC., Paris, France, publication 600)

第五步：教师点评，核对答案

填写完毕，教师随机选择一个或多个小组某一同学的作业进行集中点评，核对答案。

自我能力测评

能力形成性评价表

评 价 指 标	分 值		实 际 得 分
能读懂改证函	快速准确看懂	20 分	
	花很长时间看懂	10 分	
	基本看不懂	0~9 分	
能根据改证函审核信用证	30 分（根据实际需审核的问题算出平均分）		
能根据审核确认结果填改证申请书	50 分（每个小栏目 5 分，共 40 分，具体修改内容 10 分）		

任务五　填写信用证分析单

任务导入

香港华夏银行收到香港富华贸易有限公司的改证申请，审核无误后，于 2010 年 3 月 15 日开出信用证修改书，当日光大银行宁波分行开立信用证修改通知书（单证 1-15）连同收到的修改书一并转交给了出口商宁波光明进出口公司。宁波光明进出口公司的单证员小兰收到信用证修改通知书后，再次对信用证修改书进行审核无误后，遂根据原信用证和相关修改书的主要内容填写信用证分析单，作为缮制、审核和管理该票业务单证的依据。

单证 1-15

中国光大银行信用证修改通知书

中国光大银行
CHINA EVERBRIGHT BANK
CHINA EVERBRIGHT BANK, NINGBO BRANCH
ADDRESS: 148 JIEFANG SOUTH ROAD NINGBO
CABLE CHUNGKUO 信 用 证 修 改 通 知 书
TELEX: 34116/34127 BOCJS CN **NOTIFICATION OF DOCUMENTARY CREDIT**
SWIFT:EVERCNBJNBI 7688 148842
FAX: 4208843

TO 致: GUANGMING IMPORT & EXPORT CORPORATION 13 XINNING ROAD, NINGBO, ZHEJIANG, CHINA TEL. 0574-88896000		WHEN CORRESPONDING PLEASE QUOTE OUT REF NO.	AD94001A40576
ISSUING BANK 开证行 HUA XIA BANK CO., LTD. HONGKONG. HK		TRANSMITTED TO US THROUGH 转递行 REF NO.	
L/C NO.信用证号 006CIM000489SBRT	DATED 开证日期 2010/03/05	AMOUNT 金额 USD33 680. 00	EXPIRY PLACE 有效地 FOREIGN
EXPIRY DATE 效期 2019/05/09	TENOR 期限 SIGHT	CHARGE 未付费用 RMB0.00	CHARGE BY 费用承担人 BENE
RECEIVED VIA 来证方式 SWIFT	AVAILABLE 是否生效 VALID	TEST/SIGN 印押是否相符 YES	CONFIRM 我行是否保兑 YES
AMEND NO.修改次数 01	AMEND DATE 修改日期 2010/03/15	INCREASE AMT 增额 USD30 312 00	DECREASE AMT 减额 0

DEAR SIRS 敬启者:

WE HAVE PLEASURE IN ADVISING YOU THAT WE HAVE RECEIVED FROM THE A/M BANK AMENDMENT TO THE CAPTIONED L/C, CONTENTS OF WHICH ARE AS PER ATTACHED SHEET(S).

兹通知贵公司，我行收自上述银行信用证修改书一份，内容见附件。

THIS AMENDMENT SHOULD BE ATTACHED TO THE CAPTIONED L/C ADVISED BY US OTHERWISE THE BENEFICIARY WILL BE RESPONSIBLE FOR ANY CONSEQUENCE ARISING THEREFROM.

本修改须附于有关信用证，否则，贵公司须对因此而产生的后果承担责任。

REMARKS 备注: ______________________

THIS AMENDMENT CONSISTS OF TWO SHEET(S), INCLUDING THE COVERING LETTER AND ATTACHMENT(S). 本修改连同附信及附件共 2 页。

KINDLY TAKE NOTES PARTIAL ACCEPTANCE OF THIS AMENDMENT IS NOT ALLOWED.

本修改不能部分接受。

如本信用证中有无法办到的条款及/或错误，请径与开证申请人联系，进行必要的修改，以排除交单时可能发生的问题。

THIS AMENDMENT ADVISED SUBJECT TO ICC UCP PUBLICATION NO.600.

本信修改之通知系遵循国际商会跟单信用证统一惯例第 600 号出版物办理。

此证如有任何问题及疑虑，请与结算业务部审证科联络，电话：0592-5129696, 5129595。

YOURS FAITHFULLY
FOR CHINA EVERBRIGHT BANK

下面是香港华夏银行开来的信用证修改书（单证 1-16）：

单证 1-16

MT707 格式信用证修改书

AMENDMENT TO A DOCUMENTARY CREDIT

15/03/10-09:30:34 LocalSwiftAcks-8414-136437

…………………………………………… **Instance Type and Transmission**………………… ……....

Notification (Transmission) of Original Sent to SWIFT(ACK)

Network Delivery Status : Network Ack

Priority/Delivery : Normal

Message Input Reference : 2025 100305BKHYHK JA92A 1496 555995

…………………………………………… **Message Header**……………………………………………...

Swift Input : FIN 707 Issue of a Documentary Credit

Sender : BKHYHK JA92A 1496 555995

HUA XIA BANK CO., LTD.

HONGKONG. HK

Receiver : EVERCNBJNBI 7688 148842

CHINA EVERBRIGHT BANK

NINGBO CN

MUR : 2010030502001540

……**Message Text**………………………………

Sender's Reference *20：HX0190123

Receiver's Reference *21：AD94001A40576

Issuing Bank 's Reference 23：9708MN097542

Issuing Bank 52A：BKHYHK JA92A 1496 555995

HUA XIA BANK CO. LTD

HONGKONG. HK

DATE OF ISSUE 31C：100305

DATE OF AMENDMENT 30：100315

Number of Amendment 26E：01

Beneficiary(before this amendment) *59：GUANGMING IMPORT & EXPORT CORPORATION

13 XINNING ROAD, NINGBO, ZHEJAING, CHINA

TEL. 0574-88896123

New Date of Expiry 31E：100425

Increase of Documentary Credit Amount 32B：USD30 312, 00

New Documentary Credit Amount After 34B：USD33 680, 00

NARRATIVE 79：PLS IN FIELD 31D INSERT NOW:

CHINA

INSTEAD OF

AT OUR COUNTER

PLS IN FIELD 59 AMEND AS FOLLOWS:

GUANGMING IMPORT & EXPORT CORPORATION

XINNING ROAD, NINGBO, ZHEJAING, CHINA

TEL: 0574-88896000

PLS IN FIELD 50 AMEND AS FOLLOWS:

FUHUA TRADE CO.,LTD.,

101 QUEENS ROAD CENTRAL,HONGKONG

TEL: 852-2857777

PLS IN FIELD 32B AMEND TO READ NOW

USD33 680, 00

INSTEAD OF

USD3 368, 00

（续）

		PLS IN FIELD 43P AMEND TO READ NOW ALLOWED INSTEAD OF PROHIBITED PLS IN FIELD 43T AMEND TO READ NOW PROHIBITED INSTEAD OF ALLOWED PLS IN FIELD 46A ITEM 4 AMEND AS FOLLOWS: FOR 110 PERCENT OF THE INVOICE VALUE COVERING ALL RISKS AND WAR RISKS . ALL OTHER TERMS AND CONDITIONS REMAIN UNCHAN
Sender to Receiver Info.	72:	CREDIT IS SUBJECT TO ICC UCP PUBLICATION NO.600.
TRAILER	:	MAC: 4567TR88 CHK:78GH5R08FD68

完成上述任务的步骤如下

第一步：收到信用证修改通知书后，对照信用证审核结果单对修改书再次进行审核，如发现还有错误，应再次提出修改意见，本例中小兰审核后，确认修改书无误，随即电传接受，修改书生效。

第二步：小兰将信用证修改书与原证装订在一起。切记信用证修改书是原证不可分割的一部分，必须附在一起使用。

第三步：小兰开始结合原证和修改书，对该信用证做具体分析，并填写下列信用证分析单，为今后进一步制单做准备。

职场经验

如果你是一位新手，为了本票货物日后制单的便利，你不妨将原证复印一份，对照修改书的要求用彩笔在副本信用证上直接进行修改，这样信用证修改书和原信用证合二为一，既可避免日后制单出错，又可节省制单时间。

以下是小兰在原证副本上直接做出的修改（单证 1-17）。

单证 1-17

ISSUE OF A DOCUMENTARY CREDIT

05/03/10-09:30:34 LocalSwiftAcks-8414-136437

……………………………… **Instance Type and Transmission**………………… ……....

Notification (Transmission) of Original Sent to SWIFT(ACK)

Network Delivery Status : Network Ack

Priority/Delivery : Normal

Message Input Reference : 2025 100305BKHYHK JA92A 1496 555995

……………………………… **Message Header**……………………………………………..

Swift Input : FIN 701 Issue of a Documentary Credit

Sender : BKHYHK JA92A 1496 555995

（续）

HUA XIA BANK CO., LTD.
HONGKONG. HK

Receiver : EVERCNBJNBI 7688 148842
CHINA EVERBRIGHT BANK
NINGBO CN

MUR : 2010030502001540

……Message Text……………………………

SEQUENCE OF TOTAL *27：1 / 1

FORM OF DOC，CREDIT *40A：IRREVOCABLE

DOC. CREDIT NUMBER *20：006CIM000489SBRT

DATE OF ISSUE 31C：100305

APPLICABLE RULES *40E：UCP LATEST VERSION

DATE AND PLACE OF EXPIRY *31D：DATE100509~~AT HUA XIA BANK'S COUNTER~~(改成 IN CHINA)

APPLICAN *50：~~FUHU~~（*改成 FUHUA*）TRADE CO.,LTD., ~~105~~（*改成 101*）QUEENS ROAD CENTRAL,HONGKONG
TEL: 852-2857777

BENEFICIARY *59：GUANGMING IMPORT & EXPORT CORPORATION
13 XINNING ROAD, NINGBO, ZHEJAING, CHINA
TEL.0574-8889~~6123~~（*改成 0574-88896000*）

CURRENCY CODE,AMOUNT *32B：~~USD3268, 00~~（*改成 USD33 680,00*）

MAXIMUM CREDIT AMOUNT 39B：NOT EXCEEDING L/C AMOUT

AVAILABLE WITH / BY *41D：ANY BANK IN CHINA

BY NEGOTIATION

DRAFTS AT 42C：DRAFTS AT SIGHT

FOR FULL INVOICE COST

DRAWEE 52A：BKHYHK JA92A 1496 555995
HUA XIA BANK CO., LTD
HONGKONG. HK

PARTIAL SHIPMENTS 43P：~~PROHIBITED~~（*改成 ALLOWED*）

TRANSSHIPMENT 43T：~~ALLOWED~~（*改成 PROHIBITED*）

LOADING ON BOARD 44E：ANY PORT IN CHINA

FOR TRANSPORTATION TO …44 F：HONGKONG

LATEST DATE OF SHIPMENT 44 C：100405

DESCRIPTION OF GOODS 45A：100PCT NYLON FABRICS AS PER S/C NO. E034579
INCOTERMS：CIF HONGKONG

DOCUMENTS REQUIRED 46A：

1. SIGNED COMMERCIAL INVOICE IN TRIPLICATE AND MUST CERTIFIED BY CHINA'S CHAMBER OF COMMERCE THE GOODS ARE OF CHINESE ORIGIN ONLY.

2. FULL SET OF CLEAN ON BOARD OCEAN BILLS OF LADING, MADE OUT TO ORDER OF SHIPPER AND BLANK ENDORSED AND MARKED " FREIGHT PREPAID "AND NOTIFY APPLICANT.

3. PACKING LIST IN DUPLICATE.

4. FULL SET OF NEGOTIABLE INSURANCE POLICY OR CERTIFICATE BLANK ENDORSED FOR ~~140~~（*改成 110%*）PERCENT OF THE INVOICE VALUE COVERING ~~ALL RISKS.~~（*改成 ALL RISKS AND WAR RISKS AS PER CCIC. 1981.1.1*）

5. CERTIFICATE OF QUALITY IN 2 ORIGINALS ISSUED BY MANUFACTURER.

（续）

6. CERTIFICATE OF ORIGIN GSP IN FORM A ISSUED BY THE AUTHORITY IN TWO ORIGINALS. IN ADDITON, THE CERTIFICATE OF ORIGIN MUST STATE THAT THE COUNTRY OF ORIGIN OF GOODS SHIPPED HAS BEEN MENTIONED ON EACH CARTON OF THE CONSINGMENT.

7. SHIP'S CLASSIFICATION ISSUED BY LIOYDS' IN LONDON.

8. BENEFICIARY'S CERTIFIED COPY OF FAX DISPATCHED TO THE APPLICANT WITHIN 7 DAYS AFTER SHIPMENT ADVISING THE CONTRACT NUMBER, NAME OF COMMODITY, QUANTITY, INVOICE VALUE, BILL OF LOADING, BILL OF LOADING DATE, THE ETA DATE AND SHIPPING CO.

ADDITIONAL CONDITIONS 47A：

1. SHIPMENT MUST NOT BE MADE EARLIER THAN THE CREDIT ISSUING DATE.

2. ONE SET OF NON-NEGOTIABLE SHIPPING DOCUMENTS TO BE SENT TO THE APPLICANT THROUGH COURIER SERVICE WITHIN 02 DAY AFTER SHIPMENT AND A COURIER RECEIPT OF WHICH MUST ACCOMPANY THE ORIGINAL DOCUMENTS STATED ABOVE.

3. DISCREPANCY FEE OF USD35.00 WILL BE DEDUCTED FROM THE PROCEEDS OF EACH PRESENTATION OF DISCREPANT DOCUMENTS.

4. ALL DOCUMENTS MUST BE FORWARDED IN ONE LOT BY EXPRESS.

5. ALL DOCUMENTS MUST INDICATE L/C NO. CONTRACT NO. AND NAME OF ISSUING BANK.

CHARGES 71B： All BANKING CHARGES ~~INSIDE~~ （*改成 OUTSIDE*）THE OPENING BANK ARE FOR BENEFICIARY'S ACCOUNT.

PERIOD FOR PRESENTATION 48：

21 DAYS FROM THE DATE OF SHIPMENT,
BUT NOT LATER THAN THE CREDIT VALIDITY.

CONFIRMATION INSTRUCTION 49：CONFIRM

ADVISE THROUGH BANK 57A：EVERCNBJNBI 7688 148842
CHINA EVERBRIGHT BANK
NINGBO CN

SENDER TO RECEIVER INFORMATION 72：

PLS ADVISE US WHEN ADVISING THIS L/C TO BENEFICIARY

……………………………………MESSAGE TRAILER………………………………………………

TRAILER ORDER IS MAC PAC ENC CHK TNG PDE

MAC: CF6F97BC

CHK: F04138D93C1B

DLM：BKHYHKJAXXX 1003032233

假设你是小兰，请根据修改后的信用证（单证 1-17），填写下列信用证分析单（单证 1-18）。

单证 1-18

信用证分析单

<table>
<tr><td>银行编号</td><td></td><td rowspan="2">合同号</td><td rowspan="2">S/C NO.
E034579</td><td rowspan="2">受益人</td><td colspan="3" rowspan="2">GUANGMING IMPORT & EXPORT CORPORATION
13 XINNING ROAD, NINGBO, ZHEJAING, CHINA
TEL: 0574-88896000</td></tr>
<tr><td>信用证证号</td><td>006CIM000489SBRT</td></tr>
<tr><td>开证银行</td><td colspan="3">HUA XIA BANK CO.,LTD.
HONGKONG. HK</td><td>进口商</td><td colspan="3">FUHUA TRADE CO.,LTD.,
101QUEENS ROAD CENTRAL,
HONGKONG TEL: 852-2857777</td></tr>
<tr><td>开证日期</td><td>MAR.5,2010</td><td>信用证效期</td><td>APRIL
5,2010</td><td rowspan="2">起运
口岸</td><td rowspan="2">NINGBO</td><td rowspan="2">目的港</td><td rowspan="2">HONGKONG</td></tr>
<tr><td>修改日期</td><td>MAR.15,2010</td><td>信用证到期地</td><td>IN CHINA</td></tr>
</table>

（续）

<table>
<tr><td>信用证金额</td><td colspan="5">CIF HONGKONG USD33 680, 00
SAY U S DOLLARS THIRTY THREE THOUDAND SIX HUNDRED AND EIGHTY ONLY</td><td>可否转运</td><td colspan="2">ALLOWED</td><td colspan="2">可否分批</td><td colspan="2">PROHIBITED</td></tr>
<tr><td>汇票付款人</td><td colspan="3">HUA XIA BANK CO., LTD，HONGKONG. HK</td><td>汇票期限</td><td>AT SIGHT</td><td>装运期限</td><td colspan="6">APRIL5,2010</td></tr>
<tr><td>交单日</td><td colspan="5">Within 15 days after the date of shipment</td><td>寄单日</td><td colspan="6">装运后2天内寄副本运输单据给开证申请人</td></tr>
<tr><td>注意事项</td><td colspan="12">1．装船后2日内用快件给开证申请人寄一份副本装运单据。快件收据和正本单据附在一起提交。
2．提单上标明“FREIGHT PREPAID”。
3．商业发票上要有中国商会证明货物是中国原产的。
4. 产地证要标上“THE COUNTRY OF ORIGIN OF GOODS SHIPPED HAS BEEN MENTIONED ON EACH CARTON OF THE CONSIGNMENT”。
5．所有单据上都要标明信用证号合同号和开证行名称。</td></tr>
<tr><td>单证名称</td><td>商业发票</td><td>提单</td><td>保险单</td><td>装箱单</td><td>品质证</td><td>普惠制产地证</td><td>船级证明</td><td>装运通知</td><td>寄单邮据</td><td>受益人证明</td><td>汇票</td><td>其他</td></tr>
<tr><td>银行</td><td>3 正</td><td>3 正</td><td>1 正</td><td>2 正</td><td>2 正</td><td>2 正</td><td>1 正</td><td>1 正</td><td>1 正</td><td>1 正</td><td>2 正</td><td></td></tr>
<tr><td>客户</td><td>1 副</td><td>1 副</td><td></td><td>1 副</td><td></td><td></td><td>1 副</td><td>1 副</td><td>1 副</td><td></td><td></td><td></td></tr>
<tr><td rowspan="2">提单</td><td colspan="2">抬头人</td><td colspan="4">TO ORDER OF SHIPPER</td><td rowspan="2">保险</td><td>险别</td><td colspan="4">ALL RISKS AND WAR RISKS AS PER CCIC. 1981.1.1</td></tr>
<tr><td colspan="2">通知人</td><td colspan="4">FUHUA TRADE CO.,LTD.,
101 QUEENS ROAD CENTRAL,HONGKONG
TEL: 852-2857777</td><td>加成率</td><td colspan="4">FOR 110 PERCENT OF THE INVOICE VALUE</td></tr>
<tr><td colspan="13">其他注意事项：</td></tr>
</table>

第四步：巩固训练，结合原证和相关信用证修改书填写下列信用证分析结果单

训练导入

宁波舒普机电科技公司收到中国银行宁波分行信用证修改通知书和随附的孟加拉进出口银行开立的信用证修改书后，单证员马林再次对信用证修改书进行审核无误后，根据原信用证和相关修改书的主要内容填写信用证分析单，作为缮制、审核和管理该票业务单证的依据。

单证员马林是一位新手，他完成这一任务的步骤如下：

步骤一：找出原来审核过的信用证及相关合同，信用证审核结果单，再次对信用证修改书进行审核；

步骤二：审核无误后，为了制单便利，他将信用证修改书和原证复印了一份，根据信用证修改书的要求在原证复印件上直接用彩笔进行了修改，修改后的信用证如下所示（注：两证合二为一，为以后制单提供方便）；

步骤三：他将信用证修改书和原证装订在一起，然后对照步骤二修改的信用证填写下列信用证分析结果单。

马林根据信用证修改书的要求，在原证副本上进行修改后的信用证如下（单证 1-19）。

单证 1-19

马林修改后的信用证

Our Reference:00333-11-1725025-1 ISS 000

Sender exbkbddh001
EXPORT IMPORT BANK OF BANGLADESH LTD.
SHARIF MANSION
56-57MOTUHEE
COMMERCAIL AREA
1000DHAKA

Message Type: MT 700
27: SEQUENCE OF TOTAL
1/1
40A: FORM OF DOC，CREDIT
IRREVOCABLE
20: DOC. CREDIT NUMBER
194508011405MALL
31C: DATE OF ISSUE
081203
40E: APPLICABLE RULES
UCP LATEST VERSION
31D: DATE AND PLACE OF EXPIRY
090130 AT NEGOT IATION BANK'S COUNTER
50: APPLICANT
SOUTH EAST EXIM LTD.
476/C.D.I. ROAD MALIBAGH
DHAKA-1219, BANGLADESH
59: BENEFICIARY
NINGBO SUPPER ELECTRONIC MACHINERY CO.,LTD.
528,JINYUAN,ROAD
INVESTMENT AND ENTERPRISE CENTRAL ZONE
YINZHOU DISTRICT, NINGBO CHINA
32B: CURRENCY CODE,AMOUNT
~~HKD~~（*改成 USD*）121,500.00
41D: AVAILABLE WITH / BY
ANY BANK IN BENEFICIARY COUNTRY
BY NEGOTIATION
42C: DRAFTS AT
~~AT 90 DAYS FROM B/L DATE DRAUN ON US~~（*改成 SIGHT*）
52A: DRAWEE
EXBKBDDH001
43P: PARTIAL SHIPMENTS
~~PROHIBITED~~（*改成 ALLOWED*）
43T: TRANSSHIPMENT
ALLOWED
44E: LOADING ON BOARD
ANY PORT IN CHINA
44F: FOR TRANSPORTATION TO
CHITTAGONG
44C: LATEST DATE OF SHIPMENT
090115

（续）

45A：DESCRIPTION OF GOODS

SUPREME BRAND SEWING MACHINE ,DETAILS AS PER S/C NO . 8021

DTD25-NOV-2008

INCOTERMS：CIF CASABLANKA

46A：DOCUMENTS REQUIRED

A) SIGNED COMMERCIAL INVOICE IN EIGHT FOLD IN ENGLISH CERTIFYING MERCHANDISE TO BE OF CHINA ORIGIN QUOTING L/C NO. 194508011405MALL, ~~ALL DULY SIGNED AND COUNTER-SIGNED BY L/C APPLICANT WHOSE SIGNATURES MUST BE IN CONFORMITY WITH THE SPECIMEN SIGNATURES HELD IN EXBKBDDH001 BANK.~~ （*删除这部分*）

B) FULL SET OF CLEAN ON BOARD OCEAN BILL OF LADING, ISSUED TO ORDER OF L/C ISSUING BANK , MARKED " FREIGHT PREPAID "AND NOTIFY APPLICANT.

C) PACKING SHOULD BE EXPORT STANDARD SEA WORTHY AND FIVE COPIES OF PACKING LIST MUST ACCOMPANY THE ORIGINAL DOCUMENTS.

D) FULL SET OF NEGOTIABLE INSURANCE POLICY OR CERTIFICATE BLANK ENDORSED FOR ~~130~~（*改成 110%*）PERCENT OF THE INVOICE VALUE COVERING ~~WPA.~~ .（*改成 WPA AND WAR RISKS*）

E) NO SOLID WOOD PACKING CERTIFICATE ISSUED BY MANUFACTURER.

F) CERTIFICATE OF QUALITY ISSUED BY ~~APPLICANT~~ .（改成 *MANUFACTURE*）

G) CERTIFICATE OF ORIGIN ISSUED BY THE BENEFICIARY .

H) BENEFICIARY'S CERTIFIED COPY OF FAX DISPATCHED TO THE APPLICANT WITHIN 2 DAYS AFTER SHIPMENT ADVISING PARTICULAR OF SHIPMENT.

47A：ADDITIONAL CONDITIONS

A) TELEGRAPHIC TRANSFER REIMBURSEMENT CLAIMS ARE SPECIFICALLY PROHIBITED UNDER THIS CREDIT.

B) ONE SET OF ~~NEGOTIABLE~~（*改成 NON-NEGOTIABLE*） SHIPPING DOCUMENTS TO BE SENT TO THE APPLICANT THROUGH COURIER SERVICE WITHIN 07 WORKING DAYS AFTER SHIPMENT AND A COURIER RECEIPT OF WHICH MUST ACCOMPANY THE ORIGINAL DOCUMENTS.

C) EACH DRAFT ACCOMPANYING DOCUMENTS MUST STATE "DRAWN UNDER CREDIT NUMBER 194508011405 MALL OF EXBKBDDH001, EXPORT IMPORT BANK OF BANGLADESH LTD. SHARIF MANSION,56-57MOTUHEE, COMMERCIALAREA,1000DHAKA".

D) SHIPMENT/TRANSSHIPMENT BY ISRAEL ARE STRICTLY PROHIBITED AND A CERTIFICATE TO THIS EFFECT SHOULD ACCOMPANY EACH SET OF DOCUMENTS.

71B：CHARGES

All BANKING CHARGES OUTSIDE THE OPENING BANK ARE FOR BENEFICIARY'S ACCOUNT.

48： PERIOD FOR PRESENTATION

15 DAYS FROM THE DATE OF SHIPMENT,

BUT NOT LATER THAN THE CREDIT VALIDITY.

49： CONFIRMATION INSTRUCTION

~~WITHOUT~~（改成 *CONFIRM*）

78： INSTR TO THE PAY/ACCE/NEG BANK

A) DISCREPANT DOCUMENTS MUST NOT BE NEGOTIATED WITHOUT OUR PRIROR APPROVAL.

B) DOCUMENT SHOULD BE MAILED BY COURIER IN ONE LOTS TO EXBKBDDH001, SHARIF MANSION,56-57 MOTUHEE,COMMERCIAL AREA,1000 DHAKA".

C) WE SHALL ARRANGE REIMBURSEMENT /PAYMENT OF THE BILL AS PER THE INSTRUCTION OF THE NEGOTIATING BANK WILL UPON RECEIPT OF CREDIT CONFORM DOCUMENTS AT OUR COUNTER.

57A：ADVISE THROUGH BANK

BKNBCN2NXXX

BANK OF NINGBO

NINGBO CN

72：SENDER TO RECEIVER INFORMATION

THIS CREDIT IS SUBJECT TO UCP DC (2007 RIVISION) ICC PUBLICATION NO.600.

……………………………………END OF MESSAGE……………………………………

请你帮马林，根据上面修改后的信用证填写下列信用证分析结果单（单证 1-20）。

单证 1-20

信用证分析单

<table>
<tr><td>银行编号</td><td colspan="2"></td><td rowspan="2">合同号</td><td rowspan="2"></td><td rowspan="2">受益人</td><td rowspan="2" colspan="3"></td></tr>
<tr><td>信用证证号</td><td colspan="2"></td></tr>
<tr><td>开证银行</td><td colspan="4"></td><td>进口商</td><td colspan="3"></td></tr>
<tr><td>开证日期</td><td></td><td>信用证效期</td><td colspan="2"></td><td rowspan="2">起运口岸</td><td rowspan="2"></td><td rowspan="2">目的港</td><td rowspan="2"></td></tr>
<tr><td>改证日期</td><td></td><td>信用证到期地</td><td colspan="2"></td></tr>
<tr><td>信用证金额</td><td colspan="4"></td><td>可否转运</td><td></td><td>可否分批</td><td></td></tr>
<tr><td>汇票付款人</td><td colspan="2"></td><td>汇票期限</td><td></td><td>装运期限</td><td colspan="3"></td></tr>
<tr><td>交单日</td><td colspan="4"></td><td>寄单日</td><td colspan="3"></td></tr>
<tr><td>注意事项</td><td colspan="8"></td></tr>
<tr><td>单证名称</td><td></td><td></td><td></td><td></td><td></td><td></td><td></td><td></td></tr>
<tr><td>银行</td><td></td><td></td><td></td><td></td><td></td><td></td><td></td><td></td></tr>
<tr><td>客户</td><td></td><td></td><td></td><td></td><td></td><td></td><td></td><td></td></tr>
<tr><td rowspan="2">提单</td><td>抬头人</td><td colspan="3"></td><td rowspan="2">保险</td><td>险别</td><td colspan="2"></td></tr>
<tr><td>通知人</td><td colspan="3"></td><td>加成率</td><td colspan="2"></td></tr>
<tr><td colspan="9">其他注意事项</td></tr>
</table>

第五步：教师点评，核对答案

填写完毕，教师随机选择一个或多个小组某一同学的作业集中点评，核对答案。

自我能力测评

能力形成性评价表

评价指标	分 值		实际得分
能看懂信用证的内容	快速准确看懂	30分	
	花很长时间看懂	30分	
	基本看不懂	0~20分	
能看懂信用证修改书的内容，并根据修改书要求做出修改	快速准确看懂，并修改	40分	
	花很长时间看懂，并修改	30分	
	基本看不懂，无法修改	0~20分	
能根据信用证填写分析表	30分		
总 分			

知识拓展

一、SWIFT信用证格式

SWIFT（Society for Worldwide Interbank Financial Telecommunication）为环球银行财务电

讯协会，简称环银电协，是1973年5月根据比利时法律在布鲁塞尔成立的合作性协会，作为一种银行间的合作性的、自动的世界通信系统，它经过20多年的发展，已拥有近100个国家的4 000家左右的成员银行。中国银行于1983年2月加入该系统，其他的一些中资银行也陆续加入该系统。SWIFT每周7天，每天24小时连续不断地运行，其成员银行能在几分钟内互相传递信息。

SWIFT电讯系统的特点是电文标准化。采用SWIFT信用证，必须遵守SWIFT使用手册的规定，使用专门的格式和代号，而且信用证必须按国际商会制定的《跟单信用证统一惯例》的规定进行，在信用证中可以省去银行的承诺条款，但不能免去银行所应承担的义务。

当前银行开立信用证的主要方式是SWIFT，开立SWIFT信用证的格式代号为MT700和MT701，修改信用证的格式代号为MT707。

SWIFT信用证MT700、MT701的开立格式

M/O ①	Tag 代号	Field Name 栏目名称	Content/Options 内容
M	27	Sequence of Total 合计次序	1n/1n② 1个数字/1个数字
M	40A	Form of Documentary Credit 跟单信用证类别	24x 24个字
M	20	Documentary Credit Number 信用证号码	16x 16个字
O	23	Reference to Pre-Advice 预告的编号	16x 16个字
O	31C	Date of Issue 开证日期	6n 6个数字
M	31D	Date and Place of Expiry 到期日及地点	6n29x 6个数字/29个字
O	51A	Applicant Bank 申请人银行	A or D A 或 D
M	50	Applicant 申请人	4*35x 4行×35个字
M	59	Beneficiary 受益人	4*35x 4行×35个字
M	32B	Currency Code, Amount 币别代号、金额	3a15n 3个字母/15个数字
O	39A	Percentage Credit Amount Tolerance 信用证金额加减百分率	2n/2n 2个数字/2个数字
O	39B	Maximum Credit Amount 最高信用证金额	13x 13个字
O	39C	Additional Amounts Covered 可附加金额	4*35x 4行×35个字

（续）

M/O ①	Tag 代号	Field Name 栏目名称	Content/Options 内容
M	41A	Available With…By… 向……银行押汇，押汇方式为……	A or D A 或 D
O	42C	Drafts at… 汇票期限	3*35x 3 行×35 个字
O	42A	Drawee 付款人	A or D A 或 D
O	42M	Mixed Payment Details 混合付款指示	4*35x 4 行×35 个字
O	42P	Deferred Payment Details 延迟付款指示	4*35x 4 行×35 个字
O	43P	Partial Shipments 分批装船	1*35x 1 行×35 个字
O	43T	Transshipment 转船	1*35x 1 行×35 个字
O	44E	Loading on Board/Dispatch/Taking in Charge at/from… 由……装船/发送/接管	1*65x 1 行×65 个字
O	44F	For Transportation to… 装运至……	1*65x 1 行×65 个字
O	44C	Latest Date of Shipment 最后装船日	6n 6 个数字
O	44D	Shipment Period 装运期间	6*65x 6 行×65 个字
O	45A	Description of Goods and/or Services 货物叙述和/或各种服务	50*65x 50 行×65 个字
O	46A	Documents Required 应提示单据	50*65x 50 行×65 个字
O	47A	Additional Conditions 附加条件	50*65x 50 行×65 个字
O	71B	Charges 费用	6*35x 6 行×35 个字
O	48	Period for Presentation 提示期间	4*35x 4 行×35 个字
M	49	Confirmation Instructions 保兑期间	7x 7 个字
O	53A	Reimbursement Bank 偿付行	A or D A 或 D
O	78	Instructions to the Paying/Accepting/Negotiation Bank 对付款/承兑/议付行之指示	12*65x 12 行×65 个字
O	57A	Advise Through Bank 通过……银行通知	A,B or D A,B 或 D
O	72	Sender to Receiver Information 银行间的备注	6*35x 6 行×35 个字

注：① M/O 为 Mandatory 与 Optional 的缩写，前者是指必要项目，后者为任意项目。
② 合计次序是指本证的页次，共两个数字，前后各一，如“1/2”，其中“2”指本证共 2 页，“1”指本页为第 1 页。

具体信用证范本可见前面单证 1-6 和 1-8。

对已开出的 SWIFT 信用证进行修改，则需要采用 MT707 标准格式。

SWIFT 信用证修改书的格式代号为 MT707

代号（Tag）	栏位名称（Field Name）
20	送讯银行的编号（Sender's Reference）
21	收讯银行的编号（Receiver's Reference）
23	开证银行的编号（Issuing Bank's Reference）
52A	开证银行（Issuing Bank）
31C	开证日期（Date of Issue）
!30	修改日期（Date of Amendment）
26E	修改序号（Number of Amendment）
59	受益人（修改以前的）（Beneficiary, before this amendment）
31E	新的到期日（New Date of Expiry）
32B	信用证金额的增加（Increase of Documentary Credit Amount）
33B	信用证金额的减少（Decrease of Documentary Credit Amount）
34B	修改后新的信用证金额（New Documentary Credit Amount After）
39A	信用证金额加减百分率（Percentage Credit Amount Tolerance）
39B	最高信用证金额（Maximum Credit Amount）
39C	可附加金额（Additional Amount Covered）
44A	由……装船/发送/接管（Loading on Board/Dispatch/Taking in Charge at /from…）
44B	装运至……（For Transportation to…）
`44C	最后装船日（Latest Date of Shipment）
44D	装船期间（Shipment Period）
79	叙述（Narrative）
72	银行间备注（Sender to Receiver Information）

二、UCP600 简介

截止 2006 年 6 月，国际商会新惯例起草工作小组已经推出了 3 版完整的征求意见稿，即 UCP600。在 2006 年 10 月的国际会议上，各国国际商会国家委员会代表对 UCP600 予以表决通过，并于 2007 年 7 月 1 日生效。这次修订较之 UCP500 有较大幅度改动，将原来 UCP500 的 49 条减为现有的 39 条，格式排版参照 ISBP，不论是在逻辑安排、名词术语或是各当事人权利义务方面，都有改观，并都有更清楚明确的解释。

（一）"信用证"的含义和"相符交单"的原则

1. 第一条 UCP 的适用范围

UCP600 乃一套规则，适用于所有的其文本中明确表明受本惯例约束的跟单信用证（下称信用证）（在其可适用的范围内，包括备用信用证）。除非信用证明确修改或排除，本惯例各条文对信用证所有当事人均具有约束力。

2. UCP600 第二条定义

就本惯例而言，信用证“指一项不可撤销的安排，无论其名称或描述如何，该项安排构成开证行对相符交单予以承付的确定承诺。”从该定义可以看出。从 UCP600 起，国际贸易中的信用证都是不可撤销的，不存在可撤销的信用证。

上述定义也确立了“相符交单”的原则，UCP600“相符交单”不同于 UCP500 的“单证相符”、“单单相符”。那么何谓“相符交单”呢？UCP600 第 2 条指出，就本惯例而言，相符交单“指与信用证条款、本惯例的相关适用条款和国际标准银行实务一致的交单”。这里涉及与信用证条款、本惯例的相关适用条款和国际标准银行实务三个一致。信用证条款好理解，如讲到发票，就与信用证的发票条款一致，讲到汇票，就与信用证中的汇票条款一致，依此类推；本惯例的相关适用条款就是 UCP600 共有 39 个条款，至于相关适用，就是对号入座，到 39 个条款中去找对应的条款；国际标准银行实务（简称 ISBP）很多内容的语言表达更为清楚，操作指导性更强，对单据的制作更加详细化。信用证的受益人可以根据需要在 UCP 600 和 ISBP 中有针对性地找到某种单据的制作要求，这样就能达到相符交单。

（二）信用证与合同

（1）就其性质而言，信用证与可能作为其开立基础的销售合同或其他合同是相互独立的交易，即使信用证中含有对此类合同的任何援引，银行也与该合同无关，且不受其约束。因此，银行关于承付、议付或履行信用证项下其他义务的承诺，不受申请人基于与开证行或与受益人之间的关系而产生的任何请求或抗辩的影响。受益人在任何情况下不得利用银行之间或申请人与开证行之间的合同关系。

（2）开证行应劝阻申请人试图将基础合同、形式发票等文件作为信用证组成部分的做法。

（三）UCP600 与 UCP500 的具体区别

1. 形式方面的变化

修订版的条文编排参照了 ISP98（《国际备用证惯例》）的格式，对 UCP500 的 49 个条款进行了大幅度的调整及增删，变成现在的 39 条。

第 1～5 条为总则部分，包括 UCP 的适用范围、定义条款、解释规则、信用证的独立性等；第 6～13 条明确了有关信用证的开立、修改、各当事人的关系与责任等问题；第 14～16 条是关于单据的审核标准、单证相符或不符的处理的规定；第 17～28 条属单据条款，包括商业发票、运输单据、保险单据等；第 29～32 条规定了有关款项支取的问题；第 33～37 条属于银行的免责条款；第 38 条是关于可转让信用证的规定；第 39 条是关于款项让渡的规定。

其中第 2 条（定义条款）和第 15 条（相符交单）为新增条款；删除了原 UCP500 中 7 个不必要或过时的条款：第 5 条（开立信用证的指示）、第 6 条（可撤销与不可撤销信用证）、第 8 条（信用证的撤销）、第 12 条（不完整与不清楚的指示）、第 30 条（运输行出具的运输单据）、第 33 条（运费到付/预付运输单据）、第 38 条（其他单据）。

2. 内容方面的变化

（1）增加了专门的定义条款，体现了 UCP600 细化规定的精神，对一些术语作出定义不仅可以使概念明晰化，从而有利于条款的理解与适用，而且更可以解决一些地方法律适用的问题；引入了“Honour”（兑付）的概念；改进了议付的定义。

（2）约定了解释规则，摒弃了可撤销信用证。

（3）开证行、保兑行及指定银行的责任更清晰、确定，规范了第二通知行的做法。

（4）银行的审单标准更为明确。将审单时间从“不超过 7 个银行工作日的合理时间”改为“最多不超过 5 个银行工作日”；明确了交单期限的适用范围；将单据与信用证相符的要求细化为“单内相符、单单相符、单证相符”。

（5）将银行处理不符单据的选择增加到四种：持单听候交单人的处理；持单直到开证申请人接受不符单据；径直退单；依据事先得到交单人的指示行事。

3．概念的变化

（1）对基本概念进行了定义。UCP 自 20 世纪 30 年代问世，先后经历了六次修订。然而，不论哪一个版本，均未对诸如开证行、申请人、受益人等相关当事人及保兑、议付和交单等相关行为进行定义。对这些概念，只能通过上下文及实务中形成的习惯认识来理解。针对同一个概念，由于语言、文化，案例乃至价值取向的不同，不同国家、不同当事人、甚至不同法院往往会有不同的解释，因此就会造成对 UCP 条款的曲解与误用，出现惯例统一而标准相异的现象。

对众多概念进行定义，是一项复杂而又系统的正本清源工程，它不仅涉及概念本身，更重要的是涉及各概念之间的相互联系。统一实务中形成的不同观点，建立一套既与 ICC（国际商会）以往观点不相矛盾又能经得起实践和时间检验的清晰标准是非常有意义的。ICC 在制定 ISP98 时曾表示，概念的定义是一个“可怕的尝试”。尽管如此，UCP600 最终还是迈出了关键性的一步。

（2）删除了信用证“可撤销”的概念。按照 UCP500 第 6 条和第 8 条，信用证可分为可撤销和不可撤销两种。可撤销信用证可由开证行随时修改或撤销而无须征得受益人的同意。

可撤销信用证因早期实务的需要而得以在历次版本中保留，但其对受益人明显缺乏保护，不利于信用证业务的存在与发展。而在整个 UCP500 实施期间，鲜有银行开立该类信用证的情况。可见随着时代的发展，可撤销信用证已经退出了历史舞台。UCP600 顺应实务的需要，删除了信用证“可撤销”的概念。如果实务中确有开立该类信用证的需要，按照起草组的评述，必须在信用证中列明具体的条款以反映信用证可撤销的特性。

4．单据审核时间缩短为 5 天

关于银行审核单据以确定是否接受的时间，UCP500 为“自收到单据翌日起 7 个工作日”。然而，随着市场竞争日趋剧烈，多数银行收到单据的当日便开始审核。UCP600 为了反映实务的变化，将其修改为“收到单据翌日起最长不超过 5 个工作日”，从而加快了银行处理单据的速度，确立了新的审单标准。

另外，UCP 500 的 7 个工作日是以“reasonable time”即“合理时间”为前提的，UCP600 删除了该条件。这就意味着不论单据有多么简单，单证人员多么轻闲，拒付只要不超过 5 天这一限度，就是符合规定的。而按照 UCP500，在单据比较简单的情况下，若开证行拖到最后一天拒付，一旦引起纠纷，法院可能会援引“合理时间”这一概念，判决开证行所用时间不合理，从而宣称其拒付无效。而此类案例在以往法院的判例中是不胜枚举的。UCP 600 从根本上消除了旧惯例规定的不确定性及过于理想化给银行带来的困扰，同时也消除了法院以“不合理”为由轻易地干涉银行业务的隐患。

5. 明确了沉默不等于接受

为了兼顾申请人与受益人的利益，UCP 500 并没有强制受益人必须发出接受或拒绝修改的通知，并给予其“以最后交单表示接受或拒绝”的权利。这种对受益人的优惠，常常带来问题。比如，若欲对曾经修改过的信用证再次修改，由于尚未收到单据而不知受益人是否已接受了上次修改，在两次修改有关联的情况下，就难以确定这次修改的内容。于是，一些银行便在信用证的修改通知中加列“如果在一个规定时间内，受益人没有正式拒绝修改，修改就自动生效”等类似语句。ICC 强烈反对此类错误做法，认为这是“沉默等于接受”的翻版，称其改变了“不可撤销信用证未经开证行、保兑行及受益人的同意，不得修改和撤销的性质”。而受益人的沉默被假设为接受，这也是与许多国家的法律相违背的。因此，这类想要凌驾于 UCP 之上的企图是没有法律效力的。

鉴于这种对惯例的错误运用及 ICC 曾表达的观点，UCP 600 做出了明确的规定：如果修改中加列了接受或拒绝修改的时限，银行将不予理睬。

三、信用证的特点、种类及特别条款

信用证（Letter of Credit，L/C）是进口方所在地银行，根据进口方的申请和担保，对出口方开出的一种信函式的凭证。它通过出口方所在地银行，通知出口方，由开证行负责在出口方交付信用证规定的各种装运单据时，支付所有货款。

（一）信用证的特点

信用证的特点是“一个原则，两个凭证”。“一个原则”就是严格相符的原则；“两个凭证”就是指银行只凭信用证，不问合同，只凭单据，不管货物。

1. 开证行负第一性的付款责任

开证行支付方式是由银行自己的信用作保证，所以作为一种银行保证文件的信用证，开证行对之负第一性的付款责任。

2. 信用证是一项自足的文件

开证申请书是依据买卖合同的内容提出的，因此，信用证与合同有一定的逻辑关系。但信用证一经开出，就成为独立于买卖合同以外的另一种契约，开证银行和参与信用证业务的其他银行只按信用证的规定办事，不受买卖合同的约束。基于信用证与合同的相对独立性，信用证条款的改变并不代表合同条款有类似的修改。

3. 信用证是一项纯单据文件

在信用证业务中，银行只审查收益人所提交的单据是否与信用证条款相符，以决定其是否履行付款责任。只要收益人提交符合信用证条款规定的单据，开证行就应承担付款责任。进口人也应接受单据并向开证行付款赎单。而具体货物的完好与否，则与银行无关。进口方可凭有关的单据和合同向责任方提出损害赔偿的要求。

（二）信用证的种类

根据信用证的性质、期限、流通方式等特点加以划分，常见的信用证形式有以下几种。

1. 不可撤销的信用证（Irrevocable L/C）

不可撤销的信用证一经开出，在有效期内，未经受益人及有关当事人的同意，开证行不得片面修改和撤销。只要受益人提交了符合信用证条款的单据，开证行就必须履行付款的义务。

2．保兑信用证（Confirmed L/C）

保兑信用证是指开证行开出的信用证由另一家银行对开证行的付款承诺再次进行保证的信用证。对信用证加以保兑的银行叫做保兑银行。

3．跟单信用证（Documentary L/C）

跟单信用证是指开证行凭汇票或单据履行付款义务的信用证。国际贸易中所使用的信用证大都是跟单信用证。

4．即期信用证（Sight L/C）

即期信用证是指信用证内规定只要受益人提交了符合信用证条款的跟单单据、开证行或付款行立即履行付款义务的信用证。即期信用证是单到付款，其特点是出口人收汇迅速、安全，所以在国际贸易中大多数出口商都愿意采用这种信用证。

5．远期信用证（Usance L/C）

远期信用证是指开证行或付款行在信用证中保证，在收到符合信用证的单据时，在规定的期限内付款的信用证。远期信用证又可分为银行承兑远期信用证（Banker's Acceptance Credit），延期付款信用证（Deferred Payment Credit）和假远期信用证（Usance Credit Payable at Sight）。

6．可转让信用证（Transferable Credit）

可转让信用证是指受益人（第一受益人）可要求被授权付款，承担延期付款责任，承兑或议付的银行（转让行），或在自由议付信用证下被特别授权的转让行，将信用证的全部或部分交给一个或几个其他受益人（第二受益人）使用的信用证。

7．循环信用证（Revolving Credit）

循环信用证是指受益人在一定时间内使用了规定的金额后，其金额又恢复到原来的金额，直至达到规定的时间、次数或金额为止的信用证。

8．对开信用证（Reciprocal Credit）

对开信用证是指交易的双方都对其进口部分以对方为受益人所开立的信用证。

9．背对背信用证（Back to Back Credit）

对背信用证是指信用证的受益人要求通知行或其他银行以原证为基础另开一张内容近似的新证给实际供货人，这另开的新证称为背对背信用证。

（三）信用证的特别条款

（1）递送议付单据方法、次数和规定时间条款（Method / Number of Time / Stipulated Time of Sending Negotiable Documents）。

（2）让进口商从议付行拿取所有装船单据条款（The Clause of Taking all Shipping Documents for Importer from Negotiating Bank）。

（3）汇率条款（The Clause for Rate of Exchange）。

（4）利率和利息条款（The Clause for Rate of Interest and Interests）。

（5）生效和未生效条款（The Operative and Inoperative Clauses）。

（6）“软条款”（The Soft Clause）。

（7）自动延期条款（The Automatic Extension Clause）。

（8）不符点费用条款（The Clause of Discrepant Fee）。

（9）电索条款（The T/T Reimbursement Clause）。

（10）注销信用证条款（The Cancel L/C Clause）。

（11）不接受凭保函议付条款（The Clause for Negotiation by Letter of Indemnity is not Acceptable）。

（12）其他限制性条款（The Other Restricted Clause）。

四、信用证的费用

信用证费用一般由三部分组成：

（1）开证费用（一般由进口商承担）。

（2）中转银行费用（一般中转行越多费用越高）。

（3）通知行费用（包括通知费、修改费、议付费、不符点费用等）。

上述费用关键在于中转银行费用的减少或转嫁。

（1）尽量选择开账户的银行或直接有代理关系的银行，减少线路迂回（即使做 T/T 时也如此）这方面可请教有经验的专业银行（如中行）结算人员。

（2）一般在 L/C 附言中如不指定，开征行以外的费用就由受益人承担，在谈付款条件时必须把这点指明，开征费用由申请人承担，并要求在 L/C 中显示。

项目二

租船订舱单据的制作与审核

知识目标

了解租船订舱的流程和所需的全套单据；了解租船订舱所需各种单据的含义、种类、作用，掌握其填制方法。

能力目标

能准确列出办理租船订舱所需单据清单；能熟练缮制租船订舱所需单据；能根据需要，准确、准时提交租船订舱所需单据。

任务分析

为达到上述目标，需完成下列任务：

- 任务一：租船订舱清单列表
- 任务二：缮制商业发票并审核
- 任务三：缮制出口货物明细单并审核
- 任务四：缮制装箱单并审核
- 任务五：缮制出口托运单并审核

任务一　租船订舱清单列表

任务导入

宁波光明进出口公司与中国香港富华贸易有限公司签订了上述出口外销合同，落实信用证后，及时备货，与供应商签订好购货合同，为了能在外销合同规定的装运期限内交货，公司单证员小兰及时向宁波华润国际货运公司办理出口租船订舱手续。作为一名新手，单证员小兰首先要熟悉租船订舱的业务流程，列出办理租船订舱业务所需的单据清单。

完成任务的步骤

第一步：教师引导学生一起学习下列租船订舱流程图（图 2-1）

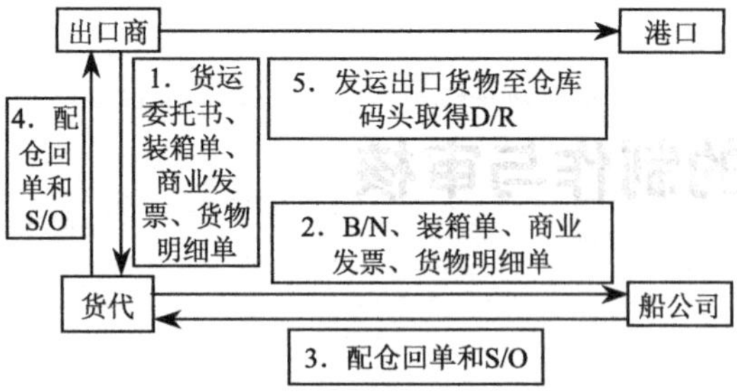

图 2-1

说明

（1）出口商货、证备齐后，缮制商业发票、货物明细单、装箱单和订舱委托书，委托货代向船公司办理订舱手续。

（2）货代接受订舱委托后，缮制集装箱托运单（B/N），随同商业发票、货物明细单、装箱单，向船公司办理订舱。

（3）船公司如接受订舱，则在托运单的几联上编上与提单（B/L）号码一致的编号，填上船名、航次，并签署，即表示确认托运人的订舱，同时把配舱回单、装货单（S/O）等托运人有关的单据退还给托运人。

（4）货代或出口商将货物运送到码头指定仓库，换取场站收据（D/R）。报关后凭海关加盖放行章的装货单（S/O）要求装货。

（5）装货后，由船长大副签署交给托运人。

（6）托运人持 M/R（大副收据）到船公司签署正本提单。

注：配舱回单、装货单（S/O）、场站收据（D/R）、大副收据（M/R）均属于托运单（B/N）中的其中一联。

第二步：要求学生根据流程图结合教师上述引导，进行小组讨论，列出办理租船订舱所要的单据清单

第三步：核对答案

完成本项目要制作并提交的单证清单：①商业发票；②货物明细单；③装箱单；④订舱委托书；⑤托运单。

自我能力测评

能力形成性评价表

评价指标	分值	实际得分
能绘制租船订舱流程图	30分	
能口头叙述租船订舱流程	30分	
能准确列出租船订舱单据清单	40分	

任务二　缮制商业发票并审核

任务导入

弄清楚了租船订舱所需的单据，宁波光明进出口公司单证员小兰就要根据清单列表，先制作商业发票。

完成任务的步骤

第一步：教师提问，制作商业发票的依据是什么

信用证支付方式下，依据信用证。托收和汇付方式下，依据外销合同。

第二步：教师引导示范，引领全体学生口头填写一份空白发票

如图 2-2 所示，教师告诉学生每一个栏目的填写要点，然后让学生根据项目一任务五中小兰在原证副本上直接做出修改后的信用证（单证 1-17）及其信用证分析单（单证 1-18），并参照任务二中的合同（单证 1-1），口头填写下列每个栏目（图 2-2）。

COMMERCIAL　INVOICE		
1）SELLER	3）INVOICE NO.	4）INVOICE DATE
	5）L/C NO.	6）DATE
	7）ISSUED BY	
2）BUYER	8）CONTRACT NO.	9）DATE
	10）FROM	11）TO
	12）SHIPPED BY	13）PRICE TERM
14）MARKS　15）DESCRIPTION OF GOOD　16）QTY.　17）UNIT PRICE　18）AMOUNT		
19)ISSUED BY 20)SIGNATURE		

> 出票人名称与地址（英文）：一般情况下为出口公司，出票人的名称和地址应与信用证的受益人的名称地址一致。

图　2-2

教师引导学生口头填写的商业发票结果如下（单证 2-1）：

单证　2-1

ISSUER GUANGMING IMPORT & EXPORT CORPORATION 13 XINNING ROAD, NINGBO, ZHEJIANG, CHINA TEL: 0574-88896000	**COMMERCIAL INVOICE**	
TO FUHUA　TRADE CO. LTD., 101 QUEENS ROAD CENTRAL, HONGKONG TEL: 852-2857777	**NO.** GM10H9141	**DATE** MAR.18,2010

（续）

<table>
<tr><td colspan="3">TRANSPORT DETAILS
FROM NINGBO TO HONGKONG BY SEA</td><td>S/C NO.
E034579
TERMS OF PAYMENT
CIF HONGKONG</td><td>L/C NO.
006CIM000489SBRT</td></tr>
<tr><td>Marks and Numbers</td><td>Description of goods</td><td>Quantity</td><td>Unit Price</td><td>Amount</td></tr>
<tr><td>FUHUA
HONGKONG
R/N0：1-1000
Total:</td><td>100PCT NYLON
FABRICS</td><td>100,000YARDS
TTL: 100,000YARDS</td><td>CIFHONGKONG
USD0.3368/YD</td><td>USD33,680.00
TTL: USD33,680.00</td></tr>
<tr><td colspan="5">SAY USDOLLARS THIRTY THREE THOUDANDSIX HUNDRED AND EIGHTY ONLY

CHINA'S CHAMBER OF COMMERCE HEREBY CERTIFY THAT THE GOODS ARE OF CHINESE ORIGIN ONLY.
IUUSING BANK：HUA XIA BANK CO.,LTD.
HONGKONG HK

GUANGMING IMPORT & EXPORT CORPORATION
XINNING ROAD, NINGBO, ZHEJAING, CHINA
XIAOLAN</td></tr>
</table>

第三步：巩固训练，学生结合一份合同或信用证独立填写一份商业发票并审核

训练任务

宁波舒普机电科技公司单证员马林根据项目一任务五中修改后的信用证（单证 1-19）及其信用证分析结果单（单证 1-20），并参照任务二中的外销合同（单证 1-3），独立填写下列商业发票（单证 2-2），商业发票的号码是 11048584。

单证 2-2

<table>
<tr><td colspan="3">ISSUER</td><td colspan="2" rowspan="2">COMMERCIAL INVOICE</td></tr>
<tr><td colspan="3">TO</td></tr>
<tr><td colspan="3" rowspan="3"></td><td>NO.</td><td>DATE</td></tr>
<tr><td colspan="3" rowspan="2">TRANSPORT DETAILS</td><td>S/C NO.</td><td>L/C NO.</td></tr>
<tr><td colspan="2">TERMS OF PAYMENT</td></tr>
<tr><td>Marks and Numbers</td><td>Description of goods</td><td>Quantity</td><td>Unit Price</td><td>Amount</td></tr>
<tr><td></td><td>Total:</td><td></td><td></td><td></td></tr>
<tr><td colspan="5">SAY

ISSUED BY</td></tr>
</table>

训练指导：学生可以根据老师的引导，示范，先尝试填写一份商业发票，如有疑问，查阅下列商业发票的填制要领；也可以先看商业发票的填制要领，再填制商业发票。

要求：填制好的商业发票要在小组中交流，然后电子文档提交到天空教室。

第四步：教师点评，核对答案

教师随机抽取每个小组制作的单据，一起批阅、点评。

知识链接

商业发票的填制要点

1．概述

商业发票，又称为发票，是进出口贸易中最重要的单据之一，是出口方对进口方签发的载有货物细节的货款价目总清单，是装运货物的总说明，并作为买卖双方交接货物和结算货款的主要单证，也是买卖双方报关、纳税、退税的依据之一，同时又是出口商缮制其他有关出口单据的依据。

2．商业发票的格式与说明

商业发票（Commercial Invoice）：可以在"商业发票"上方填写出单人的中文名称与地址。

（1）出票人（Issuer）：填写出口商的名称和地址，在信用证支付方式下，应与信用证受益人的名称和地址保持一致。

（2）受票人（To）：发票接受方的名称和地址，如属信用证方式，按信用证规定填制。一般为信用证项下的开证申请人。如有地址应与信用证一致。如属托收方式，收货人一般为合同的买方。

（3）发票号（No.）：一般由出口企业自行编制。发票作为中心票据，其他票据的号码均可与此号码相一致，如汇票号码、装箱单号码、托运单及号码等一般均与发票号码一致。

（4）运输说明（Transport details）：货物的运输信息，包括运输的起讫口岸和转运地点及运输方式（必要时加列运输工具名称）。要按信用证规定填写，并与其他运输单据保持一致。

（5）发票日期：签发发票的日期，一般应在信用证开证、改证日期之后，信用证有效期之前。发票应该是整套单据中签发日期最早的单据，不得迟于提单签发日期，最迟不能晚于议付日或汇票日。

（6）信用证号（L/C No.）：信用证号，作为出具该发票的依据。若不是信用证方式付款，本栏目留空。

（7）开证日期（Date）：信用证开立的日期。

（8）开证行（Issued by）：开立信用证的银行名称和地址。

（9）合同号（S/C No.）：销售确认书或合同号。销售确认书或合同作为出具发票的依据。

（10）合同日期（Date）：合同签订的日期。

（11）起运地（From）：起运港名称。

（12）目的地（To）：目的港名称。如货物需经转运，应把转运港的名称表示出来。如"from Ningbo to London W/T Rotterdam"。如果货物运至目的港后再转运至内陆城市，可在目的港下方打"in transit to ..."字样。

（13）运输方式（Shipped by）：填写船名和航次号。

（14）价格术语（Price Term）：跟合同或信用证一致。

（15）运输标志（Shipping Marks and Numbers）：也叫唛头，是发票的重要项目之一。如信用证有规定，应严格按照信用证的要求缮制，并与其他运输单据上的唛头保持一致。如信用证没有规定，可按合同规定填制，也可由出口商自行选定。不需要时填写 NO MARK 或 N/M 字样。

（16）货物描述、包装种类和件数（Number and Kind of Packages, Description of Goods）：这是发票的主要部分，包括商品的名称、规格、包装等内容。品名规格的应该严格按照信用证的规定或描述填写。货物的数量应该与实际装运的货物相符，同时应符合信用证的要求，如信用证没有详细的规定，必要时可以按照合同注明货物数量，但不能与来证内容有抵触。

（17）数量（Quantity）：货物的数量与计价单位连用。注意该数量和计量单位既要与实际装运货物情况一致，又要与信用证要求一致。

（18）单价（Unit Price）：计价单位的价格，包括币值、单位数额、计价单位和价格术语。如果信用证有规定，应与信用证保持一致；若信用证没规定，则应与合同保持一致。

（19）总值（Amount）：发票总金额不能超过信用证总金额。对于佣金和折扣应按信用证的规定处理。如果来证要求分别列出运费、保险费和 FOB 价，必须照办；如果来证要分别扣除佣金和折扣，必须照办。

（20）出票人（Issued by）：一般为信用证受益人，出口公司的名称。

（21）签名（Signature）：经办人签名或盖章。

（22）声名文句和其他内容（Declaration and Other Content）：位于发票下方的空白处，如图 2-2 中 18 栏和 19 栏之间的空白处，可填写根据信用证的规定或需要特别在发票上注明的内容。例如，某些参考号（L/C No），证明文句（We hereby certify that all the goods are all of Chinese origin）。

自我能力测评

能力形成性评价表

评价指标	分　值	实际得分
能看懂信用证单据条款中商业发票的要求	20 分	
能掌握商业发票各栏目填写要点	20 分	
能根据信用证对商业发票的要求独立填写各个栏目	60 分	

任务三　缮制出口货物明细单并审核

任务导入

宁波光明进出口公司单证员小兰根据项目清单，结合项目一中修改后的信用证（单证 1-17）及其信用证分析单（单证 1-18），并参照任务二中的合同（单证 1-1），制作下列出口货物明细单（单证 2-3）。

补充资料：每卷尼龙化纤织物毛重 9 公斤，净重 8.5 公斤，总体积 8.4 立方米。

单证　2-3

出口货物明细单

开证银行	HUA XIA BANK CO., LTD. HONGKONG HK	银行编号		标记唛头	
		外运编号		FUHUA HONGKONG R/NO.:1-1000	
经营单位（装船人）	GUANGMING IMPORT & EXPORT CORPORATION 13 XINNING ROAD, NINGBO, ZHEJAING, CHINA TEL: 0574-88896000	合同号	E034579		
		许可证号			
		运输方式	BY SEA		
收货人	FUHUA TRADE CO., LTD., 101 QUEENS ROAD CENTRAL, HONGKONG TEL: 852-2857777	出口口岸	NINGBO		
		目的港	HONGKONG		
		信用证号	006CIM000489SBRT		
提单或承运收据　抬头人	TO ORDER OF SHIPPER	金额	USD33 680, 00		
		开证日期	MAR.5,2010		
提单或承运收据　通知人	FUHUA TRADE CO., LTD., 101QUEENS ROAD CENTRAL, HONGKONG TEL: 852-2857777	收到日期	MAR.15,2010		
		贸易性质	一般贸易	贸易国别	中国香港
		可否转运	ALLOWED	可否分批	PROHIBITED
提单或承运收据　运费	预付　PREPAID　√	装运期限	APRIL5,2010	有效期限	APRIL 25,2010
	到付　COLLECT	提单份数	正本 3 份　√ 电放		

货物名规格及货号	件数及包装样式	数量或尺码	毛重	净重	价格（成交条件）	
					单价	总价
					CIF HONGKONG	
1100% NYLONFABRICS	1000 ROLLS	100000YARDS	9000kgs	8500kgs	USD0.3368/YD	USD33680.00

本公司注意事项		总体积		8.4CBM
		保险单	险别	ALL RISKS AND WAR RISK AS PER CCIC. 1981.1.1
		保险单	保额	FOR 110 PERCENT OF THE INVOICE VALUE
		保险单	赔款地点	HONGKONG
外运外轮注意事项		船名		
		海关编号		
		放行日期		
		制单员		

第一步：学生独立填写货物明细单

货物明细单表格是中文的，学生一看就能明白，可以直接让学生去填，如有疑问，老师个别辅导。

要求：每个同学填完后，要在小组中交流，修改后，电子文本上传到天空教室。

注：货物的毛重、净重、体积在合同和信用证中如没有具体列明，单证员应根据货物实际，填写其毛重、净重和体积。

第二步：教师点评，核对答案

教师随机抽取几个小组制作的单据，一起批阅、点评。

第三步：巩固训练

训练任务

宁波舒普机电科技公司单证员马林根据项目一任务五中，马林修改后的信用证（单证 1-19）及其信用证分析结果单（单证 1-20），并参照任务二中的外销合同（单证 1-3），独立填写下列货物明细单（单证 2-4）。

补充信息： Model CSM -430D 缝纫机每一纸箱的尺码是 120cm ×100cm ×80cm，每箱毛重 50 公斤，净重 48 公斤，Model CSM -438D 缝纫机每一纸箱的尺码是 125cm ×110cm ×85cm，每箱毛重 52 公斤，净重 50 公斤。

单证 2-4

出口货物明细单

开证银行		银行编号		标记唛头	
		外运编号			
经营单位（装船人）		合同号			
		许可证号			
		运输方式			
收货人		出口口岸			
		目的港			
		信用证号			
提单或承运收据：抬头人		金额			
		开证日期			
提单或承运收据：通知人		收到日期			
		贸易性质		贸易国别	
		可否转运		可否分批	
提单或承运收据：运费	预付	装运期限		有效期限	
	到付	提单份数	正本 3 份 √ 电放		

货物名规格及货号	件数及包装样式	数量或尺码	毛重	净重	价格（成交条件）	
			公斤		单价	总价

本公司注意事项		总体积		
		保险单	险别	
			保额	
			赔款地点	
外运外轮注意事项		船名		
		海关编号		
		放行日期		
		制单员		

知识链接

出口货物明细单填制要点

1．出货物明细单中有以下几点是必填项

（1）日期：填单日期。

（2）经营单位：××××进出口有限公司。

（3）收货人：一般填写合同的买方，如信用证另有规定，按信用证的要求填写。

（4）提单抬头人、通知人：根据信用证中提单条款上的收货人和通知人填写。

（5）运费：根据实际情况在“预付”或“到付”处打勾。

（6）提单张数：按实际情况在“正本提单3份”或“电放”处打勾。

（7）发票号：按照商业发票上的发票号填写。

（8）金额：按发票金额填写。

（9）收汇方式：按实际收汇方式填写（T/T、L/C、D/P）。

（10）货物性质：按实际情况在对应小括号内打勾。

（11）贸易国别、出口口岸、目的港：按信用证规定填写，与发票一致。报关单和提单应与此保持一致。

（12）装运期限：按实际填写，不早于提单出运日期。

（13）标记唛码、货名规格及货号、箱数、体积、毛重、净重、价格按商业发票和一些实际信息填写，提单、报关单上的内容要与此一致。

（14）结汇单证：按提交给客人或银行（信用证方式下）的实际情况在各单证名称下方的空格内打勾。

2．其他几点按实际填写，也可以不填写，根据具体情况由各代理公司自行决定

自我能力测评

能力形成性评价表

评价指标	分　值	实际得分
能掌握货物明细单格式	10分	
能掌握货物明细单各栏目填写要点	20分	
能根据信用证及补充资料独立填写各个栏目	10分	

任务四　缮制装箱单并审核

任务导入

宁波光明进出口公司单证员小兰根据项目清单，结合项目一中修改后的信用证（单证 1-17）及其信用证分析单（单证 1-18），并参照任务二中的合同（单证 1-1）和项目二中填写的商业发票（单证 2-1）及货物明细单（单证 2-3）制作装箱单。

完成上述任务的步骤如下

第一步：教师引导、示范，引领全体学生口头填写一份空白装箱单

如下图（图 2-3）所示，教师广播教学，讲解每一个栏目的填写要点，然后让学生结合项目一中修改后的信用证（单证 1-17）及其信用证分析单（单证 1-18），并参照项目二任务二中的合同（单证 1-1）和项目二中填写的商业发票（单证 2-1）及货物明细单（单证 2-3），口头填写一份空白装箱单。

出口商，信用证 BENIFICIARY

PACKING LIST

EXPORTER			INVOICE NO.		INVOICE DATE	
			FROM		TO	
			SHIPPED BY			
TO			SHIPPING MARK			
C/NOS	NO. AND KINDS OF PKGS	GOODS	QTY	G.W.	N.W.	MEAS.
TOTAL PACKAGES IN WORDS: SPECIAL CONDITIONS: ISSUED BY SIGNATURE						

图 2-3

教师引导学生口头填写的装箱单答案如下（单证 2-5）：

单证　2-5

Packing List

EXPORTER(1) GUANGMING IMPORT & EXPORT CORPORATION 13 XINNING ROAD, NINGBO, ZHEJIANG, CHINA TEL: 0574-88896000	**INVOICE NO.(3)** GM10H9141	**INVOICE DATE(4)** MAR.18,2010
	FROM(5) NINGBO	**TO(6)** HONGKONG
	SHIPPED BY(7) SEA	
TO(2) FUHUA TRADE CO., LTD., 101 QUEENS ROAD CENTRAL, HONGKONG TEL: 852-2857777	**SHIPPING MARK(8)** FUHUA HONGKONG R/NO：1-1000	

R/NOS	DESCRIPION OF GOODS	NO. AND KINDS OF PKGS	QTY	G.W.	N.W.	MEAS.
1-1000	100% NYLON FABRICS	1000 ROLLS	100,000 yards	@9kg 9000kg	@8.5kg 8500kg	@0.0084m^3 8.4m^3
TOTAL		1000 ROLLS	100,000 yards	9000kg	8500kg	8.4m^3

TOTAL PACKAGES IN WORDS: SAY ONE THOUSAND ROLLS ONLY.

L/C NO. 006CIM000489SBRT

S/C NO. E034579

ISSUING BANK: HUA XIA BANK CO., LTD.

HONGKONG HK

GUANGMING IMPORT & EXPORT CORPORATION

XINNING ROAD, NINGBO, ZHEJAING, CHINA

XIAOLAN

第二步巩固训练：学生结合一份合同或信用证独立填写一份装箱单并审核

训练任务

宁波舒普机电科技公司单证员马林根据项目一任务五中，马林修改后的信用证（单证1-19）及其信用证分析结果单（单证1-20），并参照任务二中的外销合同（单证1-3）和项目二中的商业发票（单证2-2）和货物明细单（单证2-4）独立填写下列装箱单（单证2-6）。

单证 2-6

Packing list

<table>
<tr><td colspan="3" rowspan="3">EXPORTER(1)</td><td colspan="2">INVOICE NO.(3)</td><td colspan="2">INVOICE DATE(4)</td></tr>
<tr><td colspan="2">FROM(5)</td><td colspan="2">TO(6)</td></tr>
<tr><td colspan="4">SHIPPED BY(7)</td></tr>
<tr><td colspan="3">TO(2)</td><td colspan="4">SHIPPING MARK(8)</td></tr>
<tr><td>C/NOS</td><td>DESCRIPTION OF GOODS</td><td>NO. AND KINDS OF PKGS</td><td>QTY</td><td>G.W.</td><td>N.W.</td><td>MEAS.</td></tr>
<tr><td>(9)</td><td>(10)</td><td>(11)</td><td>(12)</td><td>(13)</td><td>(14)</td><td>(15)</td></tr>
<tr><td colspan="7">TOTAL PACKAGES IN WORDS（16）
ISSUED BY :（17）
SIGNATURE（18）</td></tr>
</table>

训练指导：学生可以根据老师的引导、示范，先尝试填写一份装箱单，如有疑问，再去查阅下列装箱单的填制要领；也可以先看装箱单的填制要点，再去填制装箱单。

要求：填制好的装箱单要在小组中交流，然后电子文档提交到天空教室。

第三步：教师点评，核对答案

教师随机抽取每个小组制作的单据，一起批阅、点评。

知识链接

装箱单填制要点

装箱单无统一格式，一般由出口商自行设计，其基本内容及制单要求有：

（1）EXPORTER（出口商名称、地址）：与发票一致，信用证中的受益人（BENEFICIARY），合同中的卖方（SELLER）。

（2）TO（进口商名称、地址）：与发票一致，信用证中的开证申请人（APPLICANT），合同中的买方（BUYER）。

（3）INVOICE NO.（发票号码）：与发票号码一致。

（4）DATE（制单日期）：装箱单缮制日期。应与发票日期一致，不能迟于信用证的有效期及提单日期。

（5）FROM（装运港）：填写实际货物被装上船的港口全称。

（6）TO（目的港）：填写实际货物被最后卸离船舶所在港口的全称。

（7）SHIPPED BY（运输方式）：一般只简单地表明运输路线及运输方式，如 FROM…TO…BY SEA /AIR，必要时加注运输工具的名称。

（8）唛头（SHIPPING MARKS）：必须符合合同或信用证的规定，与发票保持一致。

（9）C/NO.（箱子顺序号）：如第一种货物装了 10 箱，其顺序号就是 1-10，第二种货物装了三箱，其顺序号就是 11-13。

（10）NO. AND KIND OF PKGS（外包装的种类和数量）：要写明包装物的名称及数量。如第一种货物装了 10 个纸箱，就填"10 CARTONS"。

（11）DESCRIPTION OF GOODS（货物描述）：按信用证要求填写，可使用统称，但不可与信用证抵触，要列明不同产品的规格，如型号、大小、花色等。

（12）计价单位的数量（QUANTITY）：要写明成交单位的名称及数量，如第一种货物有 8000 件，装了 10 箱。这里填"8000PCS"。

注：有的装箱单是将（10）和（12）栏合并在一起，如 800PCS/10CTNS。

（13）G.W.（GROSS WEIGHT)毛重：按实际情况填写每个外包装的实际毛重，并计算总量，最后在合计栏处注明总毛重，还要填写所有货物的总毛重。如第一种货物 10 箱，每箱毛重 50kgs，就可以这样填写 500kgs/50kgs，第二种货物 3 箱，每箱 60kgs，就可以填写 180/60，最后计算总毛重为 680kgs，写在合计栏里。

（14）N.W.（NET WEI GHT）净重：按实际情况填写每个外包装的实际毛重,并计算总量，该栏最下面还要填写所有货物的总净重。具体填法和（13）栏一样。

（15）MEAS（MEASURE）尺码：按实际情况填写每个外包装的尺码，并计算尺码，该栏最下面还要填写所有货物的总尺码。具体填法和（13）栏一样。

（16）包装总数大写：以大写文字写明总包装数量，必须与数字表示的包装数量一致。如："4400 纸箱 SAY FOUR THOUSAND FOUR HUNDRED CARTONS ONLY."。

（17）ISSUED BY（制单人）：出口公司的名称和地址。

（18）SIGNATURE（出口商签章）：若合同或信用证要求，则要进行签章。由出口公司的法人代表或者经办制单人员代表公司在装箱单右下方签名，上方空白栏填写公司英文名称，下方则填写公司法人英文名称。

自我能力测评

能力形成性评价表

评 价 指 标	分　值	实 际 得 分
能看懂并翻译信用证中装箱单条款	20 分	
能掌握装箱单各栏目填写要点	20 分	
能根据信用证及补充资料独立填写装箱单各个栏目	60 分	

任务五 缮制出口托运单并审核

任务导入

宁波光明进出口公司单证员小兰根据任务一中的单据清单，结合项目一中修改后的信用证（单证 1-17）及其信用证分析单（单证 1-18），并参照任务二中的合同（单证 1-1）和项目二中填写的商业发票（单证 2-1）、货物明细单（单证 2-3）和装箱单（单证 2-5），制作托运单。

第一步：教师导学、示范，引领全体学生口头填写一份空白托运单

托运单（BOOKING NOTE，B/N），俗称下货纸，是托运人根据贸易合同和信用证条款内容填制的，向承运人或其代理办理货物托运的单据。外贸公司、货代公司又将其简称为托书。托运单是出口企业向外运公司提供出口货物的必要资料，是外运公司向船公司租船订舱的依据，是日后制作提单的主要背景材料。

如果外贸公司本身开展托运业务，则需填写出口托运单（图 2-4）；如果外贸公司本身不办理运输业务，则可委托货代代理订舱，填写货物出口订舱委托书。货物出口订舱委托书的填写与托运单有关栏目相同。故这里重点介绍托运单的制作与审核。

托 运 单

SHIOPPING NOTE

托运人：
Expoter:

收货人：
Consignee

标记 Signing mark	件数 QUANTITY		尺码 MEASUREMENT
Total:			

> 信用证方式下：一般信用证提单条款都会给予以规定，应按规定填写。
> 记名收货人（记名抬头）：填“××CO.”一般是合同的买方（提单不能转让）
> 空白指示：填“TO ORDER”指示收货人（提单可背书转让）
> 记名指示：填“TO ORDER OF ××CO.”
> 托收方式下：一般填 TO ORDER 或空白不填。

可否分批 Partial shipment	:	正本 onginal B/L	:
可否转船 transshipment	:	副本 copy of B/T	:
装船期限 Latest Shipment Date	:	货存地点 coork in	:
结汇期限 Expiry Date	:	发票金额 Amourt	:
运费缴付方式	:	L/C No.	:
发票号 Invoice No.	:	合同号 S/C：No.	:
贷证情况	:		
运输方式	:		

运费吨： 运费率： 运费金额：

特殊条款：

CUANCDONC MACHINERY IMPORT
AND EXPORT CORP.（GROUP）

图 2-4

如图 2-4 所示，教师广播教学，告诉学生每一个栏目的填写要点，然后让学生结合项目一中信用证（单证 1-17）及其信用证分析单（单证 1-18），并参照任务二中的合同（单证 1-1）

和项目二中填写的商业发票（单证 2-1）、货物明细单（单证 2-3）和装箱单（单证 2-5），制作托运单。

教师引导学生口头填写的托运单答案如下（单证 2-7）：

单证　2-7

SHIPPING LETTER OF INSTRUCTION

<table>
<tr><td colspan="8">托运人：
SHIPPER:
GUANGMING IMPORT & EXPORT CORPORATION
13 XINNING ROAD, NINGBO, ZHEJIANG, CHINA
TEL. 0574-88896000</td></tr>
<tr><td colspan="4">编号：
No:GM10H9141</td><td colspan="4">船名：
S/S:</td></tr>
<tr><td colspan="4">装运港：
FROM:　NINGBO</td><td colspan="4">目的港：
TO: HONGKONG</td></tr>
<tr><td rowspan="2">标记及号码
Marks & No.</td><td rowspan="2">件数
NO.& KIND OF PKGS OR CONTAINERS</td><td colspan="2" rowspan="2">货名
Description of Goods</td><td colspan="4">重量公斤 Weight Kilos</td></tr>
<tr><td colspan="2">净 Net</td><td colspan="2">毛 Gross</td></tr>
<tr><td rowspan="2">FUHUA
HONGKONG
R/NO:1-1000</td><td rowspan="2">1000 ROLLS</td><td colspan="2" rowspan="2">100% NYLON FABRICS</td><td colspan="2">8500kg</td><td colspan="2">9000kg</td></tr>
<tr><td colspan="2">运费付款方式
Method of Freight Payment</td><td colspan="2">PREPAID</td></tr>
<tr><td colspan="4">共计件数（大写）Total Number of Packages in Writing</td><td colspan="4">SAY ONE THOUSAND ROLLS ONLY.</td></tr>
<tr><td>运费计算 Freight</td><td></td><td colspan="2">尺码 Measurement</td><td colspan="2">8.4 M^3</td><td colspan="2"></td></tr>
<tr><td>备注 Remarks</td><td colspan="7"></td></tr>
<tr><td>收货人：
CONSIGNEE</td><td>TO ORDER OF SHIPPER</td><td colspan="2">可否转船
Whether transshipment allowed</td><td>PROHIBITED</td><td colspan="2">可否分批 Whether partial shipment allowed</td><td>ALLOWED</td></tr>
<tr><td rowspan="3">通知人 Notify Party</td><td rowspan="3">FUHUA TRADE CO.,LTD.,10 1QUEENS ROAD</td><td rowspan="2">装运期
Period Of shipment</td><td rowspan="2">APRIL 5, 2010</td><td rowspan="2">有效期
Period of validity</td><td rowspan="2">APRIL 25,2010 IN CHINA</td><td>提单张数
No. of B/L</td><td>Three
（3）</td></tr>
<tr><td>提单寄送地址</td><td>宁波兴宁路 13 号</td></tr>
<tr><td colspan="4">银行编号 Bank No.</td><td colspan="2"></td></tr>
<tr><td>货存地点
GOODS IN</td><td>宁波兴宁路 13 号</td><td colspan="2">货物进栈</td><td>自送（）或货代上门取货（√）</td><td colspan="2">托运人签章</td><td></td></tr>
<tr><td>集装箱货运站地址</td><td colspan="3">宁波北仑区小港路 90 号
电话 0574-8189678</td><td>货物备妥日期</td><td colspan="3">2010 年 3 月 20 日</td></tr>
<tr><td colspan="2" rowspan="3">货物种类 TYPE OF GOODS
（√）普通货　（　）冷藏货
（　）液体　（　）散货</td><td colspan="2" rowspan="3">货物的交接方式</td><td rowspan="3">LCL/LCL</td><td>电话</td><td colspan="2">0574-88896000</td></tr>
<tr><td>传真</td><td colspan="2">0574-88896001</td></tr>
<tr><td>联系人</td><td colspan="2">小兰</td></tr>
<tr><td colspan="5">声明事项</td><td>制单日期</td><td colspan="2">MAR.18,2010</td></tr>
</table>

货代收到出口商的订舱委托书，向船公司缮制货运订舱委托书格式如下，请你以货代公司单证员的身份，填写下列托运单（单证 2-8）。

补充信息：集装箱号（TEXU2369834），封号（179576）。

单证 2-8

SHIPPER	D/R NO.	
CONSIGNEE	货代留底	
NOTIFY PARTY		第八联

PRE-CARRIAGE BY	PLACE OF RECEIPT:
OCEAN VESSEL VOY. NO.	PORT OF LOADING: NINGBO

PORT OF DISCHARGE: HONGKONG	PLACE OF DELIVERY	FINAL DESTINATION FOR THE MERCHANT'S REFERENCE

CONTAINER NO.	SEAL NO.	NO.& KIND OF PKGS OR CONTAINERS	DESCRIPTION OF GOODS	GROSS WEIGHT	MEASUREMENT
TOTAL NUMBER OF CONTAINERS OR PACKAGES (IN WORDS)		SAY ______ ONLY			

FREIGHT & CHARGE	项目	数量	费率（含转运费）
	20'		
	40'		
	BAF		
	DDC		
	附加费		

EX. RATE	PREPAID AT	PAYABLE AT	PLACE OF ISSUE
	TOTAL PREPAID	NO. OF ORIGINAL B/L THREE	

Service Type on Receiving ()CY ()CFS ()DOOR	Service Type on Delivery ()CY ()CFS ()DOOR	Reefer Temperature Required	F	C
Type of Goods	( ) Ordinary（普通） ( ) Reefer（冷藏） ( ) Dangerous（危险） ( ) Auto（裸装车辆） ( ) Liquid（液体） ( ) live Animal（活动物） ( ) Bulk（裸装）	危险品	CLASS： PROPERTY IMDG code Pade UN No.	

发货人或代理地址：			联系人：	电话：
可否转船	可否分批	装运期限	备注	集装场站名称
有效期		制单日		
海运费由： 支付				

船公司收到货代公司的货运订舱委托书后，填写船名（S.S DONGFENG V.234）、装货单（关单）号（D/R NO. HMNBJI 486888）、运费金额（USD348）后退回出口人。请以船公司单证员的名义填写下列配舱回单。

“配舱回单”是货代在取得货主的报关资料向船公司定舱后取得的单证。有时也可以用“定舱确认报文”取代。

货代负责的单证之出口托运单第十联（单证 2-9）。

单证　2-9

SHIPPER		D/R NO.		抬头	
CONSIGNEE					
NOTIFY PARTY		中国对外贸易运输公司 配舱回单（2）			第 十 联
PRE-CARRIAGE BY		PLACE OF RECEIPT			
OCEAN VESSEL VOY. NO.		PORT OF LOADING			
PORT OF DISCHARGE PLACE OF DELIVERY				FINAL DESTINATION FOR THE MERCHANT'S REFERENCE	
CONTAINER NO.	SEAL NO.	NO.& KIND OF PKGS OR CONTAINERS	DESCRIPTION OF GOODS	GROSS WEIGHT	MEASUREMENT
TOTAL NUMBER OF CONTAINERS OR PACKAGES (IN WORDS)					
FREIGHT &CHARGES	REVENUE TONS	RATE	PREPAID	COLLECT	
EX.RATE	PREPAID AT	PAYABLE AT		PLACE OF ISSUE	
	TOTAL PREPAID	NO. OF ORIGINAL B(s)/L			
SERVICE TYPE ON RECEIVING	SERVICE TYPE ON DELIVERY	REEFER TEMPERATURE REQUIRED		F	C
TYPE OF GOODS	ORDINARY , REEFER , DANGEROUS , AUTO LIQUID, LIVE ANIMAL, BULK	危险品		CLASS: PROPERTY: IMDG CODE PAGE:? UN NO.	
可否转船	可否分批				
装期	效期				
金额：					
制单日：					

第二步巩固训练：学生结合一份合同或信用证独立填写一份装箱单并审核

训练任务

宁波舒普机电科技公司单证员马林根据项目一任务五中，马林修改后的信用证（单证 1-19）及其信用证分析结果单（单证 1-20），并参照任务二中的外销合同（单证 1-3）、项目二中的商业发票（单证 2-2）、货物明细单（单证 2-4）和装箱单（单证 2-6），独立填写下列托运单各联（单证 2-10）。

单证 2-10

SHIPPING LETTER OF INSTRUCTION

托运人：					
编号： NO.			船名： S/S:		
装运港： FROM ：			目的港： TO:		
标记及号码 Marks & No.	件数 NO. OF CONTAINERS OR PKGS	货名 Description of Goods	重量公斤 Weight Kilos		
			净 Net	毛 Gross	
			运费付款方式 Method of Freight Payment		
共计件数（大写）Total Number of Packages in Writing					
运费计算 Freight		尺码 Measurement			
备注 Remarks					
收货人：CONSIGNEE		可否转船 Whether transshipment allowed		可否分批 Whether partial shipment allowed	
通知人 Notify Party		装运期 Period Of shipment	有效期 Period of validity	提单张数 No. of B/L	
				提单寄送地址	
		银行编号 Bank No.			
货存地点 GOODS IN		货物进栈	自送（）或货代上门取货（）	托运人签章	
货物种类 TYPE OF GOODS （）普通货 （）冷藏货 （）液体 （）散货		货物的交接方式		电话	
				传真	
				联系人	
声明事项				制单日期	

货代收到出口商的订舱委托书，向船公司缮制缮制缮制货运订舱委托书格式如下，请你以货代公司单证员的身份，填写下列托运单（单证 2-11）。

补充信息：集装箱号：一个 40 英尺集装箱，箱号 TEXU1399878，封号（109570）。

单证 2-11

SHIPPER			D/R NO.		
CONSIGNEE			货代留底		
NOTIFY PARTY					第八联
PRE-CARRIAGE BY		PLACE OF RECEIPT:			
OCEAN VESSEL VOY. NO.			PORT OF LOADING: NINGBO		
PORT OF DISCHARGE: HONGKONG	PLACE OF DELIVERY			FINAL DESTINATION FOR THE MERCHANT'S REFERENCE	
CONTAINER NO.	SEAL NO.	NO.& KIND OF PKGS OR CONTAINERS	DESCRIPTION OF GOODS	GROSS WEIGHT	MEASUREMENT
TOTAL NUMBER OF CONTAINERS OR PACKAGES (IN WORDS))		SAY ____ ONLY			
FREIGHT & CHARGE	项目	数量	费率（含转运费）		
	20'				
	40'				
	BAF				
	DDC				
	附加费				
EX. RATE	PREPAID AT	PAYABLE AT		PLACE OF ISSUE	
	TOTAL PREPAID	NO. OF ORIGINAL B(s)/L			
Service Type on Receiving ( )CY ( )CFS ( )DOOR	Service Type on Delivery ()CY (√)CFS (√)DOOR		Reefer Temperature Required	F	C
Type of Goods	( ) Ordinary（普通） ( ) Reefer（冷藏） ( ) Dangerous（危险） ( ) Auto（裸装车辆） ( ) Liquid（液体） ( ) live Animal（活动物） ( ) Bulk（裸装）		危险品	CLASS: PROPERTY IMDG code Page UN No.	
发货人或代理地址:			联系人:	电话:	
可否转船	可否分批	装运期限	备注	集装场站名称	
有效期		制单日			
海运费由： 支付					

船公司收到货代公司的货运订舱委托书后，填写船名（S.S hongqi V.834）、装货单（关单）号（D/R NO. HINkJt 486899）、运费金额（USD815）后退回出口人。请以船公司单证员的名义填写配舱回单。

配舱回单是货代在取得货主的报关资料向船公司定舱后取得的单证。有时也可以用定舱确认报文取代。

货代负责的单证之出口托运单第十联（单证 2-12）。

单证 2-12

SHIPPER			D/R NO.	抬头	
CONSIGNEE					
NOTIFY PARTY			中国对外贸易运输公司 配舱回单（2）		第 十 联
PRE-CARRIAGE BY			PLACE OF RECEIPT		
OCEAN VESSEL VOY. NO.			PORT OF LOADING		
PORT OF DISCHARGE PLACE OF DELIVERY			FINAL DESTINATION FOR THE MERCHANT'S REFERENCE		
CONTAINER NO.	SEAL NO.	NO.& KIND OF PKGS OR CONTAINER	DESCRIPTION OF GOODS	GROSS WEIGHT	MEASUREMENT
TOTAL NUMBER OF CONTAINERS OR PACKAGES (IN WORDS)					
FREIGHT &CHARGES	REVENUE TONS	RATE		PREPAID	COLLECT
EX.RATE	PREPAID AT		PAYABLE AT	PLACE OF ISSUE	
	TOTAL PREPAID		NO. OF ORIGINAL B(s)/L		
SERVICE TYPE ON RECEIVING	SERVICE TYPE ON DELIVERY		REEFER TEMPERATURE REQUIRED	F	C
TYPE OF GOODS	ORDINARY, REEFER, DANGEROUS , AUTO		危险品	CLASS: PROPERTY: IMDG CODE PAGE UN NO.	
	LIQUID, LIVE ANIMAL, BULK				
可否转船	可否分批				
装期	效期				
金额：					
制单日：					

训练指导：学生可以根据老师的引导、示范，先尝试填写一份托运单，有疑问时，再查阅下列托运单的填制要领；也可以先看托运单的填制要点，再去填制托运单。

要求：填制好的托运单要在小组中交流，然后将电子文档提交到天空教室。

第五步：教师点评，核对答案

填写完毕，教师随机选择一个或多个小组某一同学的作业进行集中点评，核对答案。

知识链接

海运出口托运单填制要点

一、海运出口托运单的内容

海运出口托运单（Booking Note for Cargo）是出口企业向外运公司提供出口货物的必要

资料，是外运公司向船公司订舱配载的依据。

海运出口托运单一式数份，他根据承运人或代理人的不同，有不同的名称，但大致内容基本相同。

海运出口托运单共有一式 10 联或 12 联（两张白纸联）。

第 1 联：货主（出口人）留底（Booking Note; B/N）或（Shipping Note）。

第 2 联：船代留底（B/N）。

第 3 联：运费通知（1）。

第 4 联：运费通知（2）。

第 5 联：装货单（Shipping Order;S/O），此联经船代盖章后即确认货已配定船只，可据以要求船上工作人员凭以收受货物。此联由托运人加盖“托运章”后交承运人订舱。承运人在接受订舱后填上预配船名、航次、关单号并加盖“订舱章”后交还给托运人，以确认订舱并由托运人持凭报关。报关时，海关审核后若放行，在此联上加盖“放行章”后交还报关人以确认放行并凭以装船。由此可见，此联是托运单的核心内容。

第 5 联副本：缴纳出口货物港务费申请书（由港区核算应收的港务费用）。

第 6 联（浅红色）：收货单/场站收据副本（大副联，即大副收据 M/R）。货物装上船后，大副在此联上签收，凭此向船公司或船代换取全套正本提单。

第 7 联（淡黄色）：场站收据（Dock Receipt, D/R）正本。

第 8 联：货代留底。

第 9、10 联：配舱回单①配舱回单；②船运公司在船只配定好后，在上面填写船名、装货单（关单）号后，退还给出口人。

第 11、12 联：白纸联（由货主机动使用，现已不用）

二、海运出口托运单的缮制要点

1. **托运人**（Shipper/Consignor）

填托运人的全称、街名、城市、国家名称，并填写联系电话、传真号。

（1）托运人可以是货主。

（2）托运人可以是货主的贸易代理人。

（3）托运人也可以是货主的货运代理人。

在信用证结汇方式下，托运人一般按信用证的受益人（Beneficiary）内容填写。

2. **收货人**（Consignee）

信用证方式下：一般信用证提单条款都会予以规定，应按规定填写。托收方式下：一般填“To Order”或空白不填。收货人的写法有以下几种。

记名收货人（记名抬头）：填“×× CO.”一般是合同的买方（提单不能转让）。

空白指示：填“To Order”指示收货人（提单可背书转让）。

记名指示：填“To Order of ×× CO.”（记名的一方背书转让）。

由于记名收货人的提单不能转让，给转口、中间商贸易带来了不便，因此出现了指示收货人的填法，它补充了记名收货人的缺陷，但又给船方通知货方提货带来了不便，对此，在被通知人栏作补充。

3. **被通知人**（Notify Party）

一般由买方或其代理人指定，其职责是及时接受船方发出的到货通知并将之转告真实收货人，故要求填写详细名称和地址，但他不能提货。

信用证方式下：按规定填写。

其他方式下：填写买方名称和地址。

4. **编号**（No.）

一般填写发票号码，信用证若有规定，则按信用证的规定填写。

5. **装运港、目的港**（Port of Loading、Port of Destination/Discharge）

装运港即船方收货的港口，目的港即货物最终送达的港口，一般按信用证的规定填写，注意不能用国名或地名代替，若遇重名港口，应加注国名或地名。

6. **标记及号码**（Marks & No.）

若信用证给定，则按规定填写；若信用证未规定，则一般由卖方自行设计；若无唛头，则应注明“N/M”。

若信用证规定了唛头为ABC/NEWYORK/NO.1-UP，则可使用以下两种中的任一种，但若为后一种，则只能按规定填写。

A B C	ABC
N E W Y O R K	NEWYORK
N O.1-U P	NO.1-UP

7. **货物说明**（Description of Goods）

填写货物的大类名称或统称，若同时出口不同的商品，则应分别填写。

8. **数量**（Quantity）

按最大包装的实际件数填写，如10万码花布，分别用粗胚布捆成100捆，则填“100捆”，若出口货物有多件，包装方式和材料都不同，则填每种货物的最大包装件数，如20个托盘，10个集装袋，25个捆包布匹，合计55件。分别用罗马数字小写和英文大写数字来表示。托运货物100箱，此栏填写“100CTNS”，大写栏写“SAY ONE HUNDRED CARTONS ONLY.”。

9. **毛重**（Gross Weight）

计量单位为千克（kg）。若一次装运的货物有几种不同的包装材料或者是完全不同的货物，则应分别填写，然后合计。

10. **尺码**（Measurement）

整批货的体积总数，计量单位为立方米（m^3 或 CBM）。重量和尺码是船公司计算运费的基础，应如实填写。

11. **运费付款方式**

根据合同中的价格术语填写“运费到付（Freight Collect）”或“运费预付（Freight Prepaid/Paid）”CIF、CFR术语填“Freight Prepaid/Paid”，FOB术语填“Freight Collect”。

若填了Freight Prepaid/Paid，则在Prepaid At一栏内填写装运港的名称，若填了Freight Collect，则在Collect At一栏内填目的港的名称。

12. **分批装运、转船**（Partial Shipment, Transshipment）

严格按信用证的规定，填写允许或不允许。

13. **装运期、有效期**（Date of Shipment, Date of Expiry）

按信用证规定的最迟装运期和议付有效期分别填写，一般装运期比有效期早。

若装运期空白，有效期也可空白，原因是：若托运期距装运期、信用证有效期较长，填写了，船方可能认为可以不立即安排装运，从而使托运人原定及早装运的目的落空。

14. **制单日期**

与发票日期一致。

15. **提单正本份数**（NO.OF ORIGINAL B(S)/L）

用英文和阿拉伯数字表示，一般为“THREE(3)”。

16. **货物的交接方式**（集装箱运输时）

FCL—FULL CONTAINER LOAD，LCL—LESS THAN CONTAINER LOAD，CY—CONTAINER YARD，CFS— CONTAINER FREIGHT STATION。

整箱交接—FCL/FCL；整箱接、拼箱交—FCL/LCL；拼箱接、整箱交—LCL/FCL；拼箱交接—LCL/LCL。

整箱货是在海关监督下由货主在自己仓库或工厂自行将货物装箱并加铅封，然后运交承运人，一般都送到堆场（CY）。拼箱货适用于小票货物，货主将货交承运人，由承运人或其代理人根据货物的流向、性质和重量将分属于不同货主的货物拼装在一个集装箱内发运，一般送到集散站（CFS）。

17. **货物种类**（TYPE OF GOODS）

有普通货、冷藏货、液体、散货等。

18. **特殊条款**

特殊条款主要为运输方面的特殊要求，如货物不能倒置等配货要求、立即装运等。

19. **其他**

该栏由船方填写。

20. **签字**

出口企业盖章，经办人签字。

自我能力测评

能力形成性评价表

评 价 指 标	分　值	实 际 得 分
能掌握托运单各联的用途	20 分	
能掌握托运单各联的填写规范	20 分	
能根据信用证及补充资料独立填写托运单各个栏目	60 分	

项目三

投保单据的制作与审核

知识目标

了解办理投保所需要的单据；了解投保单、保险单的种类、作用；掌握投保单、保险单的缮制要点。

能力目标

能准确列出办理投保所需单据清单；能准确缮制投保单、保险单。

任务分析

要达到上述目标，需要完成下列任务：

- 任务一：列出办理投保所需单据清单
- 任务二：缮制投保单并审核
- 任务三：缮制保险单并审核

任务一　列出办理投保所需单据清单

任务导入

宁波光明进出口公司单证员小兰办理好租船订舱手续后，根据合同和信用证保险条款的规定办理出口货物保险。作为一名新手，首先她需要弄清楚办理投保的流程及所需的单据清单。

完成该任务的步骤如下

第一步：教师引导学生一起看下列办理出口货运保险阶段的单证流程图

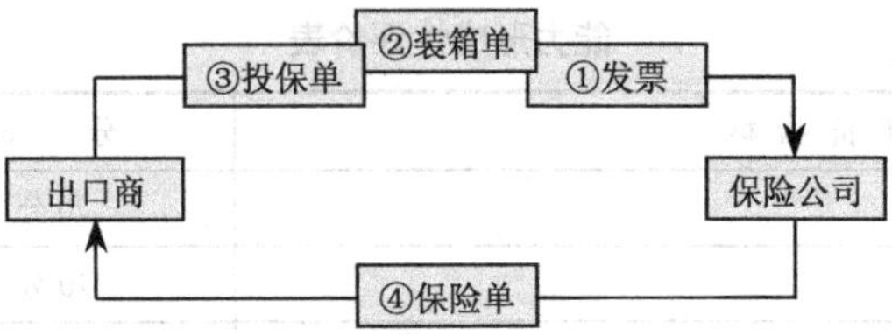

图　3-1

第二步：要求学生独自列出办理投保所需单据清单

办理投保需要的清单列表：①发票，②装箱单，③投保单，④保险单。

第三步：要求学生整理出已有的单据

对曾经制作过的单据在清单后面打√。

第四步：教师核对答案

①发票（√）；②装箱单（√）；③投保单；④保险单。

自我能力测评

能力形成性评价表

评价指标	分　值	实际得分
能绘制出口货物投保流程图	30分	
能口头叙述投保流程	30分	
能准确列出投保单据清单	40分	

任务二　缮制投保单并审核

任务导入

根据项目一清单列表，宁波光明进出口公司单证员小兰依据项目一中信用证（单证1-17）及其信用证分析单（单证1-18），并参照任务二中的合同（单证1-1）、项目二中填写的商业发票（单证2-1）、货物明细单（单证2-3）和装箱单（单证2-5），缮制投保单。

完成该任务的步骤如下

第一步：教师引导，示范，引领全体学生口头填写一份空白投保单

如下图（图3-2）所示，教师广播教学，通过课件向学生讲解每一个栏目的填写要点，然后引导学生结合项目一中信用证（单证1-17）及其信用证分析单（单证1-18），口头填写一份投保单（图3-2）。

进出口货物运输保险投保单

APPLICATION FORM I/E MARIN CARGO INSURANCE

被保险人 Assured Name			
发票号码（出口用）或合同号码（进口用）	包装数量 Quantity	保险货物项目 Description of Goods	保险金额 Amount Insured

最大包装件数，散装IN BULK，重量计价，除件数外，还标明毛重或净重

（续）

装载运输工具 Per Conveyance	航次、航班或车号 Voy.No.	开航日期 Slg.Date	
自 From	至 To	转运地 W/T at	赔款地 Claim payable at
承保险别 Condition &/or Special Coverage			
	投保人签章及公司名称、电话、地址 Applicant's Signature and Co.'s Name, Add. And TEL. No.		
备注 Remarks	投保日期 Date		

图 3-2

教师引导学生口头填写的投保单答案如下（单证 3-1）。

单证 3-1

进出口货物运输保险投保单

APPLICATION FORM I/E MARINE CARGO INSURANCE

被保险人：
Assured Name: GUANGMING IMPORT & EXPORT CORPORATION
13 XINNING ROAD, NINGBO, ZHEJIANG, CHINA
TEL. 0574-88896000

发票号码(出口用)或合同号码(进口用) **Invoice No. or Contract No.**	包装数量 **Quantity**	保险货物项目 **Description of Goods**	保险金额 **Amount Insured**
GM10H9141	1000 ROLLS	100% NYLON FABRICS	USD37,048

TOTAL AMOUNT INSURED: SAY US DOLLARS THIRTY-SEVEN THOUSAND AND FORTY-EIGHT ONLY.

装载运输工具　航次、航班或车号　开航日期
Per Conveyance S.S DONGFENG　**Voy. No.**234　**Slg. Date** as per B/L

自　至　转运地　赔款地
From NINGBO　**To** HONGKONG　**W/T at**　**Claim Payable at** HONGKONG

承保险别

Condition &/or Special Coverage

ALL RISKS AND WAR RISKS AS PER CCIC. 1981.1.1

L/C NO. 006CIM000489SBRT
S/C NO. E034579
ISSUSING BANK: HUA XIA BANK CO. LTD
HONGKONG. HK

Applicant's Signature and Co.'s Name , Add. And TEL. No.
GUANGMING IMPORT & EXPORT CORPORATION
13 XINNING ROAD, NINGBO, ZHEJAING, CHINA
TEL. 0574-88896000
XIAOLAN

Remarks　**Date : MARCH 20,2010**

第二步：巩固训练：学生结合一份合同或信用证独立填写一份投保单并审核

训练任务

宁波舒普机电科技公司单证员马林根据项目一任务五中，马林修改后的信用证（单证 1-19）及其信用证分析结果单（单证 1-20），并参照任务二中的外销合同（单证 1-3）、项目二中的商业发票（单证 2-2）、货物明细单（单证 2-4）和装箱单（单证 2-6），独立填写下列投保单（单证 3-2）。

训练指导：学生可以根据老师的引导、示范，先尝试去填写一份投保单，若有疑问，再去查阅下列投保单的填制要领；也可以先看投保单的填制要领，再去填制投保单。

要求：填制好的投保单要在小组中交流，然后电子文档提交到天空教室。

单证　3-2

进出口货物运输保险投保单

APPLICATION FORM I/E MARINE CARGO INSURANCE

被保险人： Assured Name			
发票号码（出口用）或合同号码（进口用） Invoice No. or Contract No.	包装数量 Quantity	保险货物项目 Description of Goods	保险金额 Amount Insured

TOTAL AMONT INSURED:______

装载运输工具 Per Conveyance ______ 航次、航班或车号 Voy. No. ______ 开航日期 Slg. Date ______ ______

自 From ______ 至 To ______ 转运地 W/T at ______ 赔款地 Claim Payable at ______ ______

承保险别

Condition &/or Special Coverage

Applicant's Signature and Co.'s Name , Add. And TEL. No.

Remarks　　　　Date

第三步：教师点评，核对答案

教师随机抽取每个小组制作的单据，一起评阅，点评。

知识链接

投保单填制要点

投保单由各保险公司事先印制好，是保险公司出具保险单的依据。其内容与缮制方法如下：

（1）被保险人（Insured）：若信用证有规定，应按规定填写。以 CIF 成交时，一般由出口商投保，所以此时要将保单进行背书转让。

（2）发票号码（Invoice No.）：和发票相同。

（3）标记（Marks & No.）：按信用证规定，应与发票、提单一致。

（4）包装及数量（No. of Packages, Quantity）：填写商品单件包装的件数及数量，散装应标明“In Bulk”。

（5）保险物资项目（Description）：填写品名，按信用证要求写，一般可和发票一致，届时提单也同此。

（6）保险金额（小写）（Amount）：应为发票金额加上投保加成后的金额，并按信用证要求注明货币符号，与发票上相同。注意：投保单上的保险金额的填法应该是进一取整，即，如果保险金额经计算为“US$11324.12”，则在投保单上应填“US$11325”。

（7）总保险金额（大写）：即小写保险金额的英文翻译，要注意书写的格式。

（8）装载运输工具（Per Conveyance S.S.）：要与运输单据一致，填写船名航次，航班号或车次，海运方式下可填“As Per B/L”。

（9）起运日期及起讫地点（SLG. On Or ABT, From … to …）： 可填写提单签发日，或填写“As Per B/L”。

（10）承保险别（Conditions）：按合同或信用证的规定填写，如“Covering All Risks And War Risk”。

（11）赔偿地点（Claim Payable At）：一般为目的地。

（12）保险查勘代理人（Survey By）：由保险公司自定，但要提供其地址。

（13）签发日期（Date）：签发日期须早于运输单据，这样才能证明是在装运前办理的投保。

（14）保险公司签章：保单要经签章后才能生效。

自我能力测评

能力形成性评价表

评价指标	分值	实际得分
能掌握并翻译信用证中保险条款	20分	
能掌握投保单各栏目的填写规范	20分	
能根据信用证及补充资料独立填写投保单各个栏目	60分	

任务三　缮制保险单并审核

任务导入

根据项目一清单列表，宁波光明进出口公司单证员小兰依据项目一中信用证（单证 1-17）及其信用证分析单（单证 1-18），并参照任务二中的合同（单证 1-1）、项目二中填写的商业发票（单证 2-1）、货物明细单（单证 2-3）和装箱单（单证 2-5），缮制保险单。

完成该任务的步骤如下

第一步：教师引导、示范，引领全体学生口头填写一份空白保险单

如图 3-3 所示，教师广播教学，用自制的课件告诉学生每一个栏目的填写要点，然后让学生结合项目一中小兰修改后的信用证（单证 1-14）及其信用证分析单（单证 1-15），及相关资料，说出每个栏目的填写内容。由于保险单很多栏目与投保单相同，教师重点引导学生关注不同的栏目的填写。

补充资料：保险勘察代理人名称和地址：THE PEOPLE'S INSURANCE(PROPERTY) COMPANY OF CHINA,HONGKONG BRANCH, TEL: 060-7896868。

中国人民保险公司

保　险　单　　　　保险单号次
INSURANCE POLICY　　POLICY NO.

中国人民保险公司（以下简称本公司）
THIS POLICY OR INSURANCE WI TNESSES THAT THE PEOPLE'S INSURANCE COMPANY OF CHINA (HEREINAFTER CALLED "THE COMPANY")
根据
AT THE REQUEST OF ________
（以下简称被保险人）的要求，由被保险人向本公司缴付约定的保险，按照本保险单承保险别和背面所载条款下列
(HERRINATTER CALLED "THE INSURED") ANDIN CONSIDERATION OF THE AGREED PREMTUM FAID TO THE COMPANY BY THE INSURED UNDERTAKES TO INSURE THE UNDERMENTIONED GOODS IN TRANSPORTATION SUBJECT TO THE CONDITIONS OF THIS POLICY
承保下述货物运输保险，特立本保险单
AS PER THE C… HEREON

标记 MARKS & N…	…	保险金额 AMOUNT INSURED

总保险
TOTAL AMOU… ________

> 说明：
> 保险费及保险费率（Premium and Rate）：一般由保险公司在保险单上印好"As Arranged"，可不填。若信用证要求具体列明此两栏，加盖校对章后可打上所需要的内容。

保费　PREMIUM ________　费率　RATE ________　装载运输工具　PER CONVEYANCE SS. ________
开航日期　SLG.ON OR ABT. ________　自　FROM ________　至　TO ________
承保险别：
CONDITIONS

所保货物，如遇出险，本公司凭本保险单及其他有关证件给付赔款。
CLAIMS, IF ANY, PAYABLE ON SURRENDER OF THIS POLICY TOGETHER WI TH OTHER RELEVANT DOCUMENTS
所保货物，如发生本保险单项下负责赔偿的损失或事故，

图　3-3（续）

IN THE EVENT OF ACCIDENT WHEREBY LOSS OR DAMAGE MAY RESULT IN A CLAIM UNDER THIS POLICY IMMEDLATE NOTICE
应立即通知本公司下述代理人查勘。
APPLYING FOR SURVEY MUST BE GIVEN TO THE COMPANY'S AGENT AS MENTIONED HEREUNDER:

赔款偿付地点
CLAIM PAYABLE AT/IN ______________
日期 上海
DATE ______________ SHANGHAI

THE PEOPLE'S INSURANCE CO. OF CHINA
SHANGHAI BRANCH

何立岷

地址：中国上海中山东一路 23 号 TEL:3234305 3217466-44 Telex:33122 PTCCS CN.
Address: 23Zhongshan Dong Yi Lu Shanghai,China.Cable:42001 Shanghai

____
General Manager

图 3-3

教师引导学生口头填写的保险单答案如下（单证 3-3）。

单证 3-3

进出口货物运输保险单
Insurance Policy

发票号码 保险单号次

INVOICE NO. GM10H9141 **POLICY NO.**

中国人民保险公司
This policy of insurance witness that the people's insurance company of China
根据
AT THE REQUEST OF GUANGMING IMPORT & EXPORT CORPORATION
13 XINNING ROAD, NINGBO, ZHEJIANG, CHINA
TEL. 0574-88896000

（以下简称被保险人）的要求，由被保险人向本公司约定的保险费，按照本保险单承保险别和背面所载条款与下列特殊条款承保下述货物运输保险，特立本保险单。

(HEREINAFTER CALLED THE INSURED) AND IN CONDITION OF THE AGREED PREMIUM PAID TO THE COMPANY BY THE INSURED, UNDERTAKES TO INSURE THE UNDER MENTIONED GOODS IN TRANSPORTATIOAN SUBJECT TO THE CONDITION OF THIS POLICY AS PER CLAUSES PRINTED OVERLEAF AND OTHER SPECIAL CLAUSES ATTACHED HEREOF.

货物标记 **MARKS NO.**	包装数量 **QUANTITY**	保险货物项目 **DESCRIPTION OF GOODS**	保险金额 **AMOUNT INSURED**
FUHUA HONGKONG R/N0:1-1000	1000 ROLLS	100% NYLON FABRICS	USD37,048

TOTAL AMOUNT INSURED: SAY US DOLLARS THIRTY-SEVEN THOUSAND AND FORTY-EIGHT ONLY.

保费 费率 装载运输工具
PREMIUM AS ARRANGED **RATE** AS ARRANGED **PER CONVEYANCE** S.S DONGFENG V.234

开航日期
Slg. Date AS PER B/L

自 至 转运地
From NINGBO **TO** HONGKONG **W/T at** ______

承保险别
CONDITIONS

（续）

ALL RISKS AND WAR RISKS AS PER C.C.I.C. 1981.1.1

所保货物，如遇出险，本公司凭本保险单及其他有关证件给予赔款。

CLAIMS IF ANY PAYABLE ON SURRENDER OF THIS POLICY TOGETHER WITH OTHER RELEVANT DOCUMENTS

所保货物，如发生本保险单下负责赔偿的损失或事故，

IN THE EVENT OF ACCIDENT WHEREBY LOSS OR DAMAGE MAY RESULT IN A CLAIM UNDER THIS POLICY IMMEDIATE NOTICE

应立即通知本公司下述代理勘察。

APPLING FOR SURVEY MUST BE GIVEN TO THE COMPANY'S AGENT AS MENTIONED HEREUNDER:

THE PEOPLE'S INSURANCE(PROPERTY) COMPANY OF CHINA, HONGKONG BRANCH, TEL:060-7896868

L/C NO. 006CIM000489SBRT

S/C NO. E034579

ISSUING BANK: HUA XIA BANK CO.,LTD.

HONGKONG. HK

赔款偿付地点 中国人民保险公司

Claim Payable at HONGKONG **THE PEOPLE'S INSURANCE CO. OF CHINA**

日期 地点

DATE: MARCH 21,2010 **PLACE:** NINGBO

地址：中国宁波中山东路 28 号 TEL：0574-9868789

ADRESS：28 ZHONGSHAN DONG ROAD,NINGBO ZHEJIANG CHINA TEL：0574-9868789

GENERAL MANAGER

ENDORSEMENT: GUANGMING IMPORT & EXPORT CORPORATION

13 XINNING ROAD, NINGBO, ZHEJIANG, CHINA

TEL：0574-88896000

小兰

MARCH 21,2010

第二步：巩固训练：学生结合一份合同或信用证独立填写一份保险单并审核

训练任务

宁波舒普机电科技公司单证员马林根据项目一任务五中，马林修改后的信用证（单证 1-19）及其信用证分析结果单（单证 1-20），并参照任务二中的外销合同（单证 1-3）、项目二中的商业发票（单证 2-2）、货物明细单（单证 2-4）和装箱单（单证 2-6），独立填写下列保险单（单证 3-4）。

补充资料：保险勘察代理人：THE PEOPLE'S INSURANCE(PROPERTY) COMPANY OF CHINA, BANGLADESH BRANCH, 178/B.D.F. ROAD MALIBAGH ,DHAKA-1219.

训练指导：学生可以根据刚才老师的引导、示范，先尝试去填写一份保险单，若有疑问，再去阅读下列保险单的填制要领，也可以先看保险单的填制要领，再去填制保险单。

要求：填制好的商业发票要在小组中交流，然后将电子文档提交到天空教室。

单证 3-4

进出口货物运输保险单

Insurance policy

发票号码 保险单号次

INVOICE NO. **POLICY NO.**

中国人民保险公司

This policy of insurance witness that the people's insurance company of china

根据

AT THE REQUEST OF ____________

（以下简称被保险人）的要求，由被保险人向本公司约定的保险费，按照本保险单承保险别和背面所载条款与下列特殊条款承保下述货物运输保险，特立本保险单。

(HEREINAFTER CALLED THE INSURED) AND IN CONDITION OF THE AGREED PREMIUM PAID TO THE COMPANY BY THE INSURED, UNDERTAKES TO INSURE THE UNDER MENTIONED GOODS IN TRANSPORTATIOAN SUBJECT TO THE CONDITION OF THIS POLICY AS PER CLAUSES PRINTED OVERLEAF AND OTHER SPECIAL CLAUSES ATTACHED HEREOF.

货物标记 **MAKS NO.**	包装数量 **Quantity**	保险货物项目 **Description of Goods**	保险金额 **Amount Insured**

TOTAL AMOUNT INSURED: ____________

保费 费率 装载运输工具

PREMIUM ________ **RATE** ________ **PER CONVEYANCE S.S.** ________

开航日期

Slg. Date ____________

自________ 至________ 转运地 ________

From________ **To** ________ **W/T at**________

承保险别

CONDITIONS

所保货物，如遇出险，本公司凭本保险单及其他有关证件给予赔款。

CLAIMS IF ANY PAYABLE ON SURRENDER OF THIS POLICY TOGETHER WITH OTHER RELEVANT DOCUMENTS

所保货物，如发生本保险单下负责赔偿的损失或事故，

IN THE EVENT OF ACCIDENT WHEREBY LOSS OR DAMAGE MAY RESULT IN A CLAIM UNDER THIS POLICY IMMEDIATE NOTICE

应立即通知本公司下述代理勘察。

APPLING FOR SURVEY MUST BE GIVEN TO THE COMPANY'S AGENT AS MENTIONED HEREUNDER:

赔款偿付地点 中国人民保险公司

Claim Payable at ________ **THE PEOPLE'S INSURANCE CO. OF CHINA**

日期 地点

DATE ________ **PLACE** ________

地址：中国宁波中山东路 28 号 TEL：0574-9868789

ADRESS: 28 ZHONGSHAN DONG ROAD,NINGBO **GENERAL MANAGER**

ZHEJIANG CHINA TEL: 0574-9868789

ENDORSEMENT:

第三步：教师点评，核对答案

教师随机抽取每个小组制作的单据，一起批阅，点评。

知识链接

保险单缮制要点

保险单的内容与投保单大致相同，不同栏目的缮制要点如下：

1. **保险单号次**（POLICY NO.）

按保险公司指定的编号填入。

2. **货物标记**（MARKS NO.）

应与发票的唛头相同，也可填 AS PER INVOICE NO.XXX。

3. **保险费**（PREMIUM），**费率**（RATE）

保险公司一般已印妥“AS ARRANGED”（按约定），无需填写。若信用证规定要具体列出保费等情况，则应明确填上，删除“AS ARRANGED”字样，填上具体的保险费额、费率。

4. **保险勘察代理人**（INSURANCE SURVY AGENT）

由保险公司指定，并注明详细地址，以便在货物遭受损失时，收货人可及时通知代理人进行勘察和理赔事宜。通常不接受来证中指定的理赔代理人。

5. **签发日期**（PLACE AND DATE OF ISSUE）

保险单签发日期不得晚于提单等运输单据签发日期。签发地为受益人所在地，通常已事先印在保险单上。

6. **保险公司签章**（AUTHORIZED SIGNATURE）

保险单经保险公司签章后才有效，其签章一般已事先印制在保险单的右下方，然后由授权人签名即可。

自我能力测评

能力形成性评价表

评价指标	分值	实际得分
能掌握并翻译信用证中保险条款	20分	
能掌握保险各栏目的填写规范	20分	
能根据信用证及补充资料独立填写保险单各个栏目	60分	

项目四

报检单据的制作与审核

知识目标

了解报检的流程和所需的全套单据；了解报检所需各种单据的含义、种类、作用，掌握其填制方法。

能力目标

能准确列出办理报检所需单据清单；能熟练缮制报检所需单据；能根据需要，准确、准时提交报检所需单据。

任务分析

为达到上述目标，需完成下列任务：

- 任务一：列出报检所需的单据清单并理单
- 任务二：缮制出口货物报检单并审核

任务一　列出报检所需的单据清单并理单

任务导入

宁波光明进出口公司依据有关出入境检验检疫法的规定，需要向宁波出入境检验检疫局办理出口货物报检，申请签发出境货物通关单。公司单证员小兰要备好办理报检所需全套单据。作为一名新手，单证员小兰首先要熟悉出入境检验检疫的工作程序，列明办理报检所需的单据清单，并整理好已有的单据，为下一步制单做准备。

完成任务的步骤

第一步：教师引导学生一起学习下列出境货物检验检疫工作单证流转程序图

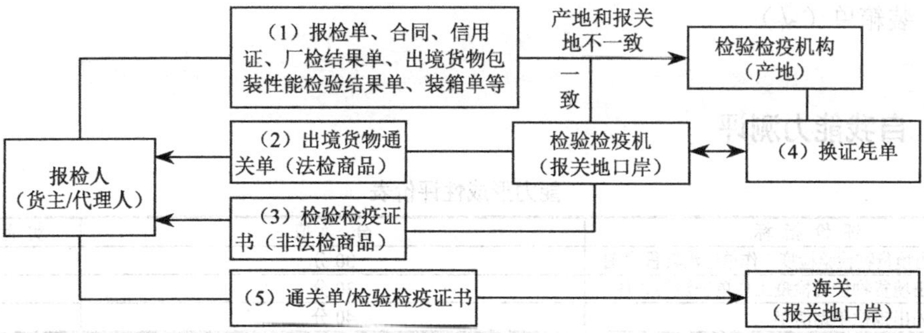

图　4-1

（1）出境货物报检时，报检人（货主或其代理人）应填写《出境货物报检单》，并提供外贸合同或销售确认书或定单；信用证、有关函电；生产经营部门出具的厂检结果单原件；检验检疫机构签发的《出境货物运输包装性能检验结果单》正本；凭样品成交的，须提供样品向产地检验检疫机构报检。

（2）、（3）产地检验检疫机构按照规定审核报检资料，符合要求的，受理报检并计收费，由施检部门实施检验检疫。对产地和报关地一致的出境货物，经检验合格后出具出境货物通关单或检验检疫证书，不合格的签发不合格通知单。

（4）产地和报关地不一致的，产地检验检疫机构检验合格后，出具换证凭单，报检人再向口岸检验检疫机关报检，换取出境货物通关单或检验检疫证书，不合格的签发不合格通知单。

（5）报检人凭检验检疫机构签发的出境货物通关单或检验检疫证书办理通关手续，海关进行验放。

第二步：要求学生独立列出报检所需的单据清单

报检所需的单据清单如下：

（1）《出境货物报检单》；

（2）外贸合同或销售确认书或定单；

（3）信用证、有关函电；

（4）生产经营部门出具的厂检结果单原件；

（5）检验检疫机构签发的《出境货物运输包装性能检验结果单》正本；

（6）产地和报关地不一致的，还应出具产地检验检疫机构签发的《出境货物换证凭单》（正本）。

第三步：要求学生整理出已有的单据

对曾经制作过的单据在清单后面打“√”。

第四步：教师核对答案

（1）《出境货物报检单》；

（2）外贸合同或销售确认书或定单；（√）

（3）信用证、有关函电；（√）

（4）生产经营部门出具的厂检结果单原件；（没有，向生产部门索要）

（5）检验检疫机构签发的《出境货物运输包装性能检验结果单》正本；（没有向生产包装容器单位索要）

（6）产地和报关地不一致的，还应出具产地检验检疫机构签发的《出境货物换证凭单》（正本）。（等待产地检验检疫机构出具）

（7）装箱单（√）

自我能力测评

能力形成性评价表

评 价 指 标	分 值	实 际 得 分
能绘制出境货物检验检疫工作单证流转程序图	30 分	
能口叙出境货物检验检疫工作单证流转程序	30 分	
能准确列出报检单据清单	40 分	

任务二　缮制出口货物报检单并审核

任务导入

宁波光明进出口公司单证员小兰列好了报检所需的单据清单，并理好了已有的单据之后，根据清单列表，接下来，她需要依据项目一中信用证（单证 1-17）及其他补充信息，缮制出境货物报检单。

第一步：教师引导、示范，引领全体学生口头填写一份空白报检单

如图 4-2 所示，教师广播教学，用自制的课件告诉学生每一个栏目的填写要点，然后让学生结合项目一中信用证（单证 1-17）及其分析结果单（单证 1-18），并参照已填写的其他单据，说出每个栏目的填写内容。

出境货物报检单					
报检单位（加盖公章）：				编　号：	
报检单位登记号：	联系人：		电话：	报检日期：	年　月　日
发货人	（中文）				
	（外文）				
收货人	（中文）				
	（外文）				
货物名称（中/外文）	H.S.编码	产地	数量/重量	货物总值	包装种类及数量
运输工具名称号码				货物存放地点	
合同号				用途	
发货日期	输往国家			许可证/审批号	
起运地				生产单位注册号	
集装箱规格、数量及					
合同、信用证订立的特 其他要求				随附单据（划“√”或补填）	
				□合同 □信用证 □发票 □换证凭单 □装箱单	□厂检单 □包装性能结果单 □许可/审批文件 □ □

货物的总值：按本批货物合同或发票上所列的总值折算成 FOB 美元价值填写，如同一报检单报检多批货物，需列明每批货物的总值。（注：如申报货物总值与国内、国际市场价格有较大差异，检验检疫机构保留核价权力。）

图　4-2

补充资料：小兰查出该商品的H.S.编码为6302.2290，取得的该批货物许可证编号为10-AB-126786，查看配仓回单，货物总海运费为USD348，查看保险单，计算出保险费为USD112。

教师引导学生口头填写的报检单答案如下（单证4-1）。

单证 4-1

中华人民共和国出入境检验检疫

出境货物报检单

报检单位（加盖公章）：宁波光明进出口公司　　*编号

报检单位登记号：331200480　联系人：小兰　电话：0574-88896000　报检日期：2010年3月24日

发货人	（中文）宁波光明进出口公司
	（外文）GUANGMING IMPORT & EXPORT CORPORATION 13XINNING ROAD, NINGBO, ZHEJIANG, CHINA TEL:574-88896000
收货人	（中文）
	（外文） FUHUA TRADE CO., LTD. 101QUEENS ROAD CENTRAL,HONGKONG TEL: 852-2857777

货物名称（中/外文）	H.S.编码	产地	数/重量	货物总值	包装种类及件数
100%尼龙织物	6302.2290	宁波象山	100 000 码	FOB ningbo USD33 220.00	1 000 卷

运输工具名称号码	S.S DONGFENG V.234	贸易方式	一般贸易	货物存放地点	宁波兴宁路13号
合同号	E034579	信用证号	006CIM000489SBRT	用途	自营内销
发货日期	2010.04.15	输往国家（地区）	中国香港	许可证/审批号	10-AB-126786
启运地	宁波	到达口岸	香港	生产单位注册号	331200480
集装箱规格、数量及号码	1×20 拼箱 TEXU2369834				

合同、信用证订立的检验检疫条款或特殊要求	标记及号码	随附单据（划“√”或补填）	
***	FUHUA HONGKONG R/NO:1-1000	☑合同 ☑信用证 ☑发票 ☐换证凭单 ☑装箱单	☑厂检单 ☐包装性能结果单 ☑许可/审批文件 ☐ ☐

需要单证名称（划“√”或补填）		*检验检疫费
☑品质证书 1正2副 ☐重量证书 ☐数量证书 ☐兽医卫生证书 ☐健康证书 ☐卫生证书	☐动物卫生证书 ☐植物检疫证书 ☐熏蒸/消毒证书 ☑出境货物换证凭单 1正2副 ☐通关单	总金额 （人民币元） 计费人 收费人

报检人郑重声明： 1. 本人被授权报验。 2. 上列填写内容正确属实，货物无伪造或冒用他人的厂名、标志、认证标志，并承担货物质量责任。 签名：小兰	领取证单 日期 签名

注：带*号的由检验检疫机构填写。

第二步巩固训练：学生结合信用证和相关单据信息独立填写一份报检单

训练任务

宁波舒普机电科技公司单证员马林根据项目一任务五中，马林修改后的信用证（单证1-19）及其信用证分析结果单（单证1-20），参照已填写的其他单据，独立填写下列报检单（单证4-2）。

到孟加拉的保险费率：水渍险0.16%，战争险0.2%，许可证编号06AB134789，报检单位登记号354820716，电话号码0574-88888888。

补充资料：马林查出两种自动缝纫机的H.S编码分别为8452.2110，8452.2190。

训练指导：学生可以根据老师的引导、示范，先去尝试填写一份报检单，若有疑问，再去查阅下列报检单的填制要领，也可以先看报检单的填制要领，再去填制报检单。

要求：填制好的报检要在小组中交流，然后将电子文档提交到天空教室。

单证 4-2

中华人民共和国出入境检验检疫
出境货物报检单

报检单位（加盖公章）： *编号______

报检单位登记号： 联系人： 电话： 报检日期： 年 月 日

发货人	（中文）	
	（外文）	
收货人	（中文）	
	（外文）	

货物名称（中/外文）	H.S.编码	产地	数/重量	货物总值	包装种类及件数

运输工具名称号码		贸易方式		货物存放地点	
合同号		信用证号		用途	
发货日期		输往国家（地区）		许可证/审批号	
启运地		到达口岸		生产单位注册号	
集装箱规格、数量及号码					

合同、信用证订立的检验检疫条款或特殊要求	标记及号码	随附单据（划“√”或补填）	
		□合同 □信用证 □发票 □换证凭单 □装箱单	□厂检单 □包装性能结果单 □许可/审批文件 □ □

需要单证名称（划“√”或补填）		*检验检疫费
□品质证书 □重量证书 □数量证书 □兽医卫生证书 □健康证书 □卫生证书	□动物卫生证书 □植物检疫证书 □熏蒸/消毒证书 □出境货物换证凭单 □通关单	总金额 （人民币元） 计费人 收费人

报检人郑重声明： 1．本人被授权报验。 2．上列填写内容正确属实，货物无伪造或冒用他人的厂名、标志、认证标志，并承担货物质量责任。 签名：______	领取证单 日期 签名

注：带*号的由检验检疫机构填写。

第三步：教师点评，核对答案

教师随机抽取每个小组制作的单据，一起批阅、点评。

知识链接

报检单缮制要点

“出境货物报检单”所列各项必须填写完整、准确、清晰，没有内容填写的栏目应该用“***”或“/”表示，不能为空。

（1）报检单位（公章）：按报检单位全称填写。报检单需加盖该报检单位的单位公章。

（2）报检单位登记号：按报检单位在检验检疫机构所办理的登记注册代码填写。

（3）联系人：填报检单位的报检员姓名。

（4）电话：填报检单位报检员的电话号码。

（5）报检日期：检验检疫机构受理报检日期。

（6）发货人：按外销合同中卖方或信用证中受益人名称填写。若无外销合同，仅有购销合同，所作的报检只是预验报检，则发货人中文名称填购销合同中的买方名称（如外贸公司的名称），外文名则用“××”表示。

（7）收货人：填外销合同中买方或信用证中的开证申请人名称。

（8）货物名称（中/外文）：按外销合同、信用证中所列货物的中/外文名称填写，根据需要还可填写型号、规格或牌号。

（9）H.S 编码：按《协调商品名称及编码制度》中的商品编码填写。

（10）产地：按生产/加工该批出口货物的省、市、县名称填写。

（11）数/重量：按实际报检货物的数量/重量填写，如计价单位为数量，就填写实际计价的数量；如计价单位为重量，重量应填实际净重量。

（12）货物总值：按外销合同或商业发票中所列货物总值折算成 FOB 美元填写。

（13）包装种类及数量：按货物运输包装种类及件数填写。

（14）运输工具名称号码：按装载货物的运输工具名称填写（如船、飞机、货柜车、火车等）及运输工具编号（如船名、飞机航班号、车牌号码等）。

（15）贸易方式：①一般贸易；②来料加工；③进料加工；④其他等。

（16）货物存放地点：填该批报检货物现在实际存放的地点（如某工厂的仓库等）。

（17）合同号：按外销合同号码、购销合同号码填写，或填形式发票的号码。

（18）信用证号：填国外开证申请人/买方开列给卖方的信用证号码。若无信用证，则用“××”表示。

（19）用途：填本批出境货物的用途。

（20）发货日期：填该批货物拟发往国外的日期。

（21）输往国家（地区）：指外贸合同中买方所在国家和地区，或合同中注明的该批货物运送最终到达的国家（地区）。若该批报检只是预验报检时，则用“××”表示。

（22）许可证/审批号：填该厂所取得的出口商品质量许可证号码或出境需审批的动植物产品的审批证明号码。若该类商品不属于此类管理范围，则用“××”表示。

（23）起运地：按该批出境货物装载后拟离境的地点。

（24）到达口岸：按该批货物运送抵达的卸货口岸填写。

（25）生产单位注册号：生产/加工本批货物的单位在检验检疫机构的注册登记编号。

（26）集装箱规格、数量及号码：按装运该批货物的集装箱的规格、数量和集装箱号码填写。若该批货物未用集装箱装运，则用“××”表示。

（27）合同、信用证订立的检验检疫条款或特殊要求：按外销合同/信用证中订立的有关检验检疫的具体条款或特殊要求填写。

（28）标记及号码：按发票装箱单（出口货物明细单）上所列的运输标记填写。货物包装为裸装/散装时应填“N/M”。若此批报检只是预验报检，无法确定唛头时，则用“暂无”表示。标记栏不够填写的，可用附单填写。

（29）随附单据（划√或补填）：将报检所附单据按此栏所列名称勾划在小方格内，并可补填所附单据。

（30）需要单证名称（划√或补填）：将报检单位需要检验检疫机构出具的有关单证按此栏所列名称勾划在小方格内并填明正、副本的份数，但最多不得超过一正二副。

（31）报检人郑重声明：报检员在认真阅读此栏后郑重签名，以承担相应的法律责任。

（32）领取单证：报检员在领取检验检疫机关所发相关单证以后，在此栏签署领取单证印刷编号、日期及姓名。

自我能力测评

能力形成性评价表

评价指标	分　值	实际得分
能掌握并翻译信用证中的检验条款	20分	
能掌握报检单各栏目的填写规范	20分	
能根据信用证及补充资料独立填写报检单各个栏目	60分	

项目五
报关单据的制作与审核

知识目标

了解报关的流程和所需的全套单据；了解报关所需各种单据的含义、种类、作用，掌握报关单据的填制方法。

能力目标

能准确列出办理报关所需单据清单；能熟练缮制报关单；能申领并填制出口许可证；能缮制并申领原产地证书；能申领并缮制外汇核销单。

任务分析

为达到上述目标，需完成下列任务：

- 任务一：列出报关所需的单据清单并理单
- 任务二：缮制出口货物报关单并审核
- 任务三：申领出口许可证及缮制相关单据
- 任务四：缮制并申领原产地证书
- 任务五：申领并缮制外汇核销单

任务一　列出报关所需的单据清单并理单

任务导入

宁波光明进出口公司依据有关合同和信用证规定的装运时间，依据海关法的有关规定，及时向宁波北仑海关办理报关手续。公司单证员小兰要备好办理报关所需全套单据。作为一名新手，单证员小兰首先要熟悉报关的工作程序，列明办理报关所需的单据清单，并整理好已有的单据，为下一步制单做准备。

完成任务的步骤

第一步：教师引导学生一起学习下列报关、装运阶段单证流转程序

出口商在货物装运前，应向当地的海关办理出口货物报关手续。海关核准无误后征收关税，并在出口货物报关单上加盖放行章。此后，船运公司才可将货物装运至船上，并签发提单。

报关、装运阶段的单证流转如图 5-1 所示。

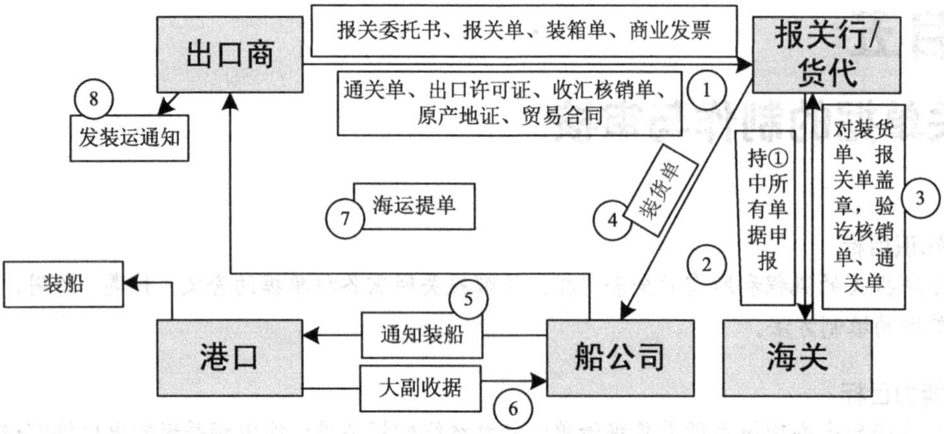

图 5-1

图 5-1 说明

① 出口商将填制好的报关委托书、报关单及发票等相关单证交报关行或货代，委托其代理报关。

② 报关行或货代整理，审核报关资料后向海关报关。

③ 海关核准无误后，收讫关税，在报关单和装货单上盖放行章，在核销单和通关单上盖验讫章。

④ 货代将盖有放行章的装货单交船公司。

⑤ 船公司凭盖有放行章的装货单通知港口装船。

⑥ 港口装船后，由船长或大副向船运公司签发大副收据（收货单）。

⑦ 船运公司凭大副收据（收货单）或通过货代向出口商签发海运提单。

⑧ 出口商拿到提单后，立即给进口商发装运通知。

①、②、③主要是报关阶段单证流转，④、⑤、⑥、⑦、⑧主要是装运阶段单证流转图。

如果是加工贸易或特定减免货物，报关时还要提交加工贸易登记手册、特定减免税证明等特殊单证。

第二步：要求学生独立列出报关所需的单据清单

报关所需的单据清单如下：

（1）主要单证就是报关单；

（2）基本单证就是商业发票、装箱单、装货单；

（3）特殊单证主要指进出口许可证、加工贸易登记手册、特定减免税证明、出口收汇核销单、原产地证明书、通关单等；

（4）备用单证主要是指进出口贸易合同、进出口企业的有关证明文件。

第三步：要求学生整理出已有的单据

对曾经制作过的单据在清单后面打“√”。

第四步：教师核对答案

（1）报关所需的主要单证：报关单；

（2）报关所需的基本单证：商业发票、装箱单、装货单（√）；

（3）报关所需的特殊单证：进出口许可证、加工贸易登记手册、特定减免税证明、出口收汇核销单、原产地证明书，通关单等；

（4）报关所需的预备单证：进出口贸易合同、进出口企业的有关证明文件（√）。

一般进出口货物不需要提交加工贸易登记手册和特定减免税证明，非法定检验货物无需提交通关单。

准备申报单证的原则是：主要单证、基本单证、特殊单证、预备单证必须齐全、有效、合法；填报报关单必须真实、准确、完整；报关单与随附单证数据必须一致。

自我能力测评

能力形成性评价表

评 价 指 标	分　值	实 际 得 分
能绘制出口报关工作单证流转程序图	30分	
能口头叙述出口报关工作单证流转程序	30分	
能准确列出口报关单据清单	40分	

任务二　缮制出口货物报关单并审核

任务导入

宁波光明进出口公司单证员小兰依据任务一中的单据清单，首先制作报关单（图5-2）。

第一步：教师引导、示范，引领全体学生口头填写一份空白报关单

中文名称及四位关区代码

中华人民共和国海关出口货物报关单

预录入编号：　　　　　　　　　　海关编号：

出口口岸 秦皇岛关（04/02）	备案	出口日期	申报日期 2010-10-12
经营单位　河北省进出口（集团）公司 130123456（1301123456789）	运输方式 江海运输	运输工具名称 SOHYA STAR/2	提运单号 1
发货单位　河北省进出口（集团）公司	贸易方式 一般贸易	征免性质	结汇方式 信用证

图　5-2（续）

许可证号	运抵国（地区）	指运港	境内货源地	
	日本　（116）	大阪	秦皇岛其他	
批准文号	成交方式	运费	保费	杂费
	CIF	20 000 000.00	1 615 597 94	
合同协议号	件数	包装种类	毛重（公斤）	净重（公斤）
TEFC00-22-01	12 500	麻袋	1 025 000	1 000 000
集装箱号	随附单据		生产厂家	
Container No./Seal No.　CBOP22222	/CTTF333333（20°）			
标记唛码及备注	B：1301002000000977			
II/II　II/II　II/II				

项号	商品编号	商品名称、规格型号	数量及单位	最终目的国（地区）	单价	总价	币制	征免
01	08024010.10	Chestnnt	500 000 千克 500 吨	日本 （116）	253 514.06	126 757 051.05	JPY 日元	
02	08024010.10	Chestnnt	300 000 千克 300 吨	日本 （116）	273 397.46	22 019 232.62	JPY 日元	
03	08024010.10	Chestnnt	200 000 千克 200 吨	日本 （116）	233 630.66	46 726 152.42	JPY 日元	
						合计：266 602 402.06	JPY 日元	

图　5-2

如图 5-2 所示，教师用自制的 PPT 向学生讲解每一个栏目的填写规范，然后让学生依据项目一中信用证（单证 1-17）及其分析结果单（单证 1-18），并参照已填写的报检单等其他单据，说出每个栏目的填写内容。

补充资料：北仑海关关区代码（3104）；经营单位的代码是 330296480；核销单编号为 031155451；该批货物投保的保险费率为 3‰，保险费=保险金额×保险费率=USD37048×3‰=USD 111.144；一个 20 英尺集装箱自重 2 275 公斤；该批货物的法定计量单位为卷/千克。

教师引导学生口头填写的报关单答案如下（单证 5-1）。

单证　5-1

中华人民共和国海关出口货物关单

预录入编号　　　　　　　　　　　　　　　　　海关编号

出口口岸	备案号	出口日期	申报日期
北仑海关 3104		20100405	20100403

经营单位	运输方式	运输工具名称	提运单号
宁波光明进出口公司 3302964801	江海运输	DONGFENG/234	

发货单位	贸易方式	征免性质	结汇方式
宁波光明进出口公司 3302964801	一般贸易	一般征税	信用证

（续）

许可证号	运抵（国地区）	指运港	境内货源地
10-AB-126786	中国香港	香港	33029

批准文号	成交方式	运费	保费	杂费
031155451	CIF	502/348/3	0.3/1	

合同协议号	件数	包装种类	毛重（公斤）	净重（公斤）
E034579	1 000	卷	9 000	8 500

集装箱号	随附单据	生产厂家
TEXU2369834/20/2275		宁波光明进出口公司

标记唛码及备注
FUHUA
HONGKONG
R/ NO.:1-1000

项号	商品编号	商品名称规格型号	数量及单位	最终目的地国（地区）	单价	总价	币制	征免
01	6302.2290	全尼龙织物	1 000 卷	中国香港	0.336 8	33 680	USD	照章征税
		100PC NYLON FABRICS	8 500 千克					
			100 000 码					

税费征收情况

录入员　　录入单位	兹声明以上申报无讹并承担法律责任	海关单批注及放行日期（签章） 审单审价
报关员		征税　　统计
申报单位（签章） 单位地址		查验 放行
邮编　　电话	填制日期	

第二步巩固训练：学生结合一份信用证和相关单据信息，独立填写一份报关单

训练任务

宁波舒普机电科技公司单证员马林根据项目一任务五中，马林修改后的信用证（单证 1-19）及其信用证分析结果单（单证 1-20），并参照已填写的报检单等其他单据，独立填写下列报关单（单证 5-2）。

补充资料：北仑海关关区代码（3104）；经营单位的代码是 330295276；核销单编号为 42155785；该批货物投保的保险费率为 3‰；一个 40 英尺集装箱自重 3 800 公斤；该批货物的法定计量单位为台。出口日期 2009 年 1 月 15 日，申报日期 2009 年 1 月 13 日。

训练指导：学生可以根据刚才老师的引导、示范，先尝试填写一份报关单，如有疑问，再查阅下列报关单的填制要领，也可以先看报关单的填制要领，再填制报关单。

要求：填制好的报关单在小组中交流，然后将电子文档提交到天空教室。

单证 5-2

中华人民共和国出口货物报关单

预录入编号：　　　　　　　　　　海关编号：

进口口岸	备案号	出口日期	申报日期	
经营单位	运输方式	运输工具名称	提运单号	
发货单位	贸易方式	征免性质	结汇方式	
许可证号	运抵（国地区）	指运港	境内货源地	
批准文号	成交方式	运费	保费	杂费
合同协议号	件数	包装种类	毛重（公斤）	净重（公斤）
集装箱号	随附单据		生产厂家	
标记唛码及备注				

项号	商品编号	商品名称规格型号	数量及单位	最终目的地国/地区	单价	总价	币制	征免

税费征收情况	
录入员　录入单位　兹声明以上申报无讹并承担法律责任	海关单批注及放行日期（签章）
报关员　　申报单位（签章）	审单审价
单位地址	征税　统计
邮编　电话　填制日期	查验 放行

第三步：教师点评，核对答案

教师随机抽取每个小组制作的单据，一起批阅、点评。

知识链接

进/出口货物报关单缮制要点

进/出口报关单（The Import& Export Declaration）是由海关总署统一格式印制，纸质进口货物报关单一式四联：分别是海关作业联、企业留存联、海关核销联、进口付汇证明联；纸质出口货物报关单一式五联：分别是海关作业联、企业留存联、海关核销联、出口付汇证明联、出口退税证明联。由进/出口企业在装运/提货前填制，经海关审核、签发后生效的法律文书。进/出口报关单是海关依法监管货物进/出口、征收关税、编制海关统计及处理其他海关业务的重要凭证。

报关单根据业务性质的不同，有一般贸易进/出口货物报关单、进料加工专用报关单、出口退税专用报关单和来料加工、补偿贸易专用报关单，其主要内容大致相同，填制方法略有差异。一般情况下，应同时采用电子和纸质两种报关单进行申报。报关单应用中文填写。具体填写说明如下。

1．预录入编号

预录入单位录入的报关单的编号，用于申报单位与海关之间引用其申报后尚未接受申报的报关单。预录入编号由接受申报的海关决定编号规则，由计算机自动打印。

2．海关编号

海关接受申报时给予报关单的顺序编号一般为18位数码，由各直属海关在接收申报时确定，应标记在报关单的每一联上。一般海关编号就是预录入号，由计算机自动打印，不需填写。

3．出口/进口口岸

注明货物实际出/进境口岸的海关名称和代码，按《海关名称及代码表》规定填制。如："上海海关2200"。倘若在我国不同出口加工区之间转让的货物，则填报对方出口加工区海关名称及代码。其他无实际进出境的货物，填报接受申报的海关名称及代码。

4．备案号

填写应向海关递交的备案审批文件的编号，如加工贸易手册编号或征、减免税证明编号、实行优惠贸易协定项下原产地证书联网管理的原产地证书编号等，一份报关单只允许填报一个备案号，备案号长度为12位数，第一个字母为备案或审批文件的标记。常见的标记及备案审批文件为：B（来料加工）、C（进料加工）、E（加工贸易电子账册）、Y（原产地证书）、Z（征免税证明）。如为一般贸易，此栏留空。

备案号的标记代码必须与报关单"贸易方式"、"征免性质"、"征免"、"用途"及"项号"栏目相协调，例如："贸易方式"为来料加工，"征免性质"也应当是来料加工，"备案号"的标记代码应为"B"，"征免"应是全免，"用途"应是加工返销，"项号"应分行填报。

5．出/进口日期

填入申报货物的运输工具出/进境的日期。本栏目为8位数字，按顺序分别为年4位、月2位、日2位，如2009年8月10日填为20090810。本栏目供海关打印报关单证明联用，预录入报关单及EDI报关单均免于填报，无实际进出境的报关单填报办理申报手续的日期，以海关接受申报的日期为准。

6．申报日期

海关接受申报的日期，其格式同出口日期。

7．经营单位

经营单位指已在海关注册登记，有权在一定的范围内从事对外经济贸易进出口活动的法人、其他组织和个人。本栏目应填报进出口企业中文名称及10位编码。签订和执行合同的如为两个单位，经营单位应填执行合同的单位。经营单位编码为10位数字。其中第一至四位为进出口单位属地的行政区划代码，第五位为市经济区划代码（"1"表示经济特区；"2"表示经济技术开发区、上海浦东新区、海南洋浦经济开发区；"3"表示高新技术开发区；"4"表示保税区、"5"表示出口加工区；"6"表示保税港区，包括已被整合到综合保税区或保税港区内的出口加工区、保税物流园区、保税区或保税物流中心；"7"表示物流园区；“9”表示其他），第六位为进出口企业经济类型编码（“1”表示有进出口经营权的国有企业；“2”表示中外合作企业；“3”表示中外合资企业；“4”表示外商独资企业；“5”表示有进出口经营权的集体企业；“6”表示有进出口经营权的私营企业；“7”表示有进出口经营权的个体工商户；“8”表示有报关权而无进出口经营权的企业；“9”表示其他，包括外国驻华企事业机构、外国驻华使领馆和临时进出口货物的企业、单位和个人），第七至第十位数为顺序编号。

8．运输方式

运输方式指载运货物进出关境所使用的运输工具的分类。根据实际运输方式并按海关规定的“运输方式代码表”，选择填报运输方式的名称或代码，常用的运输方式和代码如“水陆运输”或“2”、“铁路运输”或“3”、“汽车运输”或“4”、“航空运输”或“5”、“邮件运输”或“6”及“其他运输（驮畜、电网、管道等）”或“9”。

9．运输工具名称

将载运货物出境的运输工具的名称或运输工具编号填入此栏，一份报关单只允许填报一个运输工具名称。江海运输填报“船舶英文名”＋“/”＋“航次号”；航空运输填报“航班号”；铁路运输填报“车厢号”或“交接单号”＋“/”＋“进出境日期”；汽车运输填报“车牌号”＋“/”＋“进出境日期”。

10．提运单号

填报出口货物提单或运单编号，一票货物多个提运单时，应分单填写。江海运输：填报提运单号。如有分运单，填报“进出口提运单号”＋“*”＋“分运单号”；航空运输填报“总运单号”＋“_”（下划线）＋“分运单号”。无分运单的填报“总运单号”；邮政运输填报“包裹号”；铁路运输填报“运单号”；汽车运输免于填报。

11．收/发货单位

应填报收/发货单位的中文名称及编码，没有编码的，填报中文名称。

收货单位是指已知的进口货物在境内的最终消费、使用单位，包括自行从境外进口货物的单位、委托进出口企业进口货物的单位等。

发货单位是指出口货物在境内生产或销售的单位，包括自行出口货物的单位、委托进出口企业出口货物的单位。

12．贸易方式（监管方式）

根据实际情况并按海关规定的“贸易方式代码表”填制相应的贸易方式简称或代码。常用的贸易方式和代码如：“一般贸易”或“0110”、“易货贸易”或“0130”、“来料加工”或“0214”、“进料对口”或“0615”、“合资合作设备”或“2025”、“外资设备物品”或“2225”、“货样广告品A”或“3010”、“无代价抵偿货物”或“3100”。

本栏应与备案号栏相对应。例如：备案号栏空白时，本栏通常填“一般贸易”；备案号第一位如为“B”，本栏填“来料加工”。

13．征免性质

按海关核发的《征免税证明》中批注的征免性质或海关规定的《征免性质代码表》，填报相应的征免性质简称或其代码。如“一般征税”或“101”、“来料加工”或“502”、“进料加工”或“503”、“中外合资”或“601”、“中外合作”或“602”、“外资企业”或“603”、“鼓励项目”或“789”、“自有资金”或“799”、“其他法定”或“299”、“科教用品”或“401”。

本栏应对应贸易方式一栏。贸易方式若为“一般贸易”，则本栏为“一般征税”，贸易方式为“进料对口”，本栏填“进料加工”。

14．结汇方式/征税比例

依据合同和信用证规定，并按海关规定的“结汇方式代码表”，可选填中文名称、英文名称或代码。如“电汇”或“T/T”或“2”、“信汇”或“M/T”或“1”、“票汇”或“D/D”或“3”、“付款交单”或“D/P”或“4”、“承兑交单”或“D/A”或“5”、“信用证”或“L/C”或“6”等。出口货物报关单“结汇方式”不得为空。出口货物不需结汇的，应填其他。

进口报关单中的结汇方式及征税比例，不需填报。

15．许可证号

属于申领出口许可证的货物，必须填出口货物许可证的编号，不得为空。非许可证管理商品本栏为空，一般情况下本栏都为空。

16．运抵国（地区）/起运国（地区）

根据出口货物直接运抵的国家（地区），并按海关规定的“国别/地区代码表”填写中文名称或代码。如“日本”或“116”。如发生中转，在中转地没有发生买卖关系，起运国和运抵国不变，如在中转地发生了买卖关系，中转地为起运国或运抵国。有无发生买卖关系，可通过商业发票、提单等单证来判断。

17．指运港/装货港

填报指运港或装货港的中文名称或代码。

指运港也称目的港，填写出口货物运抵的最终目的港的中文名称，如提单中的最终目的港为“HONGKONG”，报关单指运港应填写“香港”。装货港是指进口货物在运抵我国关境前的最后一个境外装运港。

在直接运输方式下，货物实际装货的港口为装货港、直接运抵的港口为指运港；对发生运输中转的货物，最后一个中转港为装货港，指运港（亦称目的港）不发生变化。无实际进出境的货物“装货港”或者“指运港”，应填报“中国境内”。

18．境内货源地/境内目的地

按照“国内地区代码表”选择国内地区名称或代码填报，代码含义与经营单位前5位的定义相同。

境内货源地，指注明出口货物在国内的产地或始发地，及其国内地区代码。要填报具体的最小行政区域即区（县）。如“上海浦东新区或31222”。

境内目的地为已知的进口货物在我国关境内的消费、使用地区或最终运抵的地点。

19．批准文号

此栏应填报《出口收汇核销单》的编号；进口货物报关单免于填报。

20．成交方式

根据合同的成交条件，并按海关规定的《成交方式代码表》填写成交方式的名称或代码。如“FOB”或“3”、“CIF”或“1”或“CFR”或“2”等。

《Intercom 2000》通则 13 种贸易术语与报关单“成交方式”栏一般对应关系如下：

组别	E组	F组			C组				D组				
术语	EXW	FCA	FAS	FOB	CFR	CPT	CIF	CIP	DAF	DES	DEQ	DDU	DDP
成交方式	FOB				CFR		CIF						

21. **运费**

出口成交方式为 CIF、CFR，进口成交方式为 FOB，应在本栏填运费。可根据具体情况选择运费率（标记为 1）、运费单价（标记为 2）或运费总价（标记为 3）三种方式之一填报，同时注明运费标记，并按海关规定的《货币代码表》选择填报规定的币种代码。填制标准为：“货币代码”+“/”+“实际费用数字”+“/”+“费用标记”。如 5%的运费率，填报为“5/1”，24 美元的运费单价填报为“502/24/2”，7 000 美元的运费总价填报为“502/7000/3”。

我国进出口贸易中常用的货币代码分别为：美元 502，欧元 300，日元 116，英镑 303，港元 110 等。

22. **保费**

出口成交方式为 CIF，进口成交方式为 FOB、CFR，应在本栏填保费。可根据具体情况选择保费率（标记为 1）或运费总价（标记为 3）两种方式之一填报，同时注明保费标记，并按海关规定的《货币代码表》选择填报规定的币种代码。如 3‰的保费率，填报为“0.3/1”，10 000 港元保险费总价应填为“110/10000/3”。

23. **杂费**

杂费指成交价以外应计入完税价格或应从完税价格中扣除的费用，诸如手续费、佣金和回扣等，可按杂费总价（标记为 3）或杂费率（标记为 1）填报，应计入的为正，应扣除的为负。如应计入完税价格的 500 英镑杂费总价为“303/500/3”，应扣除的 1%的回扣率填报为“–1/1”。无运杂费时本栏免填。

24. **合同协议号**

注明出口货物合同（协议）的全部字头和号码。例如，“Contract No.:GM1008”，此栏填“GM1008”。

25. **件数**

按外包装的出口货物（如集装箱、托盘等）的实际件数填报，裸装、散货的货物填“1”。

26. **包装种类**

根据出口货物的实际外包装种类填报包装种类的中文名称。常见包装种类有：“Cartons=CTNS”填“纸箱”，“Pallet”填“托盘”，“Cases”填“木箱”，“Bales=BLS”填“布包”。

27. **毛重**（公斤）

按出口货物实际毛重（公斤）填，不足 1 公斤应填“1”。重量在 1 千克以上且非整数，其小数点后面保留 4 位，第 5 位及以后略去。

28. **净重**（公斤）

按出口货物实际净重（公斤）填，不足 1 公斤应填“1”。重量在 1 千克以上且非整数，其小数点后面保留 4 位，第 5 位及以后略去。

29．集装箱号

（1）填报格式："集装箱号" + "/" + "规格"+ "/" + "自重"；多个集装箱的，第一个集装箱号等信息填报在"集装箱号"栏，其他依次按相同的格式填在"标记唛码及备注"栏中。例如，一个 20 尺的集装箱，箱号为 TEXU3605231，自重是 2 275 千克，则集装箱号栏填报格式为 TEXU3605231/20/2275。

（2）非集装箱货物本栏目填报"0"（不能为空）。

30．随附单据

应填写与出口货物报关单一并向海关递交的单证的名称或代码。

（1）合同、发票、装箱单、许可证等必备的随附单证不在本栏目填报。

（2）只填报监管证件代码表中的除去进口许可证、出口许可证的监管证件代码及编号。

（3）填报方式为"监管证件代码" + ":" + "监管证件编号"。例如：××公司持 1100-2005-101256 号自动进口许可证报关，则根据名称自动进口许可证可判断其监管证件代码为"7"，故随附单据栏应填"7: 1100-2005-101256"。本栏目只填写一个监管证件的信息，多于一个监管证件的，其余的监管证件代码和编号按上述填报格式填写（原产地证书按原产地证书的格式填写）在"标记唛码及备注"栏中。多于一个监管证件的哪个证件填在随附单据栏，哪一个填在"标记唛码及备注"栏没有限制，自由选择。

（4）加工贸易内销征税报关单，本栏目填写内销征税联系单代码（c）及编号。

（5）含预归类商品报关单，本栏目填写"r" + ":" + "××关预归类书××号"。

（6）原产地证书相关内容的填报：

1）实行原产地证书联网管理的，在本栏目中填报"Y: <优惠贸易协定代码>"，同时将原产地证书编号填报在"备案号"栏，格式为"Y+原产地证书编号"。

2）未实现原产地证书联网管理的，本栏目填报"Y: <优惠贸易协定代码: 需证商品序号>"，但"备案号"栏免予填报。

3）优惠贸易协定项下出口货物，本栏目填报原产地证书代码和编号。

（7）其他填制要求：一份原产地证书只能对应一份报关单，享受协定税率和减免税的商品不能填在同一份报关单上。常用的监管证件代码表见表 5-1。

表　5-1

代　码	监管证件名称	代　码	监管证件名称
1	进口许可证	4	出口许可证
5	纺织品临时出口许可证	7	自动进口许可证
A	入境货物通关单	B	出境货物通关单
E	濒危物种允许出口证明书	F	濒危物种允许进口证明书
O	自动进口许可证（新旧机电产品）	P	固体废物进口许可证
Y	原产地证明	t	关税配额证明

31．生产厂家/用途

生产厂家：填出口货物的境内生产企业的名称，该栏仅供必要时填报。

用途：填进口货物的实际用途，按海关规定的"用途代码表"（表 5-2）填相应的名称或代码。

表 5-2

代码	名称	代码	名称	代码	名称
01	外贸自营内销	02	特区内销	03	其他内销
04	企业自用	05	加工返销	06	借用
07	收保证金	08	免费提供	09	作价提供
10	货样广告品	11	其他	13	以产顶进

32．标记唛码及备注

本栏目实际包含两部分内容，一是标记唛码，按照发票中的唛头，除图形以外的文字和数字填制，无标记唛码的免于填报；二是备注，多余的集装箱号和多余的随附单据，按照其填报要求填报在此栏。外商投资企业委托国内某家外贸公司进口的，应在备注栏填上“委托×××公司进口”。

33．项号

本栏目分两行填报及打印。

第一行打印报关单中的商品排列序号，第二行专用于加工贸易等已备案的货物在“登记手册”中的项号（此内容会在已知条件中给出。例如：××商品列手册第 2 项）。

注意：1 张报关单只允许填 5 种商品，一份报关单只允许填 20 种商品。

34．商品编号

按海关规定的商品分类编码规则填写该出口货物的商品编号，填报 8 位税则号列，以及第 9、第 10 位附加编号。

35．商品名称、规格型号

通常第一行写出口货物的中文名称，如果已知条件只有英文，需自行翻译成中文填写。第二行表示规格型号。商品名称及规格型号应按商业发票填写。

36．数量及单位

此栏分三行填报。

第一行：如果已知条件中给出一个计量单位则为第一法定计量单位。

第二行：如果已知条件中给出两个计量单位（例如：“布匹单位：公斤/米”。左侧为第一法定计量单位，右侧为第二法定计量单位）本行填写第二法定计量单位，没有第二法定计量单位，此栏为空。

第三行：成交计量单位与法定计量单位不同时，填报成交计量单位（如布匹的成交计量单位如果是码，此栏填码），成交计量单位与法定计量单位相同时，此栏为空。注明出口商品的实际数量及计量单位。

37．最终目的国（地区）

填制出口货物的最终消费或进一步加工制造国家或地区的中文名称或其国别/地区的代码。例如，最终目的国是日本，可以填“日本”或“116”。

38．单价

填报同一项号出口货物实际成交的商品单位价格，此栏目只需要填写价格数字而无须填写货币名称或者计量单位。单价非整数，其小数点后面保留 4 位，第 5 位及以后略去。

39．**总价**

填同一项号下出口货物实际成交的商品总价。此栏填法同单价。

40．**币制**

按实际成交情况根据海关规定的“币制代码表”（表 5-3）或填制名称或代码或符号。如成交货币是 USD，可填写代码“502”或符号“USD”或名称“美元”。

表　5-3

币制代码	币制符号	币制名称	币制代码	币制符号	币制名称	币制代码	币制符号	币制名称
110	HKD	港币	116	JPY	日元	142	CNY	人民币
300	EUR	欧元	303	GBP	英镑	502	USD	美元

41．**征免方式**

按海关核发的“征免税证明”和征减免税方式的代码表填写税费征收情况名称或代码。例如，全部免税填“全免”或“3”。通常为“照章征税”或“1”，手册来料加工或进料加工通常填“全免”或“3”。

42．**录入员**

用于预录入和 EDI 报关单，打印录入人员的姓名。

43．**录入单位**

用于预录入和 EDI 报关单，打印录入单位名称。

44．**申报单位**

注明向海关申报单位的全称和代码，如为委托代理报关应填报代理报关企业名称及代码，由报关员填报。

45．**填制日期**

这是指报关单的填制日期，顺序为年、月、日各 2 位。

46．**海关审单批注栏**

由海关人员填写。

自我能力测评

能力形成性评价表

评价指标	分值	实际得分
能掌握报关单每个栏目的填写规范	20 分	
能熟记备案号第一位标记码B、C、Z、Y等字母的含义	10 分	
能熟记经营单位代码第五、六位数字代表的含义	10 分	
能熟记常用运输方式、贸易方式、征免性质、结汇方式、监管证件、用途、常用币制、征免方式代码	20 分	
能根据背景资料准确填制进出口货物报关单	40 分	

任务三　申领出口许可证及缮制相关单据

任务导入

根据我国2010年《出口许可证管理商品目录》的规定，宁波光明进出口公司对外出口的货物不属于许可证管理范围内的商品，单证员小兰不需要申领出口该批货物的出口许可证。

现假设该商品属于许可证管理范围内的商品，对此，单证员小兰需备齐有关资料，向宁波市外经贸主管部门签发出口货物许可证。

完成该任务的步骤如下

第一步：弄清楚发放出口许可证的机构

商务部授权配额许可证事务局（以下简称许可证局）负责管理全国出口许可证发证机构及出口许可证的签发工作并监督检查。许可证局及商务部驻各地特派员办事处和各省、自治区、直辖市、计划单列市、新疆生产建设兵团，以及商务部授权的其他省会城市商务厅（局）、外经贸委（厅、局）负责出口许可证的具体签发工作。因此，小兰应向宁波外经贸局申请出口许可证。

第二步：弄清出口许可证的申请流程

（1）出口商填写出口许可证申请书，并随附发票、合同等文件，向发证机关提出申请；

（2）发证机关审核无误后，3日内签发出口许可证书，并通知出口商。

第三步：缮制出口许可证申请书

制单依据：宁波光明进出口公司小兰依据项目一中修改合约信用证（单证1-17）及其分析结果单（单证 1-18），并参照已填写的商业发票等其他单据，填写《出口货物许可证申请表》（单证5-3）。

填写步骤一：学生独立填写出口许可证申请表

填制指导：学生可以先尝试独立填写一份申请表，如有疑问，再查阅下列出口许可证申请书的填制要领；也可以先看出口许可证申请书的填制要领，再填制申请书。

要求：填制好的申请书要在小组中交流，然后提交到天空教室。

单证　5-3

出口许可证申请表

1. 出口商：　　　　代码： 领证人姓名：　　　　电话：	3. 出口许可证号：
2. 发货人：　　　　代码：	4. 出口许可证有效截止日期： 年　月　日
5. 贸易方式：	8. 进口国（地区）：
6. 合同号：	9. 付款方式：

（续）

7．报关口岸：			10．运输方式：		
11．商品名称：　　　　　商品编码：					
12．规格、等级	13．单位	14．数量	15．单价（币别）	16．总值（币别）	17．总值折美元
18．总　计					
19．备　注 申请单位盖章 申领日期：			20．签证机构审批（初审）： 经办人： 终审：		

填表说明：1．本表应用正楷逐项填写清楚，不得涂改、遗漏，否则无效。

2．本表内容需打印多份许可证的，请在备注栏内注明。

3．本表填写一式两份。

步骤二：老师随机抽取一组同学填制的单证，集体批阅、点评，核对答案

答案如下：

单证　5-4

出口许可证申请表

1．出口商：　　　代码： 宁波光明进出口公司　　3302187964586 领证人姓名：小兰　　电话：0574-88896000			3．出口许可证号：		
2．发货人：　　　代码： 宁波光明进出口公司　　3302187964586 电话：0574-88896000　　联系人：小兰			4．出口许可证有效截止日期： 年　月　日		
5．贸易方式：一般贸易			8．进口国（地区）： 中国香港		
6．合同号：E034579			9．付款方式：信用证		
7．报关口岸：北仑海关			10．运输方式：江海运输		
11．商品名称：全尼龙织物　　　　商品编码：6302.2290					
12．规格、等级	13．单位	14．数量	15．单价（币别）	16．总值（币别）	17．总值折美元
100%尼龙	码	100 000	USD0.3368	USD33 680	USD33 680
18．总　计		100 000		USD33 680	USD33 680
19．备　注 申领单位盖章 宁波光明进出口公司 公司法人章 申领日期：2010.03.18			20．签证机构审批（初审）： 经办人： 终审：		

第四步：主管部门签发出口货物许可证

样表如下：

单证 5-5

中华人民共和国出口许可证

EXPORT LICENSE THE PEOPLE'S REPUBLIC OF CHINA

<table>
<tr><td colspan="3">1. 出口商：
EXPORTER 宁波光明进出口公司</td><td colspan="3">3. 出口许可证号：
EXPORT LICENCESE NO.05AB122455</td></tr>
<tr><td colspan="3">2. 发货人：
CONSIGNOR 宁波光明进出口公司</td><td colspan="3">4. 出口许可证有效截止日期：
EXPORT LICENCESE EXPIRY DATE 2010.09.21</td></tr>
<tr><td colspan="3">5. 贸易方式：
TERMS OF TRADE 一般贸易</td><td colspan="3">8. 进口国（地区）：
COUNTRY /REGION OF PURCHASE 中国香港</td></tr>
<tr><td colspan="3">6. 合同号：
CONTRACT NO. E034579</td><td colspan="3">9. 付款方式：
TERMS OF PAYMENT 信用证</td></tr>
<tr><td colspan="3">7. 报关口岸：
PORT OF SHIPMENT 北仑海关</td><td colspan="3">10. 运输方式：
MEANS OF TRANSPORT 江海运输</td></tr>
<tr><td colspan="3">11. 商品名称：
DESCRIPTION OF GOODS 全尼龙织物</td><td colspan="3">商品编码：
CODE OF GOODS 6302.2290</td></tr>
<tr><td>12. 规格、等级
SPECIFICATION</td><td>13. 单位
UNIT</td><td>14. 数量
QUANTITY</td><td>15. 单价（币别）
UNIT PRICE</td><td>16. 总值（币别）
AMOUNT</td><td>17. 总值折美元
AMOUNT IN USA</td></tr>
<tr><td>100%尼龙</td><td>码</td><td>100 000</td><td>USD0.3368</td><td>USD33 680</td><td>USD33 680</td></tr>
<tr><td></td><td></td><td></td><td></td><td></td><td></td></tr>
<tr><td></td><td></td><td></td><td></td><td></td><td></td></tr>
<tr><td></td><td></td><td></td><td></td><td></td><td></td></tr>
<tr><td>18. 总计</td><td></td><td>100 000</td><td>USD0.3368</td><td>USD33 680</td><td>USD33 680</td></tr>
<tr><td colspan="3">19. 备注
SUPPLEMENTARY DETAILS</td><td colspan="3">20. 签证机构审批（初审）：
ISSUING AUTHORITY'S STAMP @SIGNATURE
宁波对外经贸局
法人章
发证日期
LICENSE DATE 2010 年 3 月 21 日</td></tr>
</table>

商务部监制本证不得涂改，不得转让。

注：出口许可证各栏目的填写与出口许可证申请表各栏目的填写基本一致。

知识链接

一、出口许可证申请表填制规范

凡申领出口许可证的单位，应按以下规范填写出口许可证申请表。

1. 出口商

（1）配额管理的出口商品，应填写出口配额指标单位的进出口企业全称；

（2）一般许可证管理的出口商品，应填写有出口经营权的各类进出口企业的全称；

（3）还贷、补偿贸易项目出口，应填写有出口经营权的代理公司全称；

（4）非外贸单位经批准出运的货物，此栏填写该单位名称；

（5）企业编码，应按外经贸部授权的发证机关编制的代码填写，13 位数。"进出口企业代码"的编码原则是：前 4 位码为企业注册地行政区代码（下同）。

2. 发货人

（1）配额招标商品（包括有偿和无偿招标）的发货人与出口商必须一致。

（2）其他出口配额管理商品的发货人原则上应与出口商一致，但与出口商有隶属关系的可以不一致。

（3）还贷出口、补偿贸易出口和外商投资企业委托代理出口时，发货人与出口商可以不一致。

3．出口许可证号

出口许可证号由发证机关编排。

4．出口许可证有效截止日期

（1）实行“一批一证”制的商品，其许可证有效期自发证之日起最长为三个月。供港澳（不包括转口）鲜活冷冻商品的许可证有效期为一个月。

（2）不实行“一批一证”制的商品、外商投资企业和补偿贸易项下的出口商品，其许可证有效期自发证之日起最长为六个月。

（3）许可证正面有效期如需跨年度时，可在当年将许可证日期填到次年，最迟至二月底。

5．贸易方式

（1）此栏内容有：一般贸易、易货贸易、补偿贸易、进料加工、来料加工、外商投资企业出口、边境贸易、出料加工、转口贸易、期货贸易、承包工程、归还贷款出口、国际展销、协定贸易、其他贸易。

（2）进料加工复出口，此栏填写进料加工。

（3）外商投资企业进料加工复出口时，贸易方式填写“外商投资企业出口”。

（4）非外贸单位出运展卖品和样品每批价值在5 000元以上的，此栏填写“国际展览”。

（5）各类进出口企业出运展卖品，此栏填写“国际展览”，出运样品填写“一般贸易”。

6．合同号

（1）合同号指申领许可证、报关及结汇时所用出口合同的编码。

（2）原油、成品油及非贸易项下出口，可不填写合同号。

（3）展品出运时，此栏应填写外经贸部批准办展的文件号。

7．报关口岸

报关口岸指出运口岸，此栏允许填写三个口岸，但仅能在一个口岸报关。

8．进口国（地区）

进口国（地区）指最终目的地，即合同目的地，不允许使用地域名（如欧洲等）。

9．支付方式

此栏的内容有：信用证、托收、汇付、本票、现金、记账和免费等。

10．运输方式

可填写海上运输、铁路运输、公路运输、航空运输、邮政运输、固定运输。

11．商品名称和编码

按外经贸部发布的出口许可证管理商品目录的标准名称填写。

12．规格等级

（1）规格等级栏，用于对所出口商品作具体说明，包括具体品种、规格（如水泥标号、钢材品种等）、等级（如兔毛等级）。同一编码商品规格型号超过四种时，应另行填写出口许可证申请表。“劳务出口物资”也应按此填写。

（2）出运货物必须与此栏说明的出口品种、规格或等级相一致。

13．单位

单位指计量单位。非贸易项下的出口商品，此栏以“批”为计量单位，具体单位在备注栏中说明。

14．数量、单价及总值

（1）数量表示该证允许出口商品的多少。此数值允许保留一位小数，凡位数超出的，一律以四舍五入进位。计量单位为“批”的，此栏均为1。

（2）单价是指与计量单位相一致的单位价格，计量单位为“批”的，此栏则为总金额。

（3）总值。填写该证允许出口商品的总金额，由单价乘以数量计算而得，应与合同、发票总金额一致。

15．备注

填写以上各栏未尽事宜。

二、出口许可证更改、延期、遗失的处理

各类进出口企业领取许可证后，因故需要对出口许可证更改、延期时，应按以下规定办理。

（1）按规定，出口许可证一经签发，任何发证机关不得更改任何证面内容；如确需更改某一项目，出口单位应填写出口许可证申请表并提供出口合同，提交原出口许可证，由发证机关换发新证。

（2）出口许可证在有效期内未使用或未使用完，出口单位可申请延期，并将原出口许可证退还原发证机关。由原发证机关按规定对未使用完的许可证做换证处理。出口许可证的有效期最迟可延期到次年的二月底。

申领单位如丢失出口许可证，应及时向发证机关和该证的报关口岸海关挂失。重新申领出口许可证时，应向发证机关提供未报关证明和遗失报告，由发证机关按规定办理。

三、申领单位的法律责任

申领单位不许伪造、变造、买卖出口许可证，对违反者，将按《中华人民共和国对外贸易法》和海关法规追究刑事责任。

自我能力测评

能力形成性评价表

评价指标	分　值	实际得分
能说出出口许可证的发证机关及申领程序	20分	
能准确列出申领出口许可证所需单据清单	20分	
能准确出口许可证申请表	60分	

任务四 申领并缮制原产地证书

任务导入

宁波光明进出口公司根据信用证的规定，应提供普惠制原产地证书。对此，单证员小兰要向宁波出入境检验检疫局主管部门申请签发普惠制产地证。

完成上述任务的步骤如下

第一步：弄清楚签发原产地证书的机构

原产地证书有多种形式，其中应用最多的是一般原产地证书（CERTIFICATE OF ORIGIN，简称 C.O.）和普惠制产地证书（GENERALIZED SYSTEM OF PREFERENCES CERTIFICATE OF ORIGIN，简称 G.S.P.），普惠制产地证书使用最广的格式为 FORM A。

1．一般原产地证书的签证机构

凡进口方要求由我官方机构签发一般原产地证的，申请单位应向商检局申请办理；凡进口方要求由我民间机构签发一般原产地证的，申请单位应向贸促会申请；未明确要求的，可向商检局或贸促会申请。

2．普惠制原产地证书的签证机构

申请单位原则上向所在地检验检疫机构申请办理签证，特殊情况需在异地申请签证时，必须提供所在地检验检疫机构注册登记的证明文件。

第二步：弄清原产地证书的申请流程

一般原产地证书和普惠制产地证书申请流程一样，只是发证机构和填写的证书格式不同。下面以普惠制产地证书申请流程为例进行说明。

（1）出口商填写普惠制产地证明申请书一份，普惠制产地证明书 FORM A 一套，随附发票一份及发证机关要求的其他文件，最迟在装运前五天，向当地商检局提出申请；

（2）发证机关审核无误后，一般在两个工作日内完成证书的签发工作，并通知出口商。

第三步：要求学生独立列出申领普惠制原产地证书的清单并理单

在已有的单据后面用√标明。

（1）普惠制产地证明申请书一份；

（2）普惠制产地证明书 FORM A 一套；

（3）发票一份（√）。

第四步：缮制普惠制产地证明书申请书

制单依据：宁波光明进出口公司小兰依据项目一中信用证（单证 1-17）及其分析结果单（单证 1-18），并参照已填写的商业发票等其他单据，填写《普惠制产地证明书申请书》（单证 5-6）。

补充资料：该单位在检验检疫局产地证签证部门注册的注册号为 87G9988。

单证 5-6

普惠制产地证明书申请书

申请单位（盖章）：

申请人郑重声明：

本人是被正式授权代表出口单位办理和签署本申请书的。本申请书及普惠制产地证格式 A 所列内容正确无误，如发现弄虚作假，冒充格式 A 所列货物，擅改证书，自愿接受签证机关的处罚及负法律责任。现将有关情况申报如下：

宁波光明进出口公司

公司法人章

现提交中国出口商业发票副本一份，普惠制产地证证明书格式 A（FORM A）一正二副，以及其他附件____份。请予审核签证。

注：凡含有进口成分的商品，必须按要求提交《含进口成分受惠商品成本明细单》。

注册号：87G9988　　证书号：

<table>
<tr><td>生产单位</td><td colspan="2"></td><td colspan="2">生产单位联系人电话</td><td colspan="2"></td></tr>
<tr><td>商品名称
（中英文）</td><td colspan="2"></td><td colspan="2">H.S.税目号
（以六位数码计）</td><td colspan="2"></td></tr>
<tr><td colspan="2">商品（FOB）总值（以美元计）</td><td colspan="2"></td><td>发票号</td><td colspan="2"></td></tr>
<tr><td>最终销售国</td><td></td><td colspan="2">证书种类划“√”</td><td>加急证书</td><td colspan="2">普通证书</td></tr>
<tr><td colspan="2">货物拟出运日期</td><td colspan="5"></td></tr>
<tr><td colspan="7">贸易方式和企业性质（请在适用处划“√”）</td></tr>
<tr><td>正常贸易</td><td>灵活贸易</td><td>中外合资
H</td><td>中外合作
Z</td><td>外商独资
D</td><td>零售
Y</td><td>展卖
M</td></tr>
<tr><td></td><td></td><td></td><td></td><td></td><td></td><td></td></tr>
<tr><td colspan="2">包装数量或毛重或其他数量</td><td colspan="5"></td></tr>
</table>

原产地标准：

本项商品系在中国生产，完全符合该给惠国给惠方案规定，其原产地情况符合以下第______条：

（1）“P”（完全国产，未使用任何进口原材料）；

（2）“W”其 H.S.税目号为__________（含进口成分或来料加工）；

（3）“F”（对加拿大出口产品，其进口成分不超过产品出厂价值的 40%）。

本批产品系：1．直接运输从________________到________________；

2．转口运输从________________中转国（地区）__________到__________。

申请人说明	领证人（签名） 电　话： 日期　　年　月　日

商检局联系记录

填制要求如下：

（1）学生先独立填写上述申请书，如有疑问，再查阅下列普惠制产地证明书申请书填写规范。

（2）填写完毕，小组交流讨论后，将结果上传到天空教室。

（3）教师随机抽取一个小组某一同学的作业进行集中点评，核对答案。

答案如下：

单证　5-7

普惠制产地证明书申请书

申请单位（盖章）：

申请人郑重声明：

宁波光明进出口公司

公司法人章

本人是被正式授权代表出口单位办理和签署本申请书的。本申请书及普惠制产地证格式 A 所列内容正确无误，如发现弄虚作假，冒充格式A 所列货物，擅改证书，自愿接受签证机关的处罚及负法律责任。现将有关情况申报如下：

现提交中国出口商业发票副本一份，普惠制产地证证明书格式 A（FORMA）一正二副，以及其他附件____份。请予审核签证。

注：凡含有进口成分的商品，必须按要求提交《含进口成分受惠商品成本明细单》。

注册号：　　　　　　　　　　　　　　　　证书号：

生产单位	宁波光明进出口公司	生产单位联系人电话	0574-88896000
商品名称（中英文）	100%尼龙织物 100% NYLON FABRICS	H.S.税目号（以六位数码计）	6302.2290

商品（FOB）总值（以美元计）	USD33 220.00	发票号	GM10H9141

最终销售国	中国香港	证书种类划“√”	加急证书	√普通证书

货物拟出运日期	2010.04.05

贸易方式和企业性质（请在适用处划“√”）

正常贸易	灵活贸易	中外合资 H	中外合作 Z	外商独资 D	零售 Y	展卖 M
√						

包装数量或毛重或其他数量	1 000 卷

原产地标准：

本项商品系在中国生产，完全符合该给惠国给惠方案规定，其原产地情况符合以下第＿（1）＿条：

（1）“P”（完全国产，未使用任何进口原材料）；

（2）“W”其 H.S.税目号为____________（含进口成分或来料加工）；

（3）“F”（对加拿大出口产品，其进口成分不超过产品出厂价值的 40%）。

本批产品系：1．直接运输从＿宁波＿到＿香港＿；

2．转口运输从＿***＿中转国（地区）＿***＿到＿***＿。

申请人说明　　***　　　　　　领证人（签名）小兰

电　　话：0574-88896000

日期　2010 年 3 月 23 日

商检局联系记录

知识链接

普惠制产地证明书申请书填写规范

（1）申请单位（盖章）栏：申请原产地证的出口企业并加盖申请单位公章。

（2）注册号：填写申请单位在检验检疫局产地证签证部门注册的注册号，如 14G001。

（3）证书号：根据签证机构的编号规则，对应于每批申报货物的编号。不得重号或跳号。编号规则：Gx/申请单位注册号/0001，x 代表年份，后四位代表流水号，如 G07/14G001/0001。

（4）申请单位：申请原产地证的出口企业。

（5）生产单位联系人电话：填写申请单位的联系电话。

（6）商品名称：填写商品品名的中英文，并且与发票证书的商品名称一致。

（7）H.S.税目号：商品的 H.S.六位数编码，海关统计编码前六位。

（8）FOB 总值：根据申报的出口货物出口发票上所列的金额以 FOB 价格填写（以美元计），如出口货物不是以 FOB 价格成交的，应换算成 FOB 价格。

（9）发票号：填写正式出口发票的号码，并与随附发票相一致。

（10）最终销售国：即货物即将运抵的最终销售国。

（11）证书种类：在此证书种类栏划“√”。

（12）拟出运日期：如实准确填写货物离开起运口岸当天的日期（年、月、日）。

（13）贸易方式和企业性质：根据实际情况选择划“√”。

（14）包装数量、毛重或其他数量：填写该批出口货物的箱数、毛重或个数等。

（15）原产地标准：根据提示及货物实际情况选择 1～4 项如实填写。

（16）本批商品系：根据货物运输路线的起运港、中转港及目的港填写本批商品运输路线，无转运港的填写“***”。

（17）申请人说明：填写具体说明，如果没有则填“***”。

（18）领证人：填写领证人姓名及日期。

第五步：缮制普惠制产地证明书

制单依据：宁波光明进出口公司小兰依据项目一中信用证（单证 1-17）及其分析结果单（单证 1-18），并参照已填写的商业发票等其他单据，填写《普惠制产地证明》。

完成上述任务的步骤如下

步骤一：教师导学、示范，引导学生口头填写一份普惠制产地证明书

如图 5-3 所示，教师广播教学，用自制的课件告诉学生每一个栏目的填写要点，然后让学生结合项目一中信用证（单证 1-17）及其分析结果单（单证 1-18），并参照已填写的商业发票等其他单据，说出每个栏目的填写内容。

ORIGINAL

<table>
<tr><td colspan="2">1. Goods consigned from (Exporter's business name, address, country)

发货人：出口方名称、详细地址及国家（地区）。一般填写合同的卖方或发票的出票人。</td><td colspan="4" rowspan="2">Reference No.
证书编号：此栏不得留空，否则，证书无效。
IZED SYSTEM OF PREFERENCES
ERTIFICATE OF ORIGIN
declaration and certificate)
FORM A
Issued in THE PEOPLE'S REPUBLIC OF CHINA
(country)
See Notes overleaf</td></tr>
<tr><td colspan="2">2. Goods consigned to (Consignee's name, address,country)</td></tr>
<tr><td colspan="2">3. Means of transport and route (as far as known)</td><td colspan="4">4. For official use</td></tr>
<tr><td>5. Item number</td><td>6. Marks and numbers of packages</td><td>7. Number and kind of packages; description of goods</td><td>8. Origin criterion (see Notes overleaf)</td><td>9. Gross weight or other quantity</td><td>10. Number and date of invoices</td></tr>
<tr><td colspan="3">11. Certification
It is hereby certified, on the basis of control carried out, that the declaration by the exporter is correct.

中华人民共和国
上海进出口商品检验局
SHANGHAI IMP. & EXP.
OMMODITY INSPECTIO

Place and date. Signature and stamp of certifying authority</td><td colspan="3">12. Declaration by the exporter
The undersigned hereby declares that the above details and statements are correct; that all the goods were produced in ________ (country)
and that they comply with the origin requirements specified for those goods in the Generalized System of Preferences for goods exported to
________ (importing country)

Place and date. Signature and stamp of certifying authority</td></tr>
</table>

图 5-3

教师引导学生口头填写的答案如下（单证 5-8）：

单证 5-8

<table>
<tr><td colspan="3">1. Goods consigned from (Exporter's name, address, country)
GUANGMING IMPORT & EXPORT CORPORATION
13 XINNING ROAD, NINGBO, ZHEJIANG, CHINA
TEL:0574-8889600</td><td colspan="3" rowspan="2">Reference No.: 1-A222/A05/0251

GENERALIZED SYSTEM OF PREFERENCES
CERTIFICATE OF ORIGIN
(Combined declaration and certificate)
FORM A
Issued in THE PEOPLE'S REPUBLIC OF CHINA
(country)
See Notes, Overleaf</td></tr>
<tr><td colspan="3">2. Goods consigned to (Consignee's name, address, country)
FUHUA TRADE CO. LTD.,
101 QUEENS ROAD CENTRAL, HONGKONG
TEL: 852-2857777</td></tr>
<tr><td colspan="3">3. Means of transport and route (as far as known)
FROM NINGBO TO HONGKONG BY SEA</td><td colspan="3">4. For official use</td></tr>
<tr><td>5. Item number

1</td><td>6. Marks and numbers of packages

FUHUA
HONGKONG
R/N0:1-1000</td><td>7. Number and kind of packages; description of goods

ONE THOUSAND (1000) ROLLS OF 100% NYLON FABRICS
******************************</td><td>8. Origin criterion (see Notes overleaf)

P</td><td>9. Gross weight or other quantity

100,000 YARDS</td><td>10. Number and date of invoices

GM10H9141
MAR18,2010</td></tr>
<tr><td colspan="3">11. Certification
It is hereby certified, on the basis of control carried out, that the declaration by the exporter is correct

Place and date. Signature and stamp of certifying authority</td><td colspan="3">12. Declaration by the exporter
The undersigned hereby declares that the above details and statements are correct, that all the goods were
Produced in ______ china ______
(country)
and that they comply with the origin requirements specified for those goods in the Generalized System of Preferences for goods exported to
______ HONGKONG ______
(importing country)

______ NINGBO, MARCH 23, 2010 ______
Place and date. Signature of certifyingauthority</td></tr>
</table>

步骤二：巩固训练：学生结合一份合同和信用证独立填写一份普惠制产地证并审核

训练任务

宁波舒普机电科技公司单证员马林根据项目一任务五中，马林修改后的信用证（单证 1-19）及其信用证分析结果单（单证 1-20），参照已填写的商业发票等其他单据，独立填写下列普惠制产地证明书（单证 5-9）。

单证　5-9

<table>
<tr><td colspan="4">1. Goods consigned from (Exporter's name, address, country)</td><td colspan="3">Reference No.: 1-A222/A05/0251</td></tr>
<tr><td colspan="4">2. Goods consigned to (Consignee's name, address, country)</td><td colspan="3">GENERALIZED SYSTEM OF PREFERENCES
CERTIFICATE OF ORIGIN
(Combined declaration and certificate)
FORM A
Issued in THE PEOPLE'S REPUBLIC OF CHINA
(country)
See Notes, Overleaf</td></tr>
<tr><td colspan="4">3. Means of transport and route (as far as known)</td><td colspan="3">4. For official use</td></tr>
<tr><td>5. Item number</td><td>6. Marks and numbers of packages</td><td colspan="2">7. Number and kind of packages; description of goods</td><td>8. Origin criterion (see Notes overleaf)</td><td>9. Gross weight or other quantity</td><td>10. Number and date of invoices</td></tr>
<tr><td colspan="3">11. Certification
It is hereby certified, on the basis of control carried out, that the declaration by the exporter is correct

Pacce and date. Signature and stamp of certifying authority</td><td colspan="4">12. Dectaration by the exporter
The undersigned hereby declares that the above details and statements are correct, that all the goods were
Produced in ____________
(country)
and that they comply with the origin requirements specified for those goods in the Generalized System of Preferences for goods exported to ____________
(importing country)

____
Place and date. Signature of certifying authority</td></tr>
</table>

训练指导：学生可以根据刚才老师的引导、示范，先尝试填写一份普惠制产地证，若有疑问可查阅下列普惠制产地证的填制要领；也可以先看普惠制产地证的填制要领，再填制普惠制产地证。

要求：填制好的普惠制产地证要在小组中交流，然后将电子文档提交到天空教室。

步骤三：教师点评，核对答案

教师随机选取某一个小组某一同学的作业进行集中点评，核对答案。

知识链接

普惠制产地证明书填制规范

普遍优惠制（简称普惠制）是发达国家对发展中国家向其出口制成品或半成品时，普遍给予的一种关税优惠待遇的制度。而享受普惠制待遇的商品，出口方一般应向给惠国提供原产地证表格 A（FORM A）。

FORM A 纹面为绿色扭索图案，由出口企业在货物出运前 5 天自行缮制好，连同 FORM

A 申请书及商业发票一份送交各地商检局审核。商检机构接受申请后，审核无误即签发正本一份进行议付（副本由出口商自己签章），除 6、8、10、11、12 栏不能更改外，其他各栏也只能改动一处，并要加盖商检局更正章。普惠制产地证的证书名称栏下方，出入境检验检疫局在印制证书时，一般已事先印妥中华人民共和国签发的英文字样，即“ISSUED IN THE PEOPLE’S REPUBLIC OF CHINA”，其他栏目的内容及填制要求如下。

1．**证书号**（Reference No.）

普惠制原产地证书标题栏（右上角），填上检验检疫机构编定的证书号。证书号编订规则：以 ZC314*/070001 为例，ZC314*指公司注册号，07 指 2007 年，0001 指企业流水号。

2．**第 1 栏：出口商名称、地址、国家**（地区）

Goods consigned from (Exporter’s name, address, country)（收货人的名称、地址、国家（地区））栏是强制性的，必须填上出口商的全称和详细地址，包括街道及门牌号码等。出口商一般为合同的卖方，信用证方式下为信用证的受益人。例如：SHENZHEN HUAYELONG IMPORTS & EXPORTS LTD. SHENZHEN, CHINA.

3．**第 2 栏：收货人的名称、地址、国家**（地区）

Goods consigned to (Consignee’s name, address, country)（收货人的名称、地址、国家（地区））中的内容一般为给惠国的最终收货人名称及地址。信用证若有特殊规定，应按规定填写。

除欧盟成员国和挪威外，此栏须填上给惠国最终收货人名称，不可填中间转口商的名称，此栏须打上国名。欧盟成员国和挪威对此栏是非强制性要求，若第二栏进口商国家和第 12 栏最终目的国都是欧盟国家，则可以与第 12 栏国家不同，也可以不填详细地址，只填上“To Order”。39 个给惠国及输入代码为：欧盟成员国（305 法国 France，303 英国 United Kingdom，306 爱尔兰 Ireland，304 德国 Germany，302 丹麦 Denmark，307 意大利 Italy，301 比利时 Belgium，309 荷兰 Netherlands，308 卢森堡 Luxembourg，310 希腊 Greece，312 西班牙 Spain，311 葡萄牙 Portugal，315 奥地利 Austria，330 瑞典 Sweden，318 芬兰 Finland，327 波兰 Poland，321 匈牙利 Hungary，350 斯洛文尼亚 Slovenia Rep，352 捷克 Czech Rep，353 斯洛伐克 Slovak Rep，334 爱沙尼亚 Estonia，335 拉脱维亚 Latvia，336 立陶宛 Lithuania，108 塞浦路斯 Cyprus，324 马耳他 Malta，保加利亚 The Repubic of Bulgaria，罗马尼亚 Romania），137 土耳其 Turkey，331 瑞士 Switzerland，326 挪威 Norway，116 日本 Japan，601 澳大利亚 Australia，609 新西兰 New Zealand，501 加拿大 Canada，344 俄罗斯 Russia，347 乌克兰 Ukraine，340 白俄罗斯 Byelorussia，341 哈萨克斯坦 Kazakhstan，列支敦士登 Principality of Liechtenstein。美国也是一个给惠国，但没有给我国普惠制优惠。

4．**第 3 栏：运输方式及路线**（就所知道而言）

Means of transport and route (as far as known)（运输方式及路线）栏一般应填上装货、到货地点（始启运港、目的港）及运输方式（如海运、陆运、空运），转运商品应加上转运港。例如：FROM DONGGUAN TO SHENZHEN BY TRUCK，THENCE TRANSSHIPPED TO HAMBURG BY SEA.

对输往内陆给惠国的商品，如瑞士、奥地利，由于这些国家没有海岸，因此如是海运，都须经第三国，再转运至该国，填证时应注明。例如：BY VESSEL FROM SHENZHEN TO HAMBURG, IN TRANSIT TO SWITZERLAND.

5．第4栏：供官方使用

For official use（供官方使用）栏由签证当局填写，正常情况下此栏空白。特殊情况下，签证当局在此栏加注。例如：①货物已出口，签证日期迟于出货日起，签发“后发”证书时，此栏盖上“ISSUED RETROSPECTIVELY”红色印章。②证书遗失、被盗或者损毁，签发“复本”证书时盖上“DUPLICATE”红色印章，并在此栏注明原证书的编号和签证日期，并声明原发证书作废，其文字是“THIS CERTIFICATE IS IN REPLACEMENT OF CERTIFICATE OF ORIGIN NO.…DATED…WHICH IS CANCELLED”。

注意：在录入后发证书时，请在申请书备注栏注明“申请后发”，否则计算机将退回。

6．第5栏：商品顺序号

Item number（商品顺序号）栏内填入有不同品种的产品的同一批出口货物，可按不同品种归类后，用阿拉伯数字按顺序编号后填入“1”，“2”，“3”等，以此类推。单项商品，此栏填“1”。

7．第6栏：唛头及包装号

Marks and numbers of packages（唛头及包装号）栏按发票上的唛头填写。填具的唛头应与货物外包装上的唛头及发票的唛头一致；唛头不得出现中国以外的地区和国家制造的字样，也不能出现香港、澳门、台湾原产地字样（例如：MADE IN TAIWAN, HONG KONG PRODUCTS 等）；如货物无唛头应填“N/M”。如唛头过多，此栏不够填则打上（SEE THE ATTACHMENT），用附页填打所有唛头（附页的纸张要与原证书一样大小），在右上角打上证书号，并由申请单位和签证当局授权签字人分别在附页末页的右下角和左下角手签、盖印。附页手签的笔迹、地点、日期均与证书第11、12栏相一致。

注意：有附页时，请在申请书备注栏注明“唛头见附页”，否则计算机将退回。

8．第7栏：包装数量、种类及品名

Number and kind of packages; description of goods（包件数量、种类及品名）栏中包装种类及件数按商业发票和装箱单填写，必须有英文和阿拉伯数字同时表示。例如：ONE HUNDRED AND FIFTY (150) CARTONS OF WORKING GLOVES。

注意：

（1）如果包装数量为一千以上，则千与百单位之间不能有“AND”连词，否则计算机将退回。应填：TWO THOUSAND ONE HUNDRED AND FIFTY (2 150) CARTONS OF WORKING GLOVES。

（2）数量、品名要求在一页内打完，如果内容过长，则可以合并包装箱数，品名。例如：ONE HUNDRED AND FIFTY (150) CARTONS OF GLOVE, SCARF, TIE, CAP.

（3）包装必须打具体的包装种类（如 POLYWOVEN BAG, DRUM, PALLET, WOODEN CASE 等），不能只填写“PACKAGE”。如果没有包装，应填写“NUDE CARGO”（裸装货），“IN BULK”（散装货）或“HANGING GARMENTS”（挂装）。

（4）商品名称必须具体填明（具体到能找到相对应的4位HS编码），不能笼统填“MACHINE”（机器）、“GARMENT”（服装）等。对一些商品，如玩具电风扇应注明为“TOYS: ELECTRIC FANS”，不能只列“ELECTRIC FANS”（电风扇）。

（5）商品的商标、牌名（BRAND）及货号（ARTICLE NUMBER）一般可以不填。商品名称等项列完后，应在下一行加上表示结束的符号，以防止加填伪造内容。国外信用证有时要求填写合同、信用证号码等，可加填在此栏空白处。

9．第 8 栏：原产地标准

Origin criterion (see Notes overleaf)（原产地标准）栏是本证书的核心内容，是国外海关审核的重点项目，必须按规定如实填写。

（1）完全原产品，不含任何非原产成分，出口到所有给惠国，填写“P”。

（2）含有非原产成分的产品，出口到欧盟、挪威、瑞士和日本，填写“W”，其后加上出口产品的 HS 商品目号，如“W”42.02。条件：①产品列入了上述给惠国的“加工清单”符合其加工条件；②产品未列入“加工清单”，但产品生产过程中使用的非原产原材料和零部件经过充分的加工，产品的 HS 品目号不同于所用的原材料和零部件的 HS 品目号。

（3）含有非原产成分的产品，出口到加拿大，填写“F”。条件：非原产成分的价值未超过产品出厂价的 40%。

（4）含有非原产成分的产品，出口到俄罗斯、乌克兰、白俄罗斯、哈萨克斯坦、捷克、斯洛伐克六国，填写“Y”，其后加上非原产成分价值占该产品离岸价格的百分比，例如“Y”38%。条件：非原产成分的价值未超过产品离岸价的 50%。

（5）输往澳大利亚、新西兰的货物，此栏可以留空。

10．第 9 栏：毛重或其他数量

Gross weight or other quantity（毛重或其他数量）栏应以商品的正常计量单位填，如“只”、“件”、“双”、“台”、“打”等。例如：“3200 doz.”或“6270 kg.”。以重量计算的则填毛重，只有净重的，则净重亦可，但要标上 N.W.（NET WEIGHT）。

11．第 10 栏：发票号码及日期

Number and date of invoices（发票号码及日期）栏不得留空。月份一律用英文（可用缩写）表示。例如：“PHK50016 Apr.6，2007”。此栏的日期必须按照正式商业发票填具，发票日期不得迟于出货日期。

12．第 11 栏：签证当局的证明

Certification（签证当局的证明）栏中证明的内容在印制单据时一般已事先印好。

本栏由出入境检验检疫局签章并由其授权签字人手签。出证日期及地点由申请单位一起填写。其日期不得早于第 10 栏的发票日期和第 12 栏的申请如期，也不能晚于提单的装运日期。签章与手签不能重叠或覆盖。检验检疫机构只签正本单据，不签署副本。

13．第 12 栏：出口商的声明

Declaration by the exporter（出口商的声明）应填写的内容包括以下几点。

（1）生产国：声明本批产品的原产地为中国，即“CHINA”，一般在印制单据时已事先印妥。

（2）进口国：填给惠国的国名，应与证书第 2 栏收货人所在国的国别一致。

（3）申报单位盖章、签字：由出口商加盖本单位中、英文对照图章，并由专人进行签字，图章名称必须与第 1 栏一致，签字应为手签，图章与签字不能重叠。

（4）申请日期、地点：日期应晚于发票日期，早于第 11 栏签证日期和装运期；地点应为出口商所在地的城市名称。

能力迁移：一般原产地证书的填制

制单依据：根据项目一中信用证（单证 1-17）及其分析结果单（单证 1-18），假设把单据中的普惠制产地证改为一般原产证书，请同学们独立填写下列单据 5-10 一般原产地证书。

单证 5-10

一般原产地证书

<table>
<tr><td colspan="2">1. Exporter</td><td colspan="3" rowspan="2">Certificate No.
CERTIFICATE OF ORIGIN
OF
THE PEOPLE'S REPUBLIC OF CHINA</td></tr>
<tr><td colspan="2">2. Consignee</td></tr>
<tr><td colspan="2">3. Means of transport and route</td><td colspan="3" rowspan="2">5. For certifying authority use only</td></tr>
<tr><td colspan="2">4. Country/region of destination</td></tr>
<tr><td>6. Marks and numbers</td><td>7. Number and kind of packages; description of goods</td><td>8. HS code</td><td>9. Quantity</td><td>10. Number and date of invoices</td></tr>
<tr><td colspan="2">11. Declaration by the exporter
The undersigned hereby declares that the above details and statements are correct; that all the goods were produced in china and that they comply with the rules of origin of the people's republic of China.

……………………………………………………………
Place and date. Signature and stamp of certifying authority</td><td colspan="3">12. Certification
It is hereby certified that the declaration by the exporter is correct.

……………………………………………………………
Place and date.Signature and stamp of certifying authority</td></tr>
</table>

知识链接

一般原产地证书填写规范

（1）出口商（Exporter）：信用证下的受益人。

（2）收货人（Consignee full name, address, country）：一般为进口商名称、地址及所在国。

（3）运输方式和路线（Means of transport and route）：信用证或合同规定，填起运地、目的地及采用的运输方式。

（4）目的地国家或地区（Country/region of destination）：一般应与最终收货人或最终目的港国别一致，不能填中间商国家的名称。

（5）供出证方使用（For certifying authority use only）：由签证机构在签发后发证书、补发证或加注其他声明时使用，一般留空不填。

（6）标记唛码（Marks and numbers）：应按发票上所列唛头填写完整，若没有唛头，则填写“N/M”，不得留空。

（7）品名及包装种类和件数（Desription of goods, number and kind of packages）：一般应按商业发票填写。填写包装种类和件数后，要一并在阿拉伯数字后加注英文表述，末行要打上表示结束的符号“*****”，以防添加内容。

（8）HS 编码（HS code）：与报关单“一致”，八位编码，不可留空。

（9）数量（Quantity）：填写商品的量值及计算单位，若无则填写重量。

（10）发票号及日期（Number and date of invoices）：和发票相同，日期中的月份用英文缩写，不要用阿拉伯数字。

（11）出口商声明（Declaration by the exporter）：已事先印好，由出口公司填写签发地点、日期并盖公章和由专人签字，且不得重合。

（12）证明（Certification）：由贸促会或商检局填写签发地、日期并盖章和手签。

自我能力测评

能力形成性评价表

评价指标	分值	实际得分
能说出一般和普惠制产地证发证机关及申领程序	20分	
能准确列出申领原产地证所需单据清单	20分	
能根据信用证或合同准确填制出口许可证	60分	

任务五 申领并缮制外汇核销单

任务导入

宁波光明进出口公司的单证员小兰依据任务一中的单据清单，获悉报关时需要提交外汇核销单。因此，在报关前她到外汇管理局申领核销单，并缮制出口收汇核销单。

完成上述任务的步骤如下

第一步：弄清向什么机构申领外汇核销单

出口收汇核销遵循属地管理原则，由出口单位向其所在地的外汇管理部门申领核销单，在何地申领就在何地办理核销手续。

第二步：弄清楚报关阶段核销单申领和使用的程序

（1）出口企业需上网向外汇管理局申请所需核销单的份数，凭操作员IC卡到外汇管理局领取有编号与“条形码”并加盖“国家外汇管理局监制章”的纸质核销单。

（2）出口企业在报关前须上网向海关进行核销单备案，并于领单90天内凭已缮制的核销单、注明核销单编号的出口报关单和其他单据向海关审核。

（3）海关核准无误后，在核销单“海关签注栏”处加盖“验讫章”，退还出口企业。

（4）在货物出口后，出口企业必须上网将已用于出口报关的核销单、出口报关单和发票向外汇管理局交单备案。

任务：要求学生根据上述文字描述，独立画报关阶段核销单申领和使用的程序图（图5-4）。

图 5-4

注意：①申领空白核销单；②报关；③验讫核销单；④交回核销单存根及附件

第三步：缮制外汇核销单

制单依据：宁波光明进出口公司小兰依据项目一中信用证（单证 1-17）及其分析结果单（单证 1-18），并参照已填写的商业发票等其他单据，填写《外汇核销单》。

补充资料：宁波光明进出口公司税务登记 9 位代码为 809776428，报关单编号为 547689219。

完成制单任务的步骤如下

步骤一：教师导学、示范，引导学生口头填写一份核销单，如图 5-5 所示范

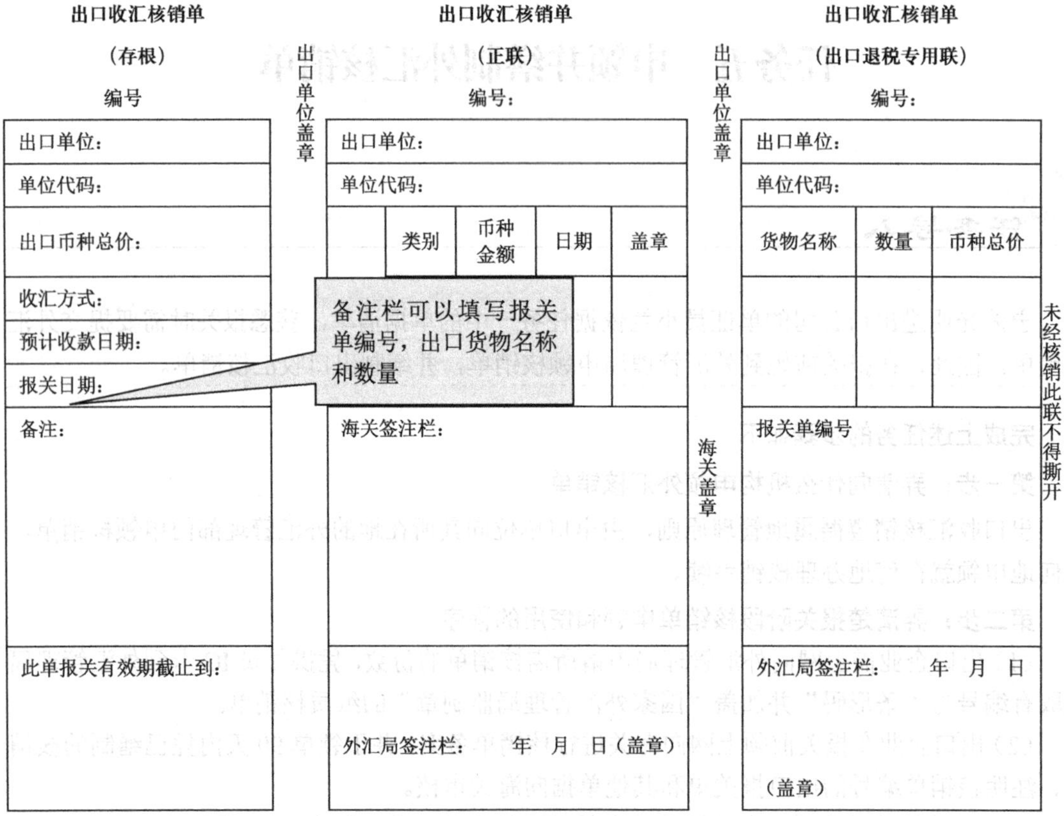

图 5-5 外汇核销单填制提示及示范

学生在教师的引导下，口头填写的外汇核销单答案如下（单证 5-11）：

单证 5-11

出口收汇核销单

出口收汇核销单 存根 编号：031155451	（出口单位盖章）
出口单位： 宁波光明进出口公司	
单位编码： 809776428	
出口币种总价： USD33 680	
收汇方式：L/C	
预计收款日期：	
报关日期：2010.04.03	
备注：	
此单报关有效期截止到 2010.04.05	

出口收汇核销单 监制章 编号：031155451					（出口单位盖章）
出口单位： 宁波光明进出口公司					
单位编码： 809776428					
银行签注栏	类别	币种金额	日期	盖章	
海关签注栏：					
外汇局签注栏 年 月 日（盖章）					

出口收汇核销单 监制章 编号：031155451		
出口单位 宁波光明进出口公司		
单位编码： 809776428		
货物名称	数量	币种总价
报关单编号：547689219		
外汇局签注栏 年 月 日（盖章）		

步骤二：巩固训练：学生结合合同或信用证填写出口收汇核销单并审核

训练任务

宁波舒普机电科技公司单证员马林根据项目一任务五中，马林修改后的信用证（单证1-19）及其信用证分析结果单（单证1-20），并参照已填写的商业发票等其他单据，独立填写下列出口收汇核销单（单证5-12）。

补充资料：宁波舒普机电科技公司税务登记 9 位代码为 608576431，报关单编号为907689276。

单证 5-12

出口收汇核销单 存根 编号：	（出口单位盖章）
出口单位：	
单位编码：	
出口币种总价：	
收汇方式：	
预计收款日期：	
报关日期：	
备注：	
此单报关有效期截止到	

出口收汇核销单 监制章 编号：					（出口单位盖章）
出口单位：					
单位编码：					
银行签注栏	类别	币种金额	日期	盖章	
海关签注栏：					
外汇局签注栏 年 月 日（盖章）					

出口收汇核销单 监制章 编号：		
出口单位		
单位编码：		
货物名称	数量	币种总价
报关单编号：		
外汇局签注栏 年 月 日（盖章）		

训练指导：学生可以根据刚才老师的引导、示范，先尝试填写一份出口收汇核销单，若有疑问，可查阅下列出口收汇核销单的填制要领；也可以先看出口收汇核销单的填制要领，再填制出口收汇核销单。

要求：填制好的出口收汇核销单在小组中交流，然后将电子文档提交到天空教室。

步骤三：教师点评，核对答案

教师随机选取某一个小组某一同学的作业进行集中点评，核对答案。

知识链接

出口收汇核单据缮制要点

出口收汇核销单，简称核销单，是指由国家外汇管理局统一管理，各分支局核发，出口单位凭以向海关办理出口报关、向银行办理出口收汇、向外汇管理机关办理出口收汇核销、向税务机关办理出口退税申报、有统一编号的重要凭证。通过这一凭证国家可以全面掌握收汇实绩，催促逾期收汇，防止外汇漏收或骗取出口退税。

（一）具体栏目

出口收汇核销单由国家外汇管理局统一印制，每张分为左、中、右联，各联都编有同一号码。

（1）左联为存根联，内容有出口单位（盖章）、出口总价、收汇方式、预计收汇日期、报关日期、发票编号、合同编号等项目。

（2）中联记载外汇指定银行结汇收账情况及外汇管理局核销情况。

（3）右联为出口退税专用联，内容有出口单位（盖章）、货名、数量、出口总价、报关单编号、外汇管理局核销情况等栏目。

（二）缮制方法

1．核销单存根联的缮制方法

核销单存根联的填制应以本套结汇单据的发票的出口报关单内容为依据，在货物发运和出口报关后交回当地外汇管理局留存备案。

（1）编号：编号事先已由国家外汇管理局统一印就。

（2）出口单位名称：注明合同的出口方全称，并加盖公章，应与出口货物报关单、发票同项内容一致。

（3）单位代码：此栏填出口单位的税务登记 9 位数代码。

（4）出口币种总价：按外汇的原币种填入该批货物的应收总额，通常与商业发票总金额相同。

（5）收汇方式：根据合同的规定填制收汇方式。如 L/C、D/D、D/A、T/T 等。

（6）预计收款日期：根据具体的收汇方式，推算出可能收到外汇的日期填入此栏。具体的推算方法有：即期信用证或托收项下的货款，属于近洋的地区，为寄单日后第 25 天，如为远洋的地区则为 35 天；远期信用证或托收项下的货款，属于近洋的地区，为付款日后

35 天，如为远洋的地区则为 45 天；分期付款要注明每次收款日期和金额；寄售项下的货款最迟在报关日起 360 天之内结汇；自寄单据项下的货款，自报关日起 50 天内结算。

（7）报关日期：报关日期是报关单上的申报日期。

（8）报关单位备注：填写收汇方面需要说明的事项。例如，委托代理方式下，代理出口企业必须注明委托单位名称，并加盖代理出口企业的公章；属于两个或两个以上单位联合出口，应注明其他单位名称及其出口金额，并加盖报关单位公章；原出口商品如发生变更，要填原核销单的编号等。

（9）此单报关有效期截止到：一般填写出口货物的装运日期。

2．核销单核销联的缮制方法

核销单核销联的内容除与存根联同项内容以外，还有下栏项目：

（1）银行签注栏：由银行填写商品的类别号、货币名称和金额，注明日期，并加盖公章。

（2）海关签注栏：此栏由海关批注有关内容，加盖公章。如“该票货物已于 2010.04.05 结关”并加盖公章。

（3）外汇局签注栏：由外汇管理局在本栏批注有关内容，填制日期，加盖公章。

3．核销单出口退税专用联的缮制方法

出口外汇核销单出口退税专用栏目除与上述两联相同以外，还有如下内容：

（1）货物名称：填实际出口货物名称，并与发票、出口货物报关单的品名一致。

（2）数量：按包装方式的件数填写，应与报关单同项内容相符。

（3）币种总价：按发票或报关单的总金额和币种填写。

（4）报关单编号：按出口货物报关单的实际编号填入。

自我能力测评

能力形成性评价表

评价指标	分　值	实际得分
能绘制核销单申领和使用流程图	20 分	
能准确列出申领核销单所需单据清单	20 分	
能根据信用证或合同和其他资料准确填制核销单	60 分	

项目六

装运单据的制作与审核

知识目标

了解出口装运的有关规定，熟悉出口装运的业务流程，掌握海运提单和装运通知的主要内容和缮制要点。

能力目标

能正确缮制并审核提单；能正确缮制装运通知书。

任务分析

- 任务一：列出装运阶段所需单据清单
- 任务二：缮制海运提单
- 任务三：缮制装运通知书

任务一　列出装运阶段所需单据清单

任务导入

宁波光明进出口公司的货物顺利报关之后，就要按照合同和信用证的规定办理装运手续。单证员小兰作为一位新手，她首先需要弄清装运需要哪些单据，并列好清单。

完成上述任务的步骤如下

第一步：教师引导学生复习任务五中报关、装运阶段单证流转程序图

① 出口商将填制好的报关委托书、报关单会同发票等相关单证交报关行或货代，委托其代理报关。

② 报关行或货代整理，审核报关资料后向海关报关。

③ 海关核准无误后，收讫关税，在报关单和装货单上盖放行章，在核销单和通关单上盖验讫章。

④ 货代将盖有放行章的装货单交船公司。

⑤ 船公司凭盖有放行章的装货单通知港口装船。

⑥ 港口装船后，由船长或大副向船运公司签发大副收据（收货单）。

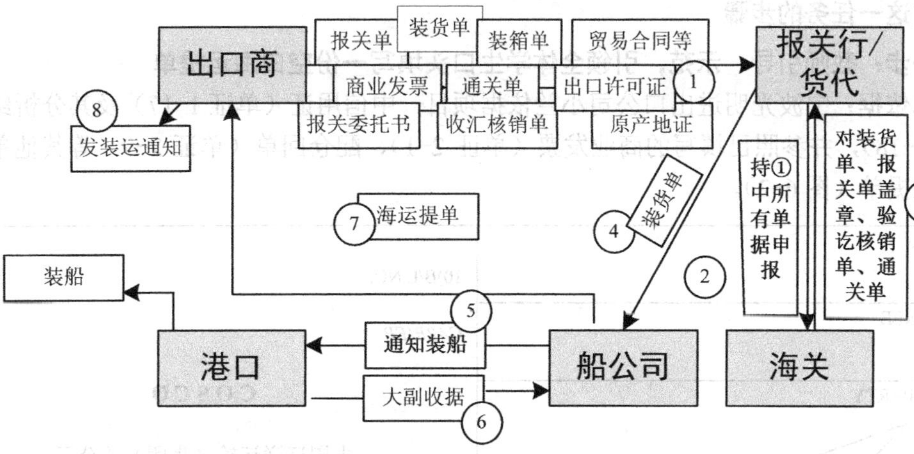

图　6-1

⑦ 船运公司凭大副收据（收货单）或通过货代向出口商签发海运提单。

⑧ 出口商拿到提单后，立即给进口商发装运通知。

①、②、③主要是报关阶段单证流程，④、⑤、⑥、⑦、⑧主要是装运阶段单证流程图。

第二步：要求学生独立列出装运所需的单据清单并理单

列出装运所需的单据清单，在已有的单据后面打"√"。

第三步：教师核对答案

（1）装货单（托运单中的一联）（√）；

（2）收货单（托运单中的一联）（√）；

（3）海运提单；

（4）装运通知。

自我能力测评

能力形成性评价表

评价指标	分　值	实际得分
能绘制报关装运阶段单据操作流程图	40分	
能准确列出转运阶段所需单据清单	60分	

任务二　缮制海运提单

任务导入

根据任务一中的单据清单，宁波光明进出口公司的单证员小兰在装运前，事先要缮制好海运提单。

完成这一任务的步骤

第一步：教师引导、示范，引领全体学生口头填写一份空白海运提单

制单依据：宁波光明进出口公司小兰依据项目一中信用证（单证 1-17）及其分析结果单（单证 1-18），并参照已填写的商业发票（单证 2-1）、配仓回单（单证 2-9）等其他单据，制作海运提单（图 6-2）。

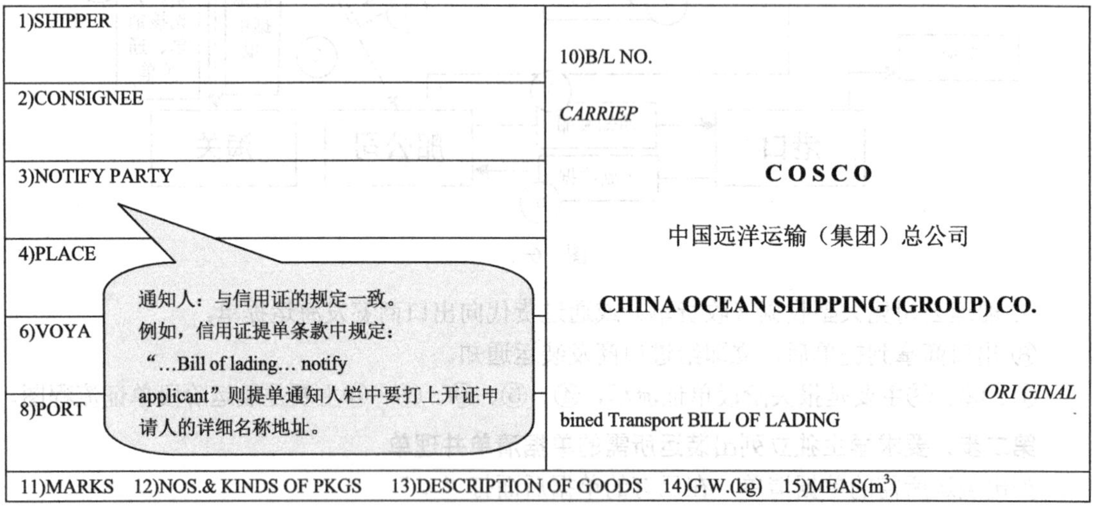

图 6-2

如图 6-2 所示，教师用自制的 PPT 引导学生学习每一个栏目的填写规范，然后让学生依据上述制单背景资料，口头填写每一个栏目。

教师引导学生口头填写的提单答案如下（单证 6-1）。

单证 6-1

<table>
<tr><td colspan="2">Shipper
GUANGMING IMPORT & EXPORT CORPORATION
13 XINNING ROAD, NINGBO, ZHEJIANG, CHINA
TEL: 0574-88896000</td><td rowspan="3">B/L NO. HMNBJI 486888
PIL
PACIFIC INTERNATIONAL LINES (PTE) LTD.
(Incorporated in Singapore)
COMBINED TRANSPORT BILL OF LADING
Received in apparent good order and condition except as otherwise noted the total number of container or other packages or units enumerated below for transportation from the place of receipt to the place of delivery subject to the terms hereof. One of the signed Bills of Lading must be surrendered duly endorsed in exchange for the goods or delivery order. On presentation of this document (duly) endorsed to the Carrier by or on behalf of the Holder, the rights and liabilities arising in accordance with the terms hereof shall (without prejudice to any rule of common law or statute rendering them binding on the Merchant) become binding in all respects between the Carrier and the Holder as though the contract evidenced hereby had been made between them.
SEE TERMS ON ORIGINAL B/L</td></tr>
<tr><td colspan="2">Consignee
TO ORDER OF SHIPPER</td></tr>
<tr><td colspan="2">Notify Party
FUHUA TRADE CO., LTD.,
101 QUEENS ROAD CENTRAL,HONGKONG
TEL: 852-2857777</td></tr>
<tr><td>Vessel and Voyage Number
S.S. DONGFENG V.234</td><td>Place of Receipt</td><td>Port of Loading
NINGBO</td></tr>
<tr><td>Port of Discharge
HONGKONG</td><td>Place of Delivery</td><td>Number of Original B/L
THREE(3)</td></tr>
</table>

（续）

PARTICULARS AS DECLARED BY SHIPPER – CARRIER NOT RESPONSIBLE			
ContainerNos/Seal Nos.Marks and/Numbers	No. of Container / Packages / Description of Goods	GrossWeight (kilos)	Measurement (cumetres)
FUHUA HONGKONG R/NO.:1-1000	1000 ROLLS OF 100% 100PCT NYLON FABRICS TEXU2369834/179576 Freght Prepaid L/C No.006CIM, 00489SBRT Issuing Bank: Huaxia Bank Co., Ltd Hongkong	9000kgs	8.4CBM

FREIGHT & CHARGES AS ARRANGED	Number of Containers/Packages (in words) SAY TOTAL ONE THOUSAND ROLLS ONLY.
	Shipped on Board Date: APRIL 5,2010
	Place and Date of Issue: NINGBO APRIL 5,2010
	In witness whereof this number of Original Bills of Lading stated Above all of the tenor and date one of which being accomplished the others to stand void. for **PACIFIC INTERNATIONAL LINES (PTE) LTD.** as Carrier

第二步巩固训练：学生结合一份合同和信用证独立填写一份提单

训练任务

宁波舒普机电科技公司单证员马林根据项目一任务五中，马林修改后的信用证（单证 1-9）及其信用证分析结果单（单证 1-20），并参照已填写的商业发票（单证 2-2）、配仓回单（单证 2-12）等其他单据，独立填写下列提单（单证 6-2）。

单证 6-2

Shipper		B/L NO. PIL **PACIFIC INTERNATIONAL LINES (PTE) LTD.** (Incorporated in Singapore) **COMBINED TRANSPORT BILL OF LADING** Received in apparent good order and condition except as otherwise noted the total number of container or other packages or units enumerated below for transportation from the place of receipt to the place of delivery subject to the terms hereof. One of the signed Bills of Lading must be surrendered duly endorsed in exchange for the goods or delivery order. On presentation of this document (duly) endorsed to the Carrier by or on behalf of the Holder, the rights and liabilities arising in accordance with the terms hereof shall (without prejudice to any rule of common law or statute rendering them binding on the Merchant) become binding in all respects between the Carrier and the Holder as though the contract evidenced hereby had been made between them. **SEE TERMS ON ORIGINAL B/L**
Consignee		
Notify Party		
Vessel and Voyage Number	Port of Loading	Port of Discharge
Place of Receipt	Place of Delivery	Number of Original B/L

（续）

<table>
<tr><th colspan="4">PARTICULARS AS DECLARED BY SHIPPER – CARRIER NOT RESPONSIBLE</th></tr>
<tr><td>ContainerNos/Seal Nos.Marks and/Numbers</td><td>No. of Container / Packages / Description of Goods</td><td>GrossWeight (kilos)</td><td>Measurement (cumetres)</td></tr>
<tr><td></td><td></td><td></td><td></td></tr>
<tr><td rowspan="4">FREIGHT & CHARGES</td><td colspan="3">Number of Containers/Packages (in words)</td></tr>
<tr><td colspan="3">Shipped on Board Date:</td></tr>
<tr><td colspan="3">Place and Date of Issue:</td></tr>
<tr><td colspan="3">In witness whereof this number of Original Bills of Lading stated Above all of the tenor and date one of which being accomplished the others to stand void.

for PACIFIC INTERNATIONAL LINES (PTE) LTD. as Carrier</td></tr>
</table>

训练指导：学生可以根据刚才老师的引导、示范，先尝试填写一份海运提单，如有疑问查阅下列提单的填制要领；也可以先看提单的填制要领，再去填制提单。

要求：填制好的提单要在小组中交流，然后将电子文档提交到天空教室。

第三步：教师随机抽取一组同学填制的单证，集体批阅、点评，核对答案

知识链接

海运提单的填制要点

海运提单的格式由各船公司自行确定，在形式上各有特色，但都包括了以下的主要内容：

（1）承运人（Carrier）：提单上必须表明以轮船公司注册的承运人，否则银行不予接受，但在制单中一般已经印制好了，不用另外打制。

（2）托运人（Shipper）：即发货人，信用证方式下为信用证受益人，一般就是出口方；托收方式下为托收的委托人。

（3）收货人（Consignee）：记名提单填收货人名称，一般为进口商；不记名提单则填“To Bearer”，指示提单填“To Order”或“To The Order Of ×××”。指示提单需背书才能转让。

（4）被通知人（Notify Party）：信用证方式下按规定填写。该栏要有详细的名称和地址。

（5）船名、港口：见表 6-1。

表 6-1

提单项目	转船	直达
PRECARRIAGE BY	第一程船船名	空白
PLACE OF RECEIPT	船方收货的港口	空白
OCEAN VESSEL VOY. NO.	第二程船船名	船名
PORT OF LOADING	转运港	装运港
PORT OF DISCHARGE(DESTINATION)	卸货港	卸货港
PLACE OF DELIVERY	最终目的地	与卸货港同则空白

（6）唛头和集装箱号（Marks And Container No.）：若信用证中有规定唛头，按信用证要求打，若没有规定按双方事先约定或卖方自定；若没有唛头的任何提示和要求则打制“N/M”。同时应标明集装箱号码。

（7）包装与件数（No. & Kind Of Packages）：单位件数与包装要与实际货物相符，并在大写合计数内填写英文大写数目，若是两种以上不同包装单位，要分开写，再合计。

（8）品名（Description Of Goods）：按信用证要求，与发票所填一致，若货物品名较多，可用总称。

（9）毛重和体积（G.W.&Mear.）：若无特别规定，只要填写总的毛重和体积就可，现在多为集装箱货物，毛重就包括货物的净重和集装箱的皮重，体积按集装箱计，一个小柜即20尺的集装箱体积为33.2cbm。

（10）运费支付（Freight & Charges）：一般有预付（Prepaid）和到付（Collect）两种支付方式。

（11）签发地与日期（Place And Date Of Issue）：签发地一般在装运港所在地，日期表示货物实际装运的日期用证要求，答发日期一般要早或与信用证规定的装运期同一天，尽量不要倒签提单。

（12）承运人签章：由承运人或其授权的代理人签章。

（13）提单签发份数（No. Of Original B/L）：信用证方式下按信用证规定，一般为三份。

（14）提单号（B/L NO.）：位于提单右上角，以便于核查。

（15）其他：提单上要注明“On Board ”字样，正本要注明“Original”，有时要表明交接方式，如CY-CY, CFS-CY 等。

自我能力测评

能力形成性评价表

评价指标	分值	实际得分
能准确翻译信用证或合同中的提单条款	20分	
能掌握提单每个栏目的填写规范	20分	
能根据相关背景资料准确填制一份提单	40分	

任务三 缮制装运通知书

任务导入

根据图 6-1，和所列的单据清单，宁波光明进出口公司的单证员小兰在货物装运后，要向进口方发装运通知。

第一步：教师引导、示范，引领全体学生口头填写一份装运通知

制单依据：宁波光明进出口公司小兰依据项目一中信用证（单证 1-17）及其分析结果单

（单证 1-18），并参照已填写的商业发票（单证 2-1）、提单（单证 6-1）等其他单据，制作装运通知。

如图 6-3 所示，教师首先用自制的 PPT 向学生演示装运通知的填写规范。并引导学生结合相关信用证等信息，口头填写一份装运通知。

步骤一：导学

SHANGHAI STATIONERY AND SPORTING GOODS IMP. AND EXP. CORP.

5-15 F. BAISHU MANSION

1230-1240 ZHONGSHAN ROAD N.1. SHANGHAI

SHIPPING ADVICE

一般与提单日期相同，可在装货后三天内

Date: 25-Jul-96

TO:______

Re:Invoice No. 96INV/M144

L/C No. A2B960046

Dear sirs:

We hereby inform you that the goods under the above mentioned credit have been shipped. The details of the shipment are stated below:

Commodity: MEN'S GLOVES AS PER CONFIRMATION NO. 96M/144

Order（contract）No.: 6413/al; 8953/al

Quantity: 22 CARTIONS

Amount: USD4,492.00

Ocean Vessel: Per s.s. JIAN HE V.9632W

Shipping Company: CHINA OCEAN SHIPPING (GROUP) CO.

Bill of Lading No.: COS961772

E.T.D.: On/or about 25-Jul-96

E.T.A.: On/or about 25-AUG-96

Port of Loading: SHANGHAI PORT

Signature: SHANGHAI STATIONERY AND SPORTING GOODS IMP. AND EXP. COR 倪志华

图 6-3

教师引导学生口头填写的装运通知答案如下（单证 6-3）：

单证 6-3

GUANGMING IMPORT & EXPORT CORPORATION

13 XINNING ROAD, NINGBO, ZHEJIANG, CHINA TEL:0574-88896000

SHIPPING ADVICE

DATE: APRIL 6, 2010

TO: **FUHUA TRADE CO.,LTD.,**
101 QUEENS ROAD CENTRAL, HONGKONG
TEL: 852-2857777

RE：INVOICE NO.：GM10H9141
L/C NO.：006CIM000489SBRT

WE HEREBY INFORM YOU THAT THE GOODS UNDER THE ABOVE MENTIONED INVOICE HAVE BEEN SHIPPED.THE DETAILS OF THE SHIPPMENT ARE AS FOLLOWS:

MARKS:

（续）

自定 COMMODITY：100PCT NYLON FABRICS QUANTITY：100000 YARDS PACKAGE：1000 ROLLS AMOUNT：USD33680.00 PORT OF LOADING：NINGBO PORT OF DESTINATION：HONGKONG DATE OF SHIPPMENT：APR.5,2010 VESSEL'S NAME: S.S DONGFENG　V.234 B/L NO.: HMNBJI 486888 ETD: APR.5,2010 ETA: APR.7,2010 GUANGMING IMPORT & EXPORT CORPORATION 小王

第二步巩固训练：学生结合一份合同和信用证和提单信息，独立填写一份装运通知书

训练任务

宁波舒普机电科技公司单证员马林根据项目一任务五中，马林修改后的信用证（单证 1-19）及其信用证分析结果单（单证 1-20），并参照已填写的商业发票（单证 2-2）、提单（单证 6-2）等其他单据，独立填写下列装运通知（单证 6-4）。

训练指导：学生可以根据刚才老师的引导、示范，先尝试填写一份装运通知，若有疑问可查阅下列装运通知填制要领；也可以先看装运通知填制要领，再去填制装运通知书。

要求：填制好的装运通知要在小组中交流，然后将电子文档提交到天空教室。

第三步：教师随机抽取一组同学填制的单证，集体批阅、点评，核对答案

单证　6-4

____ **SHIPPING　ADVICE** DATE TO： RE： DEAR SIR， WE ARE PLEASED TO INFORM YOUR ESTEEMED COMPANY THAT THE FOLLOWING MENTIONED GOODS WILL BE SHIPPED OUT ON THE JAN.18, 2005，FULL DETAILS ARE SHOWN AS FOLLOWS： 1．INVOICE NO.： 2．BILL OF LADING NO.： 3．OCEAN VESSEL： 4．PORT OF LOADING： 5．DATE OF SHIPPMENT： 6．PORT OF DESTINATION： 7．DESCRIPTION OF GOODS： 8．MARKS AND NUMBER ON B/L： 9．L/C NO.： 10．ETD： 11．ETA： …………………………………………………………… **Authorized Signature**

知识链接

装船通知填写要点

装船通知是发货人或船东在装船后三天内给买方或其指定人发送的通知，以方便买方办理保险和安排接货等事宜。若信用证有要求，该单据也能成为交单议付的单证之一。

装船通知的格式不固定，其内容有订单或合同号、信用证号、品名、数量、总计、唛头、装运口岸、装运日期、船名、开船日期及预计到达目的港时间等，制作要点如下。

（1）抬头：填写买方或其指定的人或公司。

（2）日期：发送装运通知的日期，一般在货物装船后三天内，可与提单日期相同。

（3）提单号及船名：与提单同。

（4）预计开船日期和到达日期（ETD、ETA）：按船期表填。

（5）装运港、目的港、装运期：按合同或信用证的规定填，一般与提单同。

（6）商品描述：包括品名、唛头、数量、发票总值等，与发票同。

自我能力测评

能力形成性评价表

评价指标	分值	实际得分
掌握装船通知发出的时间	20分	
能掌握装船通知每个栏目的填写规范	20分	
能根据相关背景资料准确填制一份装船通知	60分	

项目七

结汇单据的制作与审核

知识目标

了解我国出口结汇的有关规定；熟悉出口结汇的具体办法；掌握汇票的种类及主要内容。

能力目标

能正确缮制结汇清单；能正确缮制商业汇票；能正确缮制受益人证明书等其他结汇单据；能正确审核结汇单据。

任务分析

达到上述目标，需要完成下列任务：

- 任务一：缮制结汇清单
- 任务二：缮制商业汇票并审核
- 任务三：缮制受益人证明书并审核
- 任务四：缮制品质证等商检证书并审核
- 任务六：出具船级证明
- 任务七：审核全套结汇单据

任务一　缮制结汇清单

任务导入

宁波光明进出口公司在货物装船获取提单并发出装运通知后，单证员小兰根据合同和信用证的规定，整理、缮制有关结汇单据，向中国光大银行宁波分行办理结汇手续。为此，她首先需要缮制结汇清单。

完成该任务的步骤

第一步：教师引导学生再次分析信用证中单据条款

主要分析项目一中信用证（单证 1-17）单据条款并再次查看该信用证分析结果单（单证 1-18）。

第二步：要求学生独立缮制结汇清单

在已有的单据后面打“√”。

第三步：教师核对答案

结汇清单列表，见表 7-1。

表 7-1

单 据 名 称	份 数
海运提单	3 正（√）
商业发票	3 正（√）
装箱单	2 正（√）
保险单	1 正（√）
产地证	1 正（√）
汇票	2 正
品质证	2 正
受益人证明书	1 正
船及证明	1 正
寄单邮据	1 正（√）（寄单时，向邮寄部门获取）

自我能力测评

能力形成性评价表

评价指标	分值	实际得分
能准确翻译信用证中单据条款	40 分	
能按信用证要求列出结汇所需单据清单	40 分	
能整理出结汇所需，但前面已制作过的单据	20 分	

任务二 缮制商业汇票并审核

任务导入

根据上述结汇清单，宁波光明进出公司单证员小兰根据信用证要求首先缮制汇票并审核。

完成该任务的步骤

第一步：教师导学、示范，引领全体学生口头填写一份空白汇票

制单依据：项目一中信用证（单证 1-17）及其分析结果单（单证 1-18），商业发票（单证 2-1）等其他相关单据。

如图 7-1 所示，教师用自制的 PPT 引导学生学习每一个栏目的填写规范，然后让学生依据上述制单背景资料，口头填写每一个栏目。

BILL　OF　EXCHANGE

1

凭

Drawn under ....

信用证　　　　　第　　　　号

L/D　NO. ....

日期

Dated ....　　　　　　　　..........................

按　　　　　　　　　　　　　　　款

Payable w　　　　　　　　@......................%　Per　annum

一般填写此项交易的发票号码

号码　　　　　　发票金额　　　　　..........中国..........上海..........　　　年　　月　　日

No. ....Exchange for　　　　　　　　　　SHANGHAI，CHINA..............

见票　　　　　　　　　　　　　日后（本汇票之副本未付）付

At ....Sight of this FIRST of Exchange (Second of exchange being unpaid)

pay to the order of ....或其指定人

金额

The sum of

此致

To ....

....

图　7-1

教师引导学生口头填写的汇票答案如下（单证 7-1）：

单证　7-1

BILL　OF　EXCHANGE

1

凭

Drawn under HUA XIA BANK CO., LTD.　HONGKONG

信用证　　　　　第　　　　号

L/C　No. 006CIM000489SBRT

Dated　2010.03.05

按息付款

Payable　with　interest　@.....................% per　annum

号码　　　　　汇票金额　　　　　　　　　　中国，　宁波　年 月 日

No: GM10H9141Exchange　for　　USD33 680 00　　Ningbo　，China 2010.04.20

见票　　　　　　　　　　　　日 后（本 汇 票 之 副 本 未 付）

At　XXX Sight of this　FIRST　of Exchange (Second of exchange being unpaid)

pay to the order of CHINA EVERBRIGHT BANK,NINGBO BRANCH 或 其 指 定 人

付金额

The sum of　SAY USD THIRTY-THREE THOUSAND SIX HUNDRED AND EIGHTY ONLY.

To HUA XIA BANK CO. LTD　HONGKONG

GUANGMING IMPORT & EXPORT CORPORATION

13 XINNING ROAD, NINGBO, ZHEJIANG, CHINA

小兰

单证 7-2

BILL OF EXCHANGE

No. GM10H9141

For USD33 680，00 Ningbo, China 2010.04.20

(amount in figure) (place and date of issue)

At XXX sight of this FIRST Bill of exchange(SECOND being unpaid)

pay to CHINA EVERBRIGHT BANK,NINGBO BRANCH or order the sum of

SAY USD THIRTY-THREE THOUSAND SIX HUNDRED AND EIGHTY ONLY. (amount in words)

Value received for 1000 ROLLS of 100% NYLON FABRICS

(quantity) (name of commodity)

Drawn under HUA XIA BANK CO., LTD. HONGKONG

L/C No. 006CIM000489SBRT dated 2010.03.05

To: HUA XIA BANK CO., LTD. HONGKONG

For and on behalf of

GUANGMING IMPORT & EXPORT CORPORATION

13 XINNING ROAD, NINGBO, ZHEJIANG, CHINA

小兰

第二步巩固训练：学生结合一份合同或信用证独立填写两种不同格式的汇票

训练任务

宁波舒普机电科技公司单证员马林根据项目一任务五中，马林修改后的信用证(单证 1-19)及其信用证分析结果单（单证 1-20），并参照已填写的商业发票、提单等其他单据，独立填写下列两种格式的汇票（单证 7-3 和单证 7-4)。

训练指导：学生可以根据刚才老师的引导、示范，先尝试填写一份汇票，若有疑问，可查阅下列汇票的填制要领；也可以先看汇票的填制要领，再去填制汇票。

要求：填制好的汇票要在小组中交流，然后电子文档提交到天空教室。

单证 7-3

BILL OF EXCHANGE

凭

Drawn under ……………………………………………………………..

信用证 第 号

L/C No.………………………………………

日期

Dated ……………………………………

按 息 付款

Payable with interest @....…………....% per annum

号码 汇 票 金 额 中国， 宁波 年 月 日

No: ………….……Exchange for Ningbo , China…………………...…

见票 日后（本汇票之副本未付）

At……..…………………Sight of this FIRST of Exchange (Second of exchange being unpaid)

pay to the order of ……………………………………………………………或其指定人

付金额

The sum of

To……………………..

………………………………………….

单证 7-4

BILL OF EXCHANGE

No.______________________

For______________________ ______________________

(amount in figure) (place and date of issue)

At______________ sight of this FIRST Bill of exchange(SECOND being unpaid)

pay to____ or order the sum of

____

(amount in words)

Value received for______________________ of______________________

(quantity) (name of commodity)

Drawn under______________________________

L/C No. ______________ dated______________________________

To:______________________

For and on behalf of

____

(Signature)

第三步：教师随机抽取一组同学填制的单证，集体批阅、点评，核对答案

知识链接

汇票制单要点

汇票（DRAFT/BILL OF EXCHANGE）是一方向另一方签发的无条件支付命令，要求该受票人立即或在一定时间或一个固定时期支付一定金额给某人或其指定人或来人的书面凭证。它是出口商凭以向进口商要求付款的收款工具，是一种要式的有价证券。在国际贸易中，汇票一般由卖方签发，一般都签发一套，一式两份，两份具有同样的法律效力，因此在使用中常注明“付一不付二”或“付二不付一”字样。

汇票缮制要求不得有误，而且不得涂改，否则无效。汇票的格式没有一个统一的标准，卖方可向银行购买，也可以自己设计，但主要内容包括以下几点：

（1）出票依据（DRAWN UNDER）：信用证下包括开证行、信用证号及日期。信用证方式下的汇票，应根据信用证的内容进行填写：“DRAWN UNDER”栏填开证行完整的名称，L/C NO.（信用证号码）和 DATED（开证日期）。

托收方式下的汇票，出票条款留空不填或填“FOR COLLECTION”。

（2）出票地及日期：出票地为卖方所在地，出票日期为交单议付期，一般出口方向银行交单时由银行填写，也可由出口方填写其交单日期。

（3）汇票号（NO.）：此栏填写此项交易的发票号码或其他有利于识别的号码，可以填写每一笔业务的顺序编号，也可采用此项交易的商业发票号码，以使整套单据有机地联系起来，以便核对发票与汇票中相关的内容。

（4）汇票金额：分为大写与小写两部分。汇票金额应根据发票金额填写。大、小写金额保持一致，否则，汇票无效。

汇票的小写金额由货币代号和阿拉伯数字组成，小数保留两位，若小数有三位，第三位小数四舍五入。如 1003.244 美元写为：USD1003.24。

汇票大写金额由小写金额翻译而成，包括货币全称和金额书面文字两部分，要求顶格填写，不留空隙。应在“the sum of ”后按小写金额使用英文大写数字填写，大写金额前冠以货币全称的复数形式，句末加上“Only”（整）。

大写金额的小数点以下的辅币表示方法，以 0.75 美元为例，有以下几种写法：①CENTS SEVENTY FIVE ONLY；②POINT SEVENTY FIVE ONLY。

（5）付款期限：汇票的付款期限主要有两种：即期与远期。

即期付款条件下，应在“At”与“Sight”之间空白处以虚线（或“*”号，或“×”号）连接。即“At…Sight”，表示见票即付。远期汇票的付款方式，根据日内瓦《统一汇票本票法》第 33 条规定，有三种：“见票后定期付款、出票日后定期付款、定日付款”。

1）见票后定期付款：根据所规定的期限，表示为“At ××days after Sight”。

2）出票日后定期付款：根据要求，表示为“At ××days after Sight”，同时将汇票上印就的“Sight”一词划掉。

3）定日付款：若要求以提单日后第××天到期付款，则表示为“At××days after B/L date”，同时将汇票上印就的“Sight”一词划掉。

如果信用证条款并未明确汇票的付款期限，则可视为即期付款。

（6）收款人（PAY TO THE ORDER OF /PAYEE）：在我国，一般银行为受款人，若是向银行购得的空白汇票，则都已印好。

（7）付款人（DRAWEE/PAYER）：信用证下为开证行或指定的付款行，托收下为进口商。

（8）出票人（DRAWER）：填出口人名称并由负责人签字，否则无效。

自我能力测评

能力形成性评价表

评价指标	分值	实际得分
能准确翻译信用证中汇票条款	20 分	
能掌握两种不同格式的汇票填制要点	30 分	
能根据相关合同或信用证准确填制一份汇票并审核	50 分	

任务三 缮制受益人证明书并审核

任务导入

根据上述结汇清单，宁波光明进出口公司单证员小兰根据信用证要求缮制受益人证明书并审核。

完成该任务的步骤

第一步：教师导学、示范，引领全体学生口头填写一份空白受益人证明书

制单依据：项目一中信用证（单证 1-17）及其分析结果单（单证 1-18）。

如图 7-2 所示，教师用自制的 PPT 引导学生学习每一个栏目的填写规范，然后让学生依据上述制单背景资料，口头填写每一个栏目。

SHANGHAI HUAMEI CORP.

128 LIQING ROAD, SHANGHAI .P.R.OF CHINA

- date：dec.12,2009
- **Beneficiary' s Certificate**
- TO：**NATIONAL PAPER, MART**

与证明内容相吻合，而且最迟不得晚于交单日期，一般可与提单日期同

- **Dear Sirs,**
- **Re: Invoice No. A3W425　　L/C NO.0010/01/488/172**
- We hereby certify that a complete set of non-negotiable shipping documents have been sent to applicant by airmail within two days after shipment.
- **SHANGHAI HUAMEI CORP.**
- 王健

图　7-2

教师引导学生口头填写的受益人证明书答案如下（单证 7-5）：

单证　7-5

GUANGMING IMPORT & EXPORT CORPORATION

13 XINNING ROAD, NINGBO, ZHEJAING, CHINA

Beneficiary's Certificate

Date：2010.04.05--------

TO： FUHUA TRADE CO.,LTD.,

101 QUEENS ROAD CENTRAL, HONGKONG

TEL: 852-2857777

Dear Sirs,

Re:Invoice No. GM10H9141　**L/C No.** 006CIM000489SBRT

We hereby certify that one set of non-negotiable shipping documents has been sent to FUHUA TRADE CO.,LTD. 101 QUEENS ROAD CENTRAL, HONGKONG throuth courier service within two days after shipment.

GUANGMING IMPORT & EXPOR T CORPORATION

小兰

第二步巩固训练：学生结合一份合同和信用证独立缮制受益人证明书

训练任务

宁波舒普机电科技公司单证员马林根据项目一任务五中，马林修改后的信用证（单证 1-19）及其信用证分析结果单（单证 1-20）独立填写下列受益人证明书（单证 7-6）。

单证　7-6

..______________________________

____

Beneficiary's Certificate

Date: __________

TO: __________

Dear Sirs,

Re:__________

We hereby certify______________________________

____

(Signature)

____

训练指导：学生可以根据刚才老师的引导、示范，先尝试填写一份受益人证明书，若有疑问可查阅下列受益人证明书的填制要领；也可以先看受益人证明书的填制要领，再填制受益人证明书。

要求：填制好的受益人证明书要在小组中交流，然后电子文档提交到天空教室。

第三步：教师随机抽取一组同学填制的单证，集体批阅、点评、核对答案

知识链接

一、受益人证明书填制要点

受益人证明书/声明（Beneficiary's Certificate）是指进口商在信用证中要求受益人开出证明，证明其办理了某项工作或证实某件事实的单据。受益人证明多种多样，通常是证明货物的品质、唛头、包装标识、装运及其他寄单事项的单据，由受益人根据信用证的要求来缮制；有关运输方面的证明则是卖方为满足买方对货物在运输方面的特殊要求而开立的证明文件，根据情况它可以由受益人出具，也可以由相关的运输公司来出具。

此类证明一般采用函电形式，格式由出口企业按照信用证规定或买方要求的内容自行设计。

（1）单据上要有受益人证明的字样。

（2）制单日期应与证明内容相吻合，而且最迟不得晚于交单日期，一般可与提单日期相同。如提单日期为 4 月 15 日，信用证规定："Beneficiary's Certificates certify that cable copy of shipping advice dispatched to the applicant immediately after shipment"，则受益人证明的出单日期只能在 4 月 15～18 日之间，而不能是其他时间。

（3）抬头人（TO），通常采用笼统填法，如 "to whom it may concern"（至有关人），也

可填写进口公司的名称和地址。

（4）参考号应显示信用证及发票号码。

（5）证明的内容与信用证的要求相符，开头通常用"This is to certify that…"或"We hereby certify that…"。

（6）签署，注明出口公司名称并签单。

二、受益人证明书的种类

1．寄单证明

根据信用证的要求，在装运前后寄送信用证规定的单据证明。

如：We hereby certify that one set of non-negotiable shipping documents has been sent to FUHUA TRADE CO.,LTD. 101 QUEENS ROAD CENTRAL,HONGKONG through courier service within two days after shipment.

2．电抄本

根据信用证规定，在货物出运前后一定期限内，由发货人按信用证规定的内容，用电报、电传通知信用证规定的收电人，并以电报、电传书副本，或另缮制发电证明书，作为已发电证明。

如：We hereby certify that one set of non-negotiable shipping documents has been sent to FUHUA TRADE CO.,LTD. 101 QUEENS ROAD CENTRAL,HONGKONG **by telex** within two days after shipment.

3．履约证明书

证明某件事实、货物符合成交合约或来自某产地。如寄样证明、生产过程证明。

如：We hereby certify that in compliance with the terms of the relative letter of credit ,we have sent requisit shipment samples by registered airmail to the nominees.

自我能力测评

能力形成性评价表

评价指标	分　值	实际得分
能准确翻译信用证中受益人证明书条款	20分	
能掌握常见的几种受益人证明书的填制要点	30分	
能根据相关合同或信用证准确填制一份受益人证明书并审核	50分	

任务四　缮制品质证等商检证书并审核

任务导入

根据上述结汇清单，宁波光明进出口司单证员小兰还需要制作品质证书。

完成上述任务的步骤如下

第一步：再次查看信用证中品质检验证等商检证书条款

如：宁波光明进出口公司收到的信用证中品质证书条款“5. CERTIFICATE OF QUALITY IN 2 ORIGINALS ISSUED BY MANUFACTURER”要求生产商出具 2 份正本品质证。因为要求生产商出具，单证员小兰必须缮制该证并由相关人签字。

第二步，教师引导全体学生，口头填写一份品质证书

制单依据：项目一中信用证（单证 1-17）及其分析结果单（单证 1-18），商业发票（单证 2-1）等其他相关单据。

补充资料：负责该批货物检验的工厂质检员是张华。

单证 7-7

GUANGMING IMPORT & EXPORT CORPORATION
13 XINNING ROAD, NINGBO, ZHEJIANG, CHINA
CERTIFICATE OF QUALITY

DATE:
RE: INVOICE NO.:
L/C NO.:

DESCRIPTION OF GOODS:
QUANTITY:
PAKAGE:

THIS IS TO CERTIFY THAT
CERTIFIED BY :

____
INSPECTOR

SIGNATURE

单证 7-8

GUANGMING IMPORT & EXPORT CORPORATION
13 XINNING ROAD, NINGBO, ZHEJIAING, CHINA

CERTIFICATE OF QUALITY

DATE: ARIL 5,2010
RE: INVOICE NO.: GM10H9141
L/C NO.: 006CIM000489SBRT

DESCRIPTION OF GOODS: 100% NYLON FABRICS

QUANTITY: 1000,000.00 YARDS
PACKAGE:1000 ROLLS

THIS IS TO CERTIFY THAT WE HAVE INSPECTED THE CAPTIONED GOODS AND THE QUALITY ARE IN CONFORMITY WITH S/C NO. E034579.

CERTIFIED BY :
张华
INSPECTOR

宁波光明进出口公司
GUANGMING IMPORT & EXPORT CORPORATION
张华

第三步巩固训练：学生结合一份合同和信用证独立缮制品质书

训练任务

宁波舒普机电科技公司单证员马林根据项目一任务五中，马林修改后的信用证（单证 1-19）及其信用证分析结果单（单证 1-20）独立填写下列品质证书（单证 7-9）。

补充资料：工厂品质检验员：王军。

训练指导：学生可以根据刚才老师的引导、示范，先尝试填写一份品质证书，若有疑问可查阅下列品质证书的填制要领；也可以先看品质证书的填制要领，再去填制品质证书。

要求：填制好的受益人证明书要在小组中交流，然后电子文档提交到天空教室。

第四步：教师随机抽取一组同学填制的单证，集体批阅、点评、核对答案

单证　7-9

CERTIFICATE OF QUALITY

DATE:

RE: INVOICE　NO:

L/C NO.:

DESCRIPTION OF GOODS:

QUANTITY:

PACKAGE:

THIS IS TO CERTIFY THAT

CERTIFIED BY :

INSPECTOR

SIGNATURE

知识链接

一、公司和厂家出具的检验证书缮制要点

（1）填写出口厂家或出口公司的名称和地址；

（2）填写商检证书的名称，如品质检验证书、数量检验证书；

（3）填写发票号码、信用证号码（如信用证支付）；

（4）日期：不迟于提单签发日；

（5）填写商品名称；

（6）填写计算单价时使用的计量单位的数量，也可填写与提单或其他运输单据相同栏目中最大包装件数；

（7）填写净重和毛重（重量证）；

（8）按已检验结果填写详细内容；

（9）经办人签字并加盖公章。

注：

商检局商品检验证书的大部分栏目的填写方法和上面的基本一致，不同的有：

（1）编号由商检局编制；

（2）增加收货人和发货人两个栏目，发货人栏目填写受益人名称，收货人栏目与发票抬头人栏目相同；

（3）由商检局官员签字并盖商检局公章。

注意事项

1．出证机关、地点及证书名称

如来证未规定出具证书的机关，则由出口人决定。如信用证规定“COMPETENT AUTHORITY”出证，则由商检机构出具。地点除信用证另有规定外，原则上应在装船口岸。名称应与信用证规定相符。

2．证书日期

商检证书出具日期应与提单日期相同，但也不能早于提单日期，以免收货人因从检验到装运的时间太长而怀疑货物质量是否符合证书中的检验结果。信用证如规定在装船日出证（ISSUED AT THE TIME OF SHIPMENT），则商检证书的日期原则上应与提单日期相同，如证书日期与提单日期相差超过 3 天，容易遭到开证行或开证人拒付。

3．证书内容

证书表示的商检结果要与信用证上的要求和发票等各项单据所列商品的规格、状态一致。

二、商检证书及其种类

商检证书，是各种进出口商品检验证书、鉴定证书和其他证明书的统称，是对外贸易有关各方履行契约义务、处理索赔争议和仲裁诉讼举证，具有法律依据的有效证件，也是海关验放、征收关税和优惠减免关税的必要证明。商检证书的种类和用途主要有：

（1）品质检验证书（Quality Certificate），是出口商品交货结汇和进口商品结算索赔的有效凭证。法定检验商品的证书，是进出口商品报关、输出输入的合法凭证。商检机构签发的放行单和在报关单上加盖的放行章有与商检证书同等通关效力。签发的检验情况通知单与商检证书性质相同。

（2）重量或数量检验证书（Weight or Quantity Certificate），是出口商品交货结汇、签发提单和进口商品结算索赔的有效凭证。出口商品的重量证书，也是国外报关征税和计算运费、装卸费用的证件。

（3）兽医检验证书（Veterinary Certificate），是证明出口动物产品或食品经过检疫合格的证件。适用于冻畜肉、冻禽、禽畜罐头、冻兔、皮张、毛类、绒类、猪鬃、肠衣等出口商品。是对外交货、银行结汇和进口国通关输入的重要证件。

（4）卫生/健康证书（Sanitary Certificate），是证明可供人类食用的出口动物产品、食品等经过卫生检验或检疫合格的证件。适用于肠衣、罐头、冻鱼、冻虾、食品、蛋品、乳制品、蜂蜜等，是对外交货、银行结汇和通关验放的有效证件。

（5）消毒检验证书（Inspection Certificate of Disinfection），是证明出口动物产品经过消毒处理，保证安全卫生的证件。适用于猪鬃、马尾、皮张、山羊毛、羽毛、人发等商品，是对外交货、银行结汇和国外通关验放的有效凭证。

（6）熏蒸证书（Fumigation Certificate），是用于证明出口粮谷、油籽、豆类、皮张等商品，以及包装用木材与植物性填充物等，已经过熏蒸灭虫的证书。

（7）残损检验证书（Inspection Certificate on Damaged Cargo），是证明进口商品残损情况的证件。适用于进口商品发生残、短、渍、毁等情况；可作为受货人向发货人或承运人或保险人等有关责任方索赔的有效证件。

（8）积载鉴定证书（Inspection Certificate on Hatch and /or Cargo），是证明船方和集装箱装货部门正确配载积载货物，作为证明履行运输契约义务的证件。可供货物交接或发生货损时处理争议之用。

（9）产地证明书（Certificate of Origin），是出口商品在进口国通关输入和享受减免关税优惠待遇和证明商品产地的凭证。

自我能力测评

能力形成性评价表

评价指标	分　值	实际得分
能准确翻译信用证中商检证书条款	20分	
能掌握常见的几种商检证书的填制要点	30分	
能根据相关合同或信用证准确填制一份商检证书并审核	50分	

任务五　出具船级证明

任务导入

根据上述结汇清单，宁波光明进出口司单证员小兰还需要请船公司出具船级证明。

第一步：再次查看信用证中有关船级证书条款

如：宁波光明进出口公司收到的信用证中品质证书条款“7.SHIP’S CLASSIFICATION ISSUED BY LIOYDS’ IN LONDON”单据要求“英国劳埃德船级社出具的船级证明”。

第二步：弄清楚谁出具船级证明

外贸公司可以将要求在订舱的时候提交给货代，货代联系船公司，如能办理船级证书，就可以交给他们运输，否则，必须另寻其他公司运输。

第三步：弄清楚船级证明的主要内容及缮制要点

首先教师向学生展示一份已签发的船级证明（图 7-3）。

船 级 证 明

LIOYD'S REGISTER OF SHIPPING

71 Fenchurch Street, London,ec3m4bs

telephone:01-7099199 telex: 883779

Maersk line(HK)LTD,
Technical office
30-21th fl., sunning plaza
10 Bysan avenue, CAUSEWAY BAY,
HONGKONG

Please Address Further Communications To The Secretary, and quote
Our Ref CLASS/CONF
Your Ref.

Date 10th sept., 2010

CONFIRMATION OF CLASS

TO WHOM IT MAY CONCERN:

This is to certify that according to current information available in this office, the class status of the undermentioned ship/unit is as follows:

LR. NUMBER	7358801
NAME OF SHIP/UNIT	"DONGFENG"
GROSS TONNAGE	29901
DATE OF BUILD	1987-5
CLASS STATUS	THE ABOVE SHIPMAITAINS THE CLASS+100A1 and+LMC

The above ship has the notation UMS(Unattende Machinery Space)

lssuing Office MICHELL BROW

HONGKONG FOR THE SECRETARY, LIOYD'D REGITER OF SHIPPING

图 7-3

引导学生根据这份证明总结出船级证明缮制的要点：

（1）签署该证书的机构名称和地址；

（2）签发日期；

（3）证书名称，如"CONFIRMATION OF CLASS"；

（4）抬头，通常采用笼统填法，如"TO WHOM IT MAY CONCERN"（至有关人）；

（5）船名；

（6）证明内容；

（7）由证书的出具机构签署。

船级证明上的符号所代表的含义

1. 主要船级社的名称及代码：英国劳合社（LR）、德国船级社（GL）、挪威船级社（DNV）、法国船级社（BV）、日本海事协会（NK）、美国船级社（ABS），以及中国船级社（ZC）等。

2. 英国劳合社入级符号是"100AI"。凡经入级的一切船舶将根据其适用条件授予一个或多个船级符号。对多数船舶，所授予的符号将为 100AI。"100" 此船级符号数符将授予认为适于海上营运的一切船舶。"A" 表示该船的船体和机器设备是根据劳氏规范和规定建造的，"I" 表示船舶的装备如船锚、锚链和绳索等处于良好和有效的状态。

3. 英国劳合社为适宜者授予与下列机械构造和布置相应的船级标志："LMC" 表示推进机械及主要辅助机械的建造、安装及试验是在劳氏船级社特别检验下进行，且符合劳氏船级社规范和规则，则将授予此标志。"IGS" 此标志将授予拟载运散装油或散装液态化学品并装有经认可的用于液货舱的惰性气体发生系统的船舶。

知识拓展

在我国对外贸易实践中，经常会遇到进口商在信用证中提出要求船公司证明（以下称“船证”）的情形，多来自中东和非洲地区的客户，所以单证从业人员必须对此进行恰当的理解和把握。船证通常由出口商或船方用英文制作，具体内容应以信用证中要求为准，所有船证必须签署。

很多 L/C 都对船有要求，所以需要开船证明，那么，船证明通常有哪些？该怎么做呢？

1．船舶本身的证明文件

（1）集装箱船只证明（Certificate of Container Vessel）：进口商或银行在合同/信用证中规定货物须装集装箱船并出具相应证明的，可由受益人自行制作并加盖有关签发人的图章，也可在运输单据上加以注明。

（2）船龄证明：有些国家/地区来证规定装载货物的船舶的船龄不得超过 15 年，受益人必须要求船代或船公司出具载货船只的船龄证明书（Certificate to evidence the ship is not over 15 years old 或 is under 15 years of age），这样的要求主要目的在于禁止使用老龄船，保护货物运输安全。

（3）船籍证明（Certificate of Registry）：用于证明船舶所属国籍。

（4）船级证明（Confirmation of Class）：船级是表示船舶技术状态的一种指标。在国际航运界，凡注册总吨在 100 吨以上的海运船舶，必须在某船级社或船舶检验机构监督之下进行监造。在船舶开始建造之前，船舶各部分的规格须经船级社或船舶检验机构批准。每艘船建造完毕，由船级社或船舶检验局对船体、船上机器设备、吃水标志等项目和性能进行鉴定，发给船级证书。证书有效期一般为 4 年，期满后需重新予以鉴定。船舶入级可保证船舶航行安全，有利于国家对船舶进行技术监督，便于租船人和托运人选择适当的船只，以满足进出口货物运输的需要，便于保险公司决定船、货的保险费用。

2．运输和航行证明

（1）航程证明（Certificate of Itinerary）：主要说明航程中船舶停靠的港口，一些阿拉伯国家开来的信用证中，往往要求在提单上随附声明一份，明确船籍、船名、船东及途中所经港口顺序，出口方须按要求签发此类证明并按证明中所述行驶、操作船舶。

（2）转船证明书（Certificate of Transshipment）：出口方出具转船证明书，说明出口货物将在中途转船且已联系妥当，并由托运人负责将有关转船事项通知收货人。

（3）货装具名船舶证明。如信用证要求：“A certificate from the shipping company or its agent stating that goods are shipped by APL”（意思是要求出口方提供由船公司或其代理出具的货装美国总统轮船公司的证明）。

（4）船长收据（Captain's Receipt）：有的信用证规定，样品或单据副本由载货船只的船长交进口商，并提供船长收据，如委托船长带去而未取得船长收据将影响出口商收汇，这一做法常见于近洋运输。

此外船证还包括进港证明、运费已交收据、港口费用单（port charges documents）、装卸准备就绪通知书（NOR）和装卸时间事实记录等，由于政治原因，巴基斯坦和印度互不允许悬挂对方国旗的船舶靠岸，巴基斯坦港口还不接受来自南非、韩国、以色列和中国台湾的船舶，如要求出具相应证明的，出口方必须提供。

3．航运组织和公约证明

（1）班会证明（Conference Line Certificate）：信用证规定货物须装班会船只时，向银行所交单据中应包括船公司或船代出具的证明。例如，信用证要求“A certificate issued by the carrier,shipping Co or their agents certifying that shipment has been effected by conference line and/or regular line vessels only covered by institute classification clause to accompany the documents.”。其意思是：由承运人、船公司或他们的代理签发证明，证实货物业已装运在符合伦敦协会船级条款的班会船只或定期船上，该船证随单据提交”。再如，某信用证要求“Shipping company's certificate stating that the carrying vessel has entered P&I Club and should be attached with the original documents”，其要求船证应明确载货船舶系船东保赔协会成员并应随附正本证明。

（2）黑名单证明：典型的是阿拉伯国家所要求的抵制以色列证明（Certificate of Boycott Israel）。其通常规定为：“The vessel carrying the goods is not Israeli and will not call on any Israeli ports while carrying the goods and that the vessel is not banned entry to the port of the Arab States for any reasons whatever under law and the laws and regulations of such Sates allowed.（船上所装货物为非以色列原产，船不经停任何以色列港口，船只可依法自由进入阿拉伯国家法律和规则所容许进出的港口）。”

（3）SMC、DOC 和 SOLAS：这几个缩略语近年来常出现在信用证的要求中，SMC（Safety Management Certificate 船舶安全管理证书）和 DOC（Document of Compliance 安全符合证书，也有人称其为船/港保安符合证书）是按照国际安全管理规则（ISM）的规定，载货船舶应在船上拥有的必要证书。我国海事局按 ISM 的规章发给船公司 DOC，船舶则可获 SMC，如船公司没有相应证书，那么就没有办法按信用证要求来出具此类证明。信用证中的一般要求是：“The carrying vessel should comply with the provisions of the (ISM) Code which necessiates that such vessel must have on board, copies of the two (SMC and DOC)valid Certificates and copies of such certificate must be presented with the original documents.”也可体现为“Certificate issued,signed and stamped by the owner/carrier/ master of the carrying vessel holds valid ISM certificate and ISPS (International Shipping And Port Security Safety Code《国际船舶和港口设施保安规则》。）”；SOLAS 指的是《1974 年国际海上人命安全公约》（简称 SOLAS 公约）。“9・11”事件后国际海事组织于 2002 年 12 月召开缔约国大会通过对 SOLAS 公约的修正案，并在 2004 年 7 月 1 日起开始实施。按上述有关规定，船舶应持有“安全管理证书”正本，其船名与国籍证书一致，所载公司名称与“符合证明”中的公司名称相一致。

4．正确理解船证制作要求

（1）某信用证中要求：“Certificate from the shipping agents issued at the port of shipment stating that cargo and/or interests are carried by a mechanically self propelled seaworthy vessel classified under Lloyd's register of shipping as 100AI or equivalent provided such vessels are not over fifteen years of age or over fifteen years but not over twenty five years of age and have established and maintained a regular pattern of trading on an advertised schedule to load and unload at specific ports or equivalent.”船证由船代在装运港制作，明确货物是由英国劳合社或其他相应机构确认的 100AI 级、机械驱动、适航的船舶运输，船龄应 15 年以下，或能按预先公布的船期表在特定港口持续定期投入装卸货物的商业运营的船舶，船龄也可在 15 年以上 25 年以下。证明内容以证内文字及船舶的实际情况加以叙述即可。

（2）A certificate from the shipping company or their agent stating that the goods are shipped on vessels：

-that are exempted from the “solas” convention certification requirement and is not required to have a certificate of conformity to the ISM code or that have a current ISM code certificate if the carrying vessel is subject to “solas”.

-covered by the institution classification clause.

-that are allowed by the Arab authorities to call at arabian ports and not scheduled to call at any israel port during its voyage to the U.A.E.

-under 15 years of age.

该船证要求来自阿拉伯联合酋长国开的信用证，船证由船公司或其代理签发，证明载货的船舶：如适用“SOLAS”公约则必须持有有效的 ISM 证明，否则可以豁免相关证明；船舶符合协会船级条款；经阿拉伯国家授权，船舶可挂靠所有阿拉伯口岸，船舶在驶往阿联酋途中不停靠任何以色列港口；船龄 15 年以下。

自我能力测评

能力形成性评价表

评价指标	分值	实际得分
能准确翻译信用证中船证条款	30 分	
能掌握办理船证的方法	40 分	
能了解船证的内容、掌握船证的制作要点	30 分	

任务六　审核全套结汇单据

任务导入

根据结汇清单，宁波光明进出口公司的单证员小兰根据信用证要求备齐了全套结汇单据后，需要对这些单据认真审核，确保无误后，向宁波银行交单结汇。

完成此任务的步骤

第一步：根据结汇清单，汇集信用证项下要求的所有单据，不可遗留

第二步：对每一份单据的项目、格式、内容、文字、签发日期、签字及其他事项进行认真审核，确保与信用证的要求一致（纵向审核）

第三步：以商业发票为中心，对全套单据的一致性进行审核（横向审核）

第四步：如果审核单据过程中发现任何错误，必须注意更改过程中涉及的一系列具体问题，如同一内容出现在不同的单据上；有些内容的更改必须得到相关部门的同意

职场经验

外贸单证常规审核指南

单证的审核是对已经缮制，备妥的单据对照信用证（在信用证付款情况下）或合同（非信用证付款方式）的有关内容进行单单、单证的及时的检查和核对，发现问题，及时更正，达到安全收汇的目的。

一、单证审核的基本要求

（1）及时性。及时审核有关单据可以对一些单据上的差错做到及时发现，及时更正，有效地避免因审核不及时造成的各项工作的被动。

（2）全面性。应当从安全收汇和全面履行合同的高度来重视单据的审核工作，一方面，我们应对照信用证和合同认真审核每一份单证，不放过任何一个不符点；另一方面，要善于处理所发现的问题，加强与各有关部门的联系和衔接，使发现的问题得到及时、妥善的处理。

（3）按照“严格符合”的原则，做到“单单相符，单证相符”。“单单相符，单证相符”是安全收汇的前提和基础，所提交的单据中存在的任何不符哪怕是细小的差错都会造成一些难以挽回的损失。

二、单证审核的基本方法

单证审核的基本方法概括起来有以下几种：

（1）纵向审核法。这是指以信用证或合同（在非信用证付款条件下）为基础对规定的各项单据进行一一审核，要求有关单据的内容严格符合信用证的规定，做到“单证相符”。

（2）横向审核法。在纵向审核的基础上，以商业发票为中心审核其他规定的单据，使有关的内容相互一致，做到“单单相符”。

上述审核一般由制单员或审单员进行，为第一道审核；为安全起见，应当对有关单据进行复审。

三、单证审核的要点

（一）综合审核的要点

（1）检查规定的单证是否齐全，包括所需单证的份数。

（2）检查所提供的文件名称和类型是否符合要求。

（3）有些单证是否按规定进行了认证。

（4）单证之间的货物描述、数量、金额、重量、体积、运输标志等是否一致。

（5）单证出具或提交的日期是否符合要求。

（二）分类审核的要点

1．汇票

（1）汇票的付款人名称、地址是否正确；

（2）汇票上金额的大小写必须一致；

（3）付款期限要符合信用证或合同（非信用证付款条件下）规定；

（4）检查汇票金额是否超出信用证金额，如有信用证金额前有“大约”一词可按10%的增减幅度掌握；

（5）出票人、收款人、付款人都必须符合信用证或合同（非信用证付款条件下）的规定；

（6）币制名称应与信用证和发票上的相一致。

2．商业发票

（1）抬头人必须符合信用证规定；

（2）签发人必须是受益人；

（3）商品的描述必须完全符合信用证的要求；

（4）商品的数量必须符合信用证的规定；

（5）单价和价格条件必须符合信用证的规定；

（6）提交的正副本份数必须符合信用证的要求；

（7）信用证要求表明和证明的内容不得遗漏；

（8）发票的金额不得超出信用证的金额，如数量、金额均有“大约”，可按10%的增减幅度掌握。

3．保险单据

（1）保险单据必须由保险公司或其代理出具；

（2）投保加成必须符合信用证的规定；

（3）保险险别必须符合信用证的规定并且无遗漏；

（4）保险单据的类型应与信用证的要求相一致，除非信用证另有规定，保险经纪人出具的暂保单银行不予接受；

（5）保险单据的正副本份数应齐全，如保险单据注明出具一式多份正本，除非信用证另有规定，所有正本都必须提交；

（6）保险单据上的币制应与信用证上的币制相一致；

（7）包装件数、唛头等必须与发票和其他单据相一致；

（8）运输工具、起运地及目的地，都必须与信用证及其他单据相一致；

（9）如转运，保险期限必须包括全程运输；

（10）除非信用证另有规定，保险单的签发日期不得迟于运输单据的签发日期；

（11）除信用证另有规定，保险单据一般应作成可转让的形式，以受益人为投保人，由投保人背书。

4．运输单据

（1）运输单据的类型须符合信用证的规定；

（2）起运地、转运地、目的地须符合信用证的规定；

（3）装运日期/出单日期须符合信用证的规定；

（4）收货人和被通知人须符合信用证的规定；

（5）商品名称可使用货物的统称，但不得与发票上货物说明的写法相抵触；

（6）运费预付或运费到付须正确表明；

（7）正副本份数应符合信用证的要求；

（8）运输单据上不应有不良批注；

（9）包装件数须与其他单据相一致；

（10）唛头须与其他单据相一致；

（11）全套正本都须盖妥承运人的印章及签发日期章；

（12）应加背书的运输单据，须加背书。

5．其他单据

其他单据如装箱单、重量单、产地证书、商检证书等，均须先与信用证的条款进行核对，再与其他有关单据核对，保证单证一致、单单一致。

6．单证审核的重点

单证审核是保障安全收汇的关键环节，单证审核的重点是：

（1）检查L/C规定的单证份数（比如多或者少，是否是全套等）；

（2）检查附加条款对单证的特别要求（比如是否要求注明L/C号码、合同号码等）；

（3）检查所提供的文件名称和类型是否符合要求（比如是否需要认证、出单人是否符合要求等）；

（4）单证之间的各类描述是否完全一致（比如大小写、计量单位等）；

（5）单证出具或提交的日期是否符合要求（比如保单日期、FORM A出单期等）。

四、出单中比较常见的问题

（1）对于信用证溢短装条款的误解，造成单证金额、数量错误。

一般来说，如果信用证对金额和数量溢短装有明确规定要按照要求出具；如果信用证没有明确规定，可以有5%溢短装。这里要说的是根据UCP600条款，如果计量单位是个、只等，则此项规定不适用。

（2）汇票大、小写金额打错；汇票的付款人名称、地址打错。

（3）发票的抬头人打错；发票中受益人名称、地址等与信用证描述不一致；发票上的货物描述不符合信用证的规定。

（4）有关单据如汇票/发票/保险单等的币制名称不一致或不符合信用证的规定；多装或短装。

（5）要求认证或证实单据的类型、出单人等不符合信用证要求。

（6）单单之间商品名称/数量/件数/唛头/毛净重等不一致。

（7）正本单据没有显示正本字样或提交份数不足。

（8）未按信用证要求对有关单据如发票/产地证等进行认证。

（9）提单、保险单缺少有关签字或印章。

（10）汇票/运输提单/保险单据上未按要求进行背书。

（11）提单中的卸货港、目的地签发错误，以及存在不良批注等。

五、有问题单据的具体处理

通过对有关单据的认真审核，对于有问题的单据可根据具体情况做如下处理：

（1）对有问题的单据必须进行及时更正和修正。否则，将影响安全收汇。在规定的有效期和交单期内，将有问题的单据全部改妥。

（2）有些单据由于种种原因不能按期更改或无法修改，可以向银行出具一份保函（通常称为担保书），保函中交单人要求银行向开证行寄单并承诺如果买方不接受单据或不付款，银行有权收回已偿付给交单人的款项。对此银行方面虽然可能会接受，但建议还是不要做。因为出具保函后，收不到货款的风险依然存在。同时要承担由此产生的其他费用。交单人向银行出具保函一般应事先与客户联系并取得客人接受不符单据的确认文件。

（3）请银行向开证行拍发要求接受不符点并予付款的电传（俗称“打不符电”）。有关银行在收到开证银行的确认接受不符单据的电传后再寄送有关单据，收汇一般有保证，此种方式可以避免未经同意盲目寄单情况的发生。但要求开证行确认需要一定的时间同时要冒开证行不确认的风险并要承担有关的电传费用。

（4）改用托收方式。由于单据中存在不符点，原先信用证项下的银行信用已经变为商业信用，如果客人信用较好且急需有关文件提取货物，为减少一些中间环节可采用托收方式。

上述各项措施主要是从有效控制货物所有权的前提下，以积极、稳妥的方式处理不符合有关规定的单据，避免货款两空情况的发生。因为只要掌握了代表物权的运输单据，买方就不能提取货物。如果买方仍然需要这批货物，那么买方也会接受有不符点的单据的。这里必须切记的是，不符单据是有很大风险的，对不符单据的接受与否完全取决于买方。

自我能力测评

能力形成性评价表

评价指标	分　值	实际得分
能掌握外贸单据审核的要点和重点	40分	
能根据出单常见的错误进行重点审核	30分	
能对单据审核的问题进行正确处理	30分	

项目八

出口收汇核销与退税单据的制作与审核

知识目标

了解出口收汇核销与退税的有关规定；熟悉出口退税与收汇的流程；掌握出口退税申报表的主要内容、出口收汇核销单的内容及作用。

能力目标

能正确审核出口退税单据；能正确填写出口收汇核销单；能正确审核出口收汇核销单据。

任务分解

达到上述目标，需要完成下列任务：

- 任务一：备齐并审核出口收汇核销单据
- 任务二：备齐并审核出口退税单据

任务一　备齐并审核出口收汇核销单据

任务导入

宁波光明进出口公司单证员小兰根据我国出口收汇核销制度，在银行交单结汇后，接下来备齐并审核全套出口收汇核销单据，交公司财务部门，由他们在出口日期 210 天内凭三单三票（报关单、核销单、结汇水单、外销发票、增值税发票或出口货物完税发票）到外汇管理局办理出口收汇核销业务。

完成上述任务的步骤如下

第一步：教师引导学生学习下列收汇核销流程图

出口核销程序有四个阶段：

（1）货物报关前申领核销单；

（2）货物报关时使用核销单；

（3）货物报关后交回核销单存根及其附件，货款收妥交回核销单正本及其附件；

（4）审核有关单证，办理核销手续。

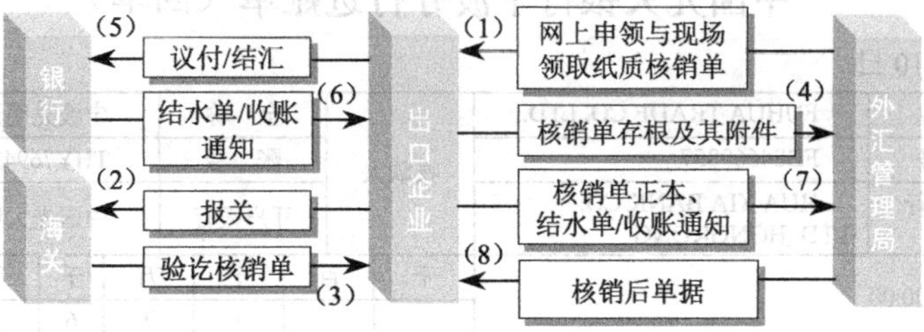

图　8-1

说明：

（1）出口企业提前到外汇管理部门领取出口收汇核销单。

（2）出口企业报关时，向海关提交事先从外汇管理部门领取的有顺序编号的外汇核销单。

（3）海关审核无误，在核销单和与核销单有相同编号的报关单上盖“验讫章”。

（4）报关后，出口企业在规定期限将核销单存根送回外汇管理局接受外汇管理部门对企业出口收汇情况的监督。

（5）货物出口后，出口企业将海关退给的核销单、报关单和有关单据送交银行收汇。

（6）货款汇交至出口地银行以后，银行向出口单位出具结汇水单或收账通知并在结汇水单或收账通知上填写有关核销单编号。

（7）出口单位凭出口收汇核销单和出口收汇核销专用联的结汇水单或收账通知及其他规定的单据，到国家外汇管理部门办理核销手续。

（8）国家外汇管理部门按规定办理核销后，在核销单上加盖“已核销”章，并将其中的出口退税专用联退还给出口单位作为日后退税依据。

第二步：学生根据上述流程图，独立缮制出口收汇核销清单、理单

在已有的单据后面打“√”。

第三步：教师核对答案

办理出口收汇核销所需单据：

（1）出口收汇核销单正本（√）；

（2）银行结汇水单/收账通知（银行已签发√）；

（3）报关单出口收汇证明联（√）；

（4）出口商业发票（√）；

（5）购进货物的增值税发票（税款抵扣联）或普通发票（√）；

（6）税收（出口货物专用）缴款书（第二联）或出口货物完税分割单（第二联）（√）。

第四步：审单、交单

上述单据整理齐全后，以发票为中心进行审核，审核无误后，交公司财务部门，由他们去外管局办理收汇核销手续。

中国光大银行宁波分行开立的结汇水单（图 8-2）、收汇核销单（图 8-3）如下。

中国光大银行宁波分行进账单（回单）

2007年8月10日　　　　第060611号

出票人	全　称	FUHUA TRADE CO.,LTD.,	收款人	全　称	宁波光明进出口贸易公司
	账　号	FB84669857		账　号	THY7694366318
	开户银行	HUA XIA BANK CO. LTD ,HONGKONG		开户银行	中国光大银行宁波分行

美元：USD 126 000.00	千	百	十	万	千	百	十	元	角	分
			1	2	6	0	0	0	0	0

票据种类	BP XT173	申报号码：No.0606775588
票据张数	核销单号：031155451	
中国光大银行国际结算专用章		出口收汇核销专用章

图　8-2

出口收汇核销单核销联和退税联

宁波光明进出口公司	出口收汇核销单 监制章 编号：031155451				
	出口单位： 宁波光明进出口公司				
	单位编码： 809776428				
	银行签注栏	类别	币种金额	日期	盖章
		全尼龙织物	USD33,680.	2010.04.20	中国光大银行
出口单位盖章	海关签注栏：该票货物已于2010．04．05结关				
	外汇管理局章 外汇局签注栏 2010年7月5日（盖章）				

宁波光明进出口公司	出口收汇核销单 监制章 编号：031155451		
	出口单位 宁波光明进出口公司		
	单位编码： 809776428		
	货物名称	数量	币种总价
出口单位盖章	海关验讫章 报关单编号：547689219		
	外汇局签注栏 年　月　日（盖章）		

图　8-3

自我能力测评

能力形成性评价表

评价指标	分　值	实际得分
能绘制出口收汇核销的基本流程图	30分	
准确列出出口收汇核销所需的单据	20分	
能在规定的时间收齐并审核“三单三票”交财务部门办理核销	50分	

任务二 备齐并审核出口退税单据

任务导入

宁波光明进出口公司在货物出运后到中国光大银行宁波分行办理了交单结汇业务，到外汇管理局办理了出口收汇核销业务，单证员小兰接下来要备齐并审核五单一票一书一收据（报关单、核销单、结汇水单、提单（复印件）、货物明细单、外销发票、托书（托运单）、场站收据等，交公司财务部门，在货物出运日起60天内，由他们到宁波税务局办理出口退税申报手续。

完成上述任务的步骤

第一步：了解出口退税的有关规定

（一）出口退税的含义与原则

（1）含义：出口退税是指已报关离境的产品，由税务机关将其出口前在生产和流通环节中已征收的中间税款返还给出口企业，从而使出口商品以不含税价格进入国际市场，参与国际竞争的一种政策制度。

（2）原则："征多少，退多少，不征不退和彻底退税"。

（二）出口退税企业范围

凡发生出口业务的出口企业，均可申报办理出口退税。

享有出口退税的企业有：

（1）具有进出口经营权的企业（包括外商投资企业）。

（2）委托出口企业。一是无进出口经营权的工厂或企业委托有进出口经营权的企业代理出口业务。二是本身有进出口经营权但委托另一家有进出口权的企业代理出口业务。代理出口企业收取代理费，委托出口企业自负盈亏，并申报办理出口退税。

（3）特定企业。如外轮公司、远洋运输公司等单位发生的一些特定业务，也可办理出口退税。

（三）出口退税的货物

只有同时具备下列条件的出口货物，才可办理出口退税。

（1）属于增值税或消费税征税范围的出口货物；

（2）已报关离境的货物；

（3）已收妥货款并结汇的货物；

（4）财务已做出口商品销售处理的货物；

（5）按规定提供全套退税单据。

（四）出口退税程序

出口退税的基本流程如图 8-4 所示：

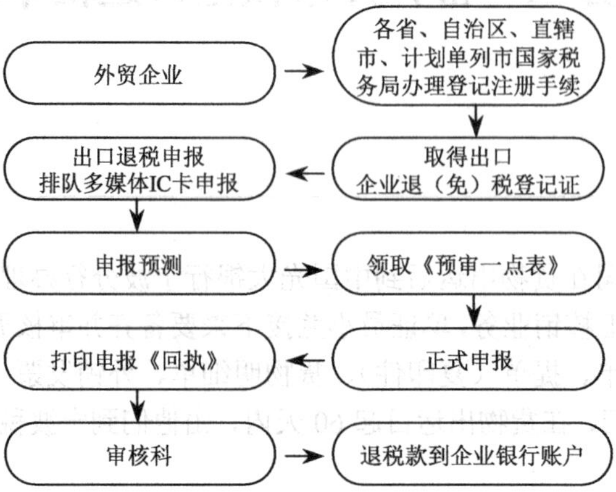

图 8-4

1. 出口退税登记

凡经批准有出口经营权，实行独立经济核算的企业单位，均应持工商营业执照，填写“出口企业退税登记表”，向所在地主管退税业务的税务机关办理出口企业退税登记。新开业、拆并、变更的出口企业，应当自变更之日起 30 天内办理退税登记。登记之后，方可申请退税。

2. 出口产品的退税鉴定

凡经营出口产品的企业，均应填写“出口产品退税鉴定表”，报经所在地主管出口退税业务的税务机关审核批准后执行。

出口企业的贸易性质、经营方式和经营品种若有变更，应在变更后 30 天内向税务机关申报退税鉴定的税种、税目、税率和计退依据。当有关退税政策须调整时，主管退税业务的税务机关应及时通知出口企业，出口企业在接到税务机关通知 30 日内，重新修订出口产品退税鉴定，并报税务机关核准后执行。

3. 出口产品的费用扣除

出口企业采购出口商品，应在库存出口商品账上将产品的出厂金额与购进等各项费用分开记账。产品出口后，出口商品销售账能反映出厂金额的，应按账上记载的出厂金额经税务机关审核后据以计算退税；出口商品销售账不能反映出厂金额的，应按库存出口商品账上记载的各项费用采取核定费用扣除率的办法经税务机关审核后予以扣除。

4. 出口产品的退税申报

出口企业在产品报关出口并在财务上做销售处理后，按月、旬或按批如实填写“出口产品退税申请表”，并随附盖有海关验讫章的“出口货物报关单”原件和“出口销售发票”，报税务机关申请退税。退税后，税务机关应在“出口货物报关单”上盖“已退税”章。

5. 出口退税审核

出口退税的审批权原则上集中在省级和计划单列市国家税务局，也可根据出口退税审核工作的实际情况，由地（市）一级国家税务局参与出口退税的具体审核工作。在上述国家税务局，设立有进出口收税管理处（分局），直接办理出口退税业务。

负责出口退税审核的税务机关在接到出口企业的退税申报表时，亦必须严格按照出口退税规定认真审核，确认无误后，逐级报请有权审批的税务机关审批，只有在批准后，才可填写《收入退还书》，送当地银行办理退税。

出口退税审核的主要内容有：出口报关单原始单据、进项税额原始单据、出口货物销售账簿和应交税金账簿等。

6．税款退付与退税清算

税款退付是在出口退税申报和审批之后，银行依据《收入退还书》将出口退税款从国库退付到出口企业的开户银行账户的行为。出口货物在办理退税手续后，如发生退关、国外退货或转为内销，企业必须向所在地主管出口退税的税务机关办理申报手续，补交已退（免）的税款。

退税清算是指出口企业要于年度终了后三个月内，进行上一年度出口退税的清算，按规定期限向主管退税机关报送“清算表”及相关资料，由主管税务机关进行全面清查。主管退税机关在出口企业清算结束后两个月内，对企业上报清算报表的清算资料进行清算核查，并向出口企业发出《清算情况通知书》说明以下问题：①出口企业的性质和清算范围，出口货物的品种、数量及销售额，清算后出口企业应退税款、已退税款。②清算中发现的问题，多退、少退、错退的金额。③清算处理结果及意见。

第二步：熟悉外贸企业出口退税申报流程

（1）下载外贸企业出口退税申报系统和出口退税网软件，安装后通过系统维护进行企业信息设置。

（2）通过退税系统完成出口明细申报数据的录入、审核。

（3）取得增值税发票后在发票开票日期 30 天内，在“发票认证系统”或国税局进行发票信息认证。

（4）通过退税系统完成进货明细申报数据的录入、审核。

（5）通过系统中“数据处理”的“进货出口数量关联检查”和“换汇成本检查”生成预申报数据。

（6）网上预申报和察看预审反馈。

（7）在申报系统中录入单证备案数据。

（8）预审通过后，进行正式申报，把预申报数据确认到正式申报数据中。

（9）打印出口明细申报表、进货明细申报表、出口退税申报汇总表各 2 份，并生成退税申报软盘，软盘中应该有 12 个文件，并在生成好的退税软盘上写上企业的名称和海关代码。

（10）准备退税申报资料，到退税科正式申报退税（需要在出口日期算起 90 天内进行正式申报）。所需资料如下：

1）打印好的专用封面纸；

2）《外贸企业出口退税进货明细申请表》；

3）《外贸企业出口退税出口明细申请表》；

4）出口退税专用核销单；

5）税收（出口货物专用）缴款书；

6）增值税票抵扣联及专用货物清单；

7）代理出口证明（如属代理出口的）；

8）出口退税专用报关单；

9）资料封底。

以上单据在装订时请按关联号排列，所有单据竖着放，靠右侧在上方装订，装订成一册。另外应附两套退税申报表（退税汇总申报表；退税进货明细表；退税出口申报明细表）并加盖公章。

企业到退税机关办理退税正式申报，退税机关审核软盘及报表和资料合格以后，企业将软盘和资料及一套退税申报表交给退税机关，退税机关会将一张退税汇总申报表签字盖章后返还给企业。正式申报退税即完成。

(11) 税款的退还。税务局得到退税的批复之后，会将数据上传到税网，同时系统自动发送电子邮件。企业看到后，可以到"数据管理"—"退税批复"栏目中查看。点击某条批复的数据，显示注意事项。点击"下一步"，会显示"出口货物税收退还申请书"的内容，企业应仔细核对开户行与账号是否准确，打印 3 份。根据注意事项的相关内容，在打印出的表单中盖章，交到退税科，由退税机关办理退库。

第三步：出口退税所需单据清单

1．两单三票

两单即：

(1) 出口货物报关单（退税联）。

(2) 出口收汇核销单（出口退税专用）。

三票即：

(1) 购进货物的增值税发票（税款抵扣联）或普通发票。

(2) 税收（出口货物专用）缴款书（第二联）（应退消费税的）或出口货物完税分割单（第二联）（从外贸企业将购进货物的）。

(3) 出口商业发票。

注明："两单三票"指的是专业外贸公司应提供的单据，非专业外贸企业委托其他外贸企业出口的，还应提供由受托方主管出口退税的税务机关签章的"代理出口货物证明"，即"二单三票一证明"。

职场经验

退税时单证员交给财务的单据清单

外销商业发票两份，报关单两联（核销联、退税联）、货物明细单一份、提单复印件一份、核销单（出口退税联）银行水单一份、场站收据一份、托书一份，简称五单、一票、一书、一收据。

2．出口货物退（免）税申报表

(1) 出口退税进货凭证申报表（一式两份）。

（2）出口货物退税申报明细表（一式四份）。

（3）出口退税汇总申报表（一式四份），并经商务主管部门稽核盖章。

3．出口货物销售明细账

仅在需要时提供。

4．退税申报软盘（一张）

软盘中申报数据的顺序、内容与申报资料、申报表一致。

注明：外贸单证员小兰主要负责备齐并审核“五单、一票、一书、一收据”，交公司财务部门，财务部门负责填制其余的表格，具体申报。

自我能力测评

能力形成性评价表

评价指标	分　值	实际得分
了解出口退税的有关规定	20分	
熟悉出口退税的流程	20分	
能在规定的时间收齐并审核“三单三票”交财务部门办理退税	60分	

项目九

信用证支付方式下出口单证的综合训练

业务背景

张明先生毕业于宁波城市职业技术学院，现应聘于宁波远大进出口公司。该公司是一家专业进出口贸易公司，公司主营各类玩具、各种童车、中国工艺品、旅游纪念品等进出口业务，深受欧洲、北美和亚洲地区国家的客户欢迎。

近日，宁波远大进出口公司利用公司网站发布供货信息，得知英国 QUA IMPORTS CO., LTD.对童车感兴趣。于是，宁波远大进出口公司业务员张明先生与 QUA IMPORTS CO., LTD.公司的 SMITH 经理进行交易磋商，同意信用证支付方式，随即签订销售合同，落实信用证。当宁波远大进出口公司收到 QUA IMPORTS CO., LTD.开立的信用证后，选择生产厂商，委托金友国际货代公司办理托运、报检和报关手续，并向当地保险公司办理投保，确保合同的履行。

任务一　草拟合同、落实信用证

工作任务一　根据成交记录填制外销合同

成交记录见表 9-1，外销合同见单证 9-1。

表 9-1

宁波远大进出口公司与英国 QUA IMPORTS CO., LTD.就童车的交易条件用电子邮件进行磋商。经过多次交易磋商，这两家公司就童车的各项交易条件达成共识，概括如下：

1．卖方（Seller）

宁波远大进出口公司

NINGBO YUANDA IMP.& EXP.CO., LTD.

152 ZHONGSHAN ROAD，NINGBO, CHINA

2．买方（Buyer）

QUA IMPORTS CO., LTD，LONDON

AKEDSANTERINK AUTO P.O.BOX9，ENGLAND

3．货号品名规格

GOOD CHILDREN　BRAND CHILDREN'S VEHICLES

ART. NO.	QUANTITY	UNIT PRICE
TR-3U-A	500 SETS	USD 64.2
TR-31-A	400 SETS	USD 55.3
TR-32-A	300 SETS	USD 58.9
TR-33-A	200 SETS	USD 44.2

4．唛头

出货前客户通知。

（续）

5．成交价格条件
CIFLONDON
6．包装条件
纸箱包装，每辆一箱。
7．交货/装运条件
装运期为2010年8月，允许分批装运及转运。
8．出口港
BEILUN
9．进口港
LONDON
10．保险条件
由卖方按CIF成交金额的110%投保中国人民保险公司海运货物一切险和战争险。
11．付款条件
保兑的即期信用证支付，7月15号前开到。
12．合同签订时间及地点
2010年6月3日于宁波。
请根据上述成交记录，填写下列外销合同。

单证　9-1

销 售 合 同
SALES CONTRACT

卖方 Seller:		编号 NO.:	NY010808
		日期 DATE:	
		地点 SIGNED IN:	
买方 Buyer:			

买卖双方同意按以下条款达成交易：
This contract is made by and agreed between the Buyer and Seller, in accordance with the terms and conditions stipulated below.

1．品名及规格 Commodity & Specification	2．数量 Quantity	3．单价及价格条款 Unit Price & Trade Terms	4．金额 Amount
Total:			

允许 With		溢短装，由卖方决定 More or less of shipment allowed at the sellers' option
5．总值 Total Value		
6．包装 Packing		
7．唛头 Shipping Marks		
8．装运期及运输方式 Time of Shipment & Means of Transportation		
9．装运港及目的地 Port of Loading & Destination		
10．保险 Insurance		
11．付款方式 Terms of Payment		

（续）

12．Documents Required	1．SIGNED COMMERCIAL INVOICE IN TRIPLICATE. 2. FULL SET OF CLEAN ON BOARD OCEAN BILLS OF LADING, MADE OUT TO ORDER OF SHIPPER AND BLANK ENDORSED AND MARKED “FREIGHT PREPAID”AND NOTIFY APPLICANT. 3．PACKING LIST IN DUPLICATE. 4．FULL SET OF NEGOTIABLE INSURANCE POLICY OR CERTIFICATE BLANK ENDORSED FOR 110 PERCENT OF THE INVOICE VALUE COVERING ALL RISKS AND WAR RISK. 5．CERTIFICATE OF QUALITY IN 2 ORIGINALS ISSUED BY COMPETENT AUTHORITY. 6．CERTIFICATE OF ORIGIN ISSUED BY THE CHINA’S CHAMBER OF COMMERCE IN TWO ORIGINALS. 7．BENEFICIARY’S CERTIFIED COPY OF FAX DISPATCHED TO THE APPLICANT WITHIN 7 DAYS AFTER SHIPMENT ADVISING THE CONTRACT NUMBER, NAME OF COMMODITY, QUANTITY, INVOICE VALUE, BILL OF LADING, BILL OF LADING DATE, THE ETA DATE AND SHIPPING CO. ALL DOCUMENTS SHOULD BE MARKED L/C NO. AND CONTRACT NO.
13．备注 Remarks	
The Buyer	The Seller
（signature）	(signature)

工作任务二

英国 QUA IMPORTS CO., LTD.单证员 MARY 申请开证

2010年6月10日，英国 QUA IMPORTS CO., LTD.收到宁波远大进出口公司的邮电及随附的外销合同，对该合同进行仔细审核发现无误后，随即会签并回寄了一份合同供对方存档。合同生效后，英国 QUA IMPORTS CO., LTD.单证员 MARY 立即对照合同条款，填写开证申请书（单证 9-2），向英国劳埃德银行伦敦分行申请开立信用证（LLOYDS BANK，LONDON BRANCH）。

单证 9-2

IRREVOCABLE DOCUMENTARY CREDIT APPLICATION

TO:			**Date:**
Beneficiary (Full name and address)		**L/C No.**	
		Ex-Card No.	
		Contract No.	
		Date and place of expiry of the credit	
Partial shipments	**Transhipment**	☐ **Issue by airmail** ☐ **With brief advice by teletransmission**	
☐ **allowed** ☐ **not allowed**	☐ **allowed** ☐ **not allowed**	☐ **Issue by express delivery**	
Loading on board/dispatch/taking in charge at/from		☐ **Issue by teletransmission (which shall be the operative instrument)**	
		Amount	
not later than			
For transportation to:			
		Credit available with	

（续）

	☐ by sight payment ☐ by acceptance ☐ by negotiation
Description of goods:	☐ by deferred payment at
	against the documents detailed herein
	☐ and beneficiary's draft(s) for % of invoice value
	at
	on
Packing:	☐ FOB ☐ CFR ☐ CIF
	☐ or other terms

Documents required: (marked with X)

1. ( ) Signed commercial invoice in ____ originals indicating L/C No. and Contract No.
2. ( ) Full set of clean on board Bills of Lading made out ____ and [ ] blank endorsed, marked "freight [ ] to collect / [ ] prepaid.
3. ( ) Airway bills showing "freight [ ] to collect/[ ] prepaid [ ] indicating freight amount" and consigned to ____ . consigned to____.
4. ( ) Insurance Policy/Certificate in ____ originals for____ % of the invoice value showing claims payable in china in currency of the draft, blank endorsed, covering [ ] Ocean Marine Transportation / [ ] Air Transportation / [ ] Over land Transportation [ ] All Risks, War Risks.
5. ( ) Certificate of Quantity / Weight in______originals issued by an independent surveyor at the loading port, indicating the actual surveyed quantity / weight of shipped goods as well as the packing condition.
6. ( ) Certificate of Quality in ____ originals issued by [ ] manufacturer/ [ ] public recognized surveyor/ [ ].
7. ( ) Beneficiary's Certified copy of cable / telex dispatched to the accountees within_____hours after shipment advising [ ] name of vessel / [ ] fight No. / [ ] wagon No., date, quantity, weight and value of shipment.
8. ( ) Beneficiary's Certificate Certifying that extra copies of the documents have been dispatched according to the contract terms.
9. ( ) Shipping Co's certificate attesting that the carrying vessel is chartered or booked by accountee or their shipping agents:
10. ( ) Other documents, if any ______.

Additional instructions:

1. ( ) All banking charges outside the opening bank are for beneficiary's account.
2. ( ) Documents must be presented within ____ days after date of issuance of the transport documents but within the validity of this credit.
3. ( ) Third party as shipper is not acceptable, Short Form/Blank back B/L is not acceptable.
4. ( ) Both quantity and credit amount ____ % more or less are allowed.
5. ( ) Prepaid freight drawn in excess of L/C amount is acceptable against presentation of original charges voucher issued by shipping Co / Air Line / or it's agent.
6. ( ) All documents to be for warded in one cover, unless otherwise stated above.
7. ( ) Other terms, if any

Account No.		**with** ______________ (name of bank)
Transacted by:		
Telephone No.:		(Applicant: name signature of authorized person)

(with seal)

工作任务三

宁波远大进出口公司单证员方玲审核信用证

宁波远大进出口公司单证员方玲于7月2日收到中国银行宁波分行的信用证通知书和随附的英国劳埃德银行伦敦分行开立的信用证（单证 9-3），随即对照合同条款仔细审核下列信用证，并填写信用证审核表（单证 9-4）。

单证 9-3

MT700 格式信用证

ISSUE OF A DOCUMENTARY CREDIT

……………………………… Message Header ………………………………

Swift Input: FIN 700 Issue of a Documentary Credit

Sender: LBLB JA92A 1496 555995
Lloyds Bank,LONDON BRANCH

Receiver: CBNB 7688 148842
CHINA BANK NINGBO BRANCH

MUR: 2010030502001540

……………………………… Message Text ………………………………

SEQUENCE OF TOTAL *27 : 1 / 1

FORM OF DOC, CREDIT *40 A : IRREVOCABLE

DOC. CREDIT NUMBER *21 : 0186BTY000489SBRT

DATE OF ISSUE 31 C : 100630

DATE AND PLACE OF EXPIRY *31 D : DATE 101130 AT OUR COUNTER

APPLICANT *50 : QUEEN IMPORTS CO., LTD, LONDON
AKEDSANTERINK AUTO P.O.BOX9, ENGLAND

BENEFICIARY ….*59 : NINGBO YUANDA IMP.& EXP.CO., LTD.
152 ZHONGSHAN ROAD, NINGBO, CHINA

CURRENCY CODE,AMOUNT *32 B : USD88030,00

MAXIMUM CREDIT AMOUNT 39B : NOT EXCEEDING L/C AMOUNT

AVAILABLE WITH / BY *41 D : ANY BANK IN CHINA BY NEGOTIATION

DRAFTS AT 42 C : DRAFTS AT 30 DAYS AFTER B/L FOR FULL INVOICE COST

DRAWEE 52 A : LBLB JA92A 1496 555995
Lloyds Bank,LONDON BRANCH

PARTIAL SHIPMENTS 43 P : PROHIBITED

TRANSSHIPMENT 43 T : ALLOWED

LOADING ON BOARD 44 A : ANY PORT IN CHINA

FOR TRANSPORTATION TO …44 B : LONDON

LATEST DATE OF SHIPMENT 44 C : 100831

DESCRIPT OF GOODS 45 A : GOOD CHILDREN BRAND CHILDREN'S VEHICLES OTHER DETAILS AS PER S/C NO. NY010808
INCOTERM : CIF HONGKONG

DOCUMENTS REQUIRED 46 A :

1. SIGNED COMMERCIAL INVOICE IN TRIPLICATE AND MUST CERTIFIED BY CHINA'S CHAMBER OF COMMERCE THE GOODS ARE OF CHINESE ORIGIN ONLY.

2. FULL SET OF CLEAN ON BOARD OCEAN BILLS OF LADING, MADE OUT TO ORDER OF SHIPPER AND BLANK ENDORSED AND MARKED "FREIGHT COLLECT"AND NOTIFY APPLICANT.

3. PACKING LIST IN DUPLICATE .

（续）

4. FULL SET OF NEGOTIABLE INSURANCE POLICY OR CERTIFICATE BLANK ENDORSED FOR 140 PERCENT OF THE INVOICE VALUE COVERING ALL RISKS.

5. CERTIFICATE OF QUALITY IN 2 ORIGINALS ISSUED BY COMPETENT AUTHORITY.

6. CERTIFICATE OF ORIGIN ISSUED BY THE CHINA'S CHAMBER OF COMMERCE IN TWO ORIGINALS. IN ADDITION, THE CERTIFICATE OF ORIGIN MUST STATE THAT THE COUNTRY OF ORIGIN OF GOODS SHIPPED HAS BEEN MENTIONED ON EACH CARTON OF THE CONSIGNMENT.

7. BENEFICIARY'S CERTIFIED COPY OF FAX DISPATCHED TO THE APPLICANT WITHIN 2 DAYS AFTER SHIPMEMT ADVISING THE CONTRACT, NAME OF COMMODITY, QUANTITY, INVOICE VALUE, BILL OF LADING, BILL OF LADING DATE, THE ETA DATE AND SHIPPING CO.

ADDITIONAL CONDITIONS 47A：

1. SHIPMENT MUST NOT BE MADE EARLIER THAN THE CREDIT ISSUING DATE.

2. ONE SET OF NEGOTIABLE SHIPPING DOCUMENTS TO BE SENT TO THE APPLICANT THROUGH COURIER SERVICE WITHIN 07 WORKING DAYS AFTER SHIPMENT AND A COURIER RECEIPT OF WHICH MUST ACCOMPANY THE ORIGINAL DOCUMENTS.

3. DISCREPANCY FEE OF USD35.00 WILL BE DEDUCTED FROM THE PROCEEDS OF EACH PRESENTATION OF DISCREPANT DOCUMENTS.

4. ALL DOCUMENTS MUST BE FORWARDED IN ONE LOT BY EXPRESS.

5. ALL DOCUMENTS MUST INDICATE L/C NO. CONTRACT NO.

CHARGES 71B：

All BANKING CHARGES INSIDE THE OPENING BANK ARE FOR BENEFICIARY'S ACCOUNT.

PERIOD FOR PRESENTATION 48:

21 DAYS FROM THE DATE OF SHIPMENT,

BUT NOT LATER THAN THE CREDIT VALIDITY.

CONFIRMATION INSTRUCTION 49: WITHOUT

+ADVISE THROUGH BANK 57A：CBNB 7688 148842

CHINA BANK NINGBO BRANCH

SENDER TO RECEIVER INFORMATION 72:

PLS ADVISE US WHEN ADVISING THIS L/C TO BENEFICIARY.

.... MESSAGE TRAILER..

TRAILER ORDER IS 《MAC:》 《PAC:》 《ENC:》 《CHK:》 《TNG:》 《PDE:》

MAC: CF6F97BC

CHK: F04138D93C1B

DLM：BKHYHKJAXXX 1003032233

单证 9-4

信用证审核结果

信用证号	
合同号	
审证结果	

工作任务四

英国 QUA IMPORTS CO., LTD.单证员 MARY 填写改证申请书

2010 年 7 月 10 日，英国 QUA IMPORTS CO., LTD.收到宁波远大进出口公司根据上述审证结果写来的改证函，单证员 MARY 立即对照合同条款再次仔细审核了信用证，确认对方改证要求是合理的，随即填写改证申请书，向原开证行提出改证申请。

请对照上述信用证审核结果单，填写下列改证申请书（单证 9-5）。

单证 9-5

改证申请书

APPLICATION FOR AMENDMENT TO LETTER OF CREDIT

To:	Amendment to L/C NO.______________
Date of APPLICATION:______________	No. of Amendment :______________
Applicant:	Advising Bank:
Beneficiary:	Amount:

Please amend the above L/C by Swift/Telex as follows

All other terms and conditions remain unchanged.

Stamp and signature(s) of the applicant:

The above-mentioned Documentary Credit is subject to the Uniform and Practice for Documentary Credits(2007revision, ICC., Paris, France, Publication 600)

工作任务五

宁波远大进出口公司单证员方玲填写信用证分析单

英国劳埃德银行伦敦分行收到英国 QUA IMPORTS CO., LTD.的改证申请书，审核无误后，于 2010 年 7 月 8 日开出信用证修改书（单证 9-6），当日中国银行宁波分行开立信用证修改通知书连同收到的修改书一并转交给了出口商宁波远大进出口公司。宁波远大进出口公司的单证员方玲收到信用证修改通知书后，再次对下列信用证修改书进行审核，审核无误后，结合原信用证和下列修改书的主要内容填写信用证分析单，作为缮制、审核和管理该票业务单证的依据。

单证　9-6

MT707 格式信用证修改书

AMENDMENT TO A DOCUMENTARY CREDIT

08/07/10-09:30:34　　　　LocalSwiftAcks-8414-136437

……………………………………

……Message Text……………………………………

ISSUING BANK　　52A：LBLB JA92A 1496 555995
LLOYDS BANK,LONDON BRANCH

DATE OF ISSUE　　31 C：　100630
DATE OF AMENDMENT　　30：　100708
NUMBER OF AMENDMENT　　26E：　01
BENEFICIARY(BEFORE THIS AMENDMENT)　　*59　：NINGBO YUANDA IMP.& EXP.CO. LTD
152 ZHONGSHAN ROAD，NINGBO　，CHINA

NEW DATE OF EXPIRY　　31E:　101130
INCREASE OF DOCUMENTARY CREDIT AMOUNT　32B:　USD700, 00
NEW DOCUMENTARY CREDIT AMOUNT AFTER　34B:　USD80730, 00
NARRATIVE　　79:　PLS IN FIELD 31D INSERT NOW:
CHINA
INSTEAD OF
AT OUR COUNTER

PLS IN FIELD59 AMEND AS FOLLOWS:
QUA IMPORTS CO. LTD，LONDON
AKEDSANTERINK AUTO P.O.BOX9，ENGLAND

PLS IN FIELD 32B AMEND TO READ NOW
USD80730, 00
INSTEAD OF
USD80030, 00

PLS IN FIELD 43P AMEND TO READ NOW
ALLOWED
INSTEAD OF
PROHIBITED

PLS IN FIELD 46A ITEM 1&4AMEND AS FOLLOWS:
1.DELETE "AND MUST CERTIFIED BY CHINA'S CHAMBER OF COMMERCE THE GOODS ARE OF CHINESE ORIGIN ONLY"
3 .MARKED "FREIGHT PREPAID" INSTEAD OF "FREIGHT COLLECT".
4.FOR 110 PERCENT OF THE INVOICE VALUE COVERING WPA, RISK OF CLASHING AND BREAKAGE AND WAR RISK INSTEAD OF FOR 140 PERCENT OF THE INVOICE VALUE COVERING ALL RISKS PLS IN FIELD 47A ITEM2 AMEND AS FOLLOWS:
NO-NEGOTIABLE SHIPPING DOCUMENTS
INSTEAD OF
NEGOTIABLE SHIPPING DOCUMENTS

PLS IN FIELD 49 ITEM 2 AMEND AS FOLLOWS
WITH
INSTEAD OF
WITHOUT
ALL OTHER TERMS AND CONDITIONS REMAIN UNCHANGE

SENDER TO RECEIVER INFO.　72:　CREDIT IS SUBJECT TO ICC UCP PUBLICATION NO.600.
TRAILER　　MAC: 4567TR88　　CHK:78GH5R08FD68

步骤一：为了今后制单的方便，方玲首先将信用证修改书和原来审核过的信用证装订在一起，并根据修改书的要求在原证上用彩笔做出修改。请你帮忙在原证（单证 9-7）上做出修改。

单证 9-7

ISSUE OF A DOCUMENTARY CREDIT

……………………………… Message Header ……………………………………………..

Swift Input : FIN 700 Issue of a Documentary Credit
Sender : LBLB JA92A 1496 555995
Lloyds Bank,LONDON BRANCH
Receiver : CBNB 7688 148842
CHINA BANK NINGBO BRANCH
MUR : 2010030502001540

……………………………… Message Text………………………………….

SEQUENCE OF TOTAL *27 : 1 / 1
FORM OF DOC，CREDIT *40 A : IRREVOCABLE
DOC. CREDIT NUMBER *21：0186BTY000489SBRT
DATE OF ISSUE 31 C： 100630
DATE AND PLACE OF EXPIRY *31 D : DATE 101130 **AT OUR COUNTER**
APPLICANT *50 : **QUEEN** IMPORTS CO. LTD，LONDAN
AKEDSANTERINK AUTO P.O.BOX9，ENGLAND
BENEFICIARY ….*59：NINGBO YUANDA IMP.& EXP.CO. LTD
152 ZHONGSHAN ROAD，NINGBO ，CHINA
CURRENCY CODE,AMOUNT *32 B : **USD88030,00**
MAXIMUM CREDIT AMOUNT 39B：NOT EXCEEDING L/C AMOUNT
AVAILABLE WITH / BY *41 D：ANY BANK IN CHINA BY NEGOTIATION
DRAFTS AT 42 C : DRAFTS AT **30 DAYS AFTER B/L FOR FULL INVOICE COST**
DRAWEE 52 A : LBLB JA92A 1496 555995
Lloyds Bank,LONDON BRANCH
PARTIAL SHIPMENTS 43 P : **PROHIBITED**
TRANSSHIPMENT 43 T : ALLOWED
LOADING ON BOARD 44 A : ANY PORT IN CHINA
FOR TRANSPORTATION TO …44 B : LONDON
LATEST DATE OF SHIPMENT 44C：100831
DESCRIPTION OF GOODS 45A：GOOD CHILDREN BRAND CHILDREN'S VEHICLES OTHER DETAILS AS PER S/C NO. NY010808
INCOTERM：CIF HONGKONG
DOCUMENTS REQUIRED 46A：

1．SIGNED COMMERCIAL INVOICE IN TRIPLICATE AND MUST CERTIFIED BY CHINA'S CHAMBER OF COMMERCE THE GOODS ARE OF CHINESE ORIGIN ONLY .

2．FULL SET OF CLEAN ON BOARD OCEAN BILLS OF LADING, MADE OUT TO ORDER OF SHIPPER AND BLANK ENDORSED AND MARKED **" FREIGHT COLLECT "**AND NOTIFY APPLICANT.

3．PACKING LIST IN DUPLICATE .

4．FULL SET OF NEGOTIABLE INSURANCE POLICY OR CERTIFICATE BLANK ENDORSED FOR **140 PERCENT** OF THE INVOICE VALUE COVERING ALL RISKS.

5．CERTIFICATE OF QUALITY IN 2 ORIGINALS ISSUED BY THE COMPETENT AUTHORITY.

6．CERTIFICATE OF ORIGIN ISSUED BY THE CHINA'S CHAMBER OF COMMERCE IN TWO ORIGINALS. IN ADDITION，THE CERTIFICATE OF ORIGIN MUST STATE THAT THE COUNTRY OF ORIGIN OF GOODS SHIPPED HAS BEEN MENTIONED ON EACH CARTON OF THE CONSIGNMENT.

7．BENEFICIARY'S CERTIFIED COPY OF FAX DISPATCHED TO THE APPLICANT WITHIN 7 DAYS AFTER SHIPMEMT ADVISING THE CONTRACT NUMBER, NAME OF COMMODITY, QUANTITY, INVOICE VALUE, BILL OF LOADING, BILL OF LOADING DATE, THE ETA DATE AND SHIPPING CO.

ADDITIONAL CONDITIONS 47A：

1．SHIPMENT MUST NOT BE MADE EARLIER THAN THE CREDIT ISSUING DATE.

2．ONE SET OF **NEGOTIABLE** SHIPPING DOCUMENTS TO BE SENT TO THE APPLICANT THROUGH COURIER SERVICE WITHIN 07 WORKING DAY AFTER SHIPMENT AND A COURIER RECEIPT OF WHICH MUST ACCOMPANY THE ORIGINAL DOCUMENTS.

（续）

3. DISCREPANCY FEE OF USD35.00 WILL BE DEDUCTED FROM THE PROCEEDS OF EACH PRESENTATION OF DISCREPANT DOCUMENTS.

4. ALL DOCUMENTS MUST BE FORWARDED IN ONE LOT BY EXPRESS.

5. ALL DOCUMENTS MUST INDICATE L/C NO. CONTRACT NO.

CHARGES　　71B:

All BANKING CHARGES INSIDE THE OPENING BANK ARE FOR BENEFICIARY'S ACCOUNT.

PERIOD FOR PRESENTATION　48:

21 DAYS FROM THE DATE OF SHIPMENT,

BUT NOT LATER THAN THE CREDIT VALIDITY.

CONFIRMATION INSTRUCTION　**49: WITHOUT**

+ADVISE THROUGH BANK　　57A: CBNB 7688 148842

CHINA BANK NINGBO BRANCH

SENDER TO RECEIVER INFORMATION　72:

PLS ADVISE US WHEN ADVISING THIS L/C TO BENEFICIARY.

……………………………………… MESSAGE TRAILER………………………………………………………………

TRAILER ORDER IS 《MAC:》《PAC:》《ENC:》《CHK:》《TNG:》《PDE:》

MAC: CF6F97BC

CHK: F04138D93C1B

DLM: BKHYHKJAXXX 1003032233

步骤二：为了今后制单、审单的方便，方玲依据修改后的信用证 9-7 填写下列信用证分析结果单（单证 9-8）。

单证　9-8

信用证分析单

银行编号			合同号		受益人						
信用证证号											
开证银行					进口商						
开证日期		信用证效期			起运口岸			目的港			
改证日期		信用证到期地									
信用证金额					可否转运			可否分批			
汇票付款人		汇票期限			装运期限						
交单日					寄单日						
注意事项											
单证名称											
银行											
客户											
提单	抬头人				保险			险别			
	通知人							加成率			
其他注意事项：											

任务二 履行合同和信用证的规定——备货

业务导入

宁波远大进出口公司没有自己的生产实体，在收到信用证改证书经审核无误后，必须寻找合适的加工生产企业履行交货义务。为此，业务员张明先生通过对多家童车的生产规模和生产能力的调查，选择了江苏昆山陆家童车厂作为好孩子童车出口货物的加工企业，并与其签订采购合同，确保出口货物按时按质顺利完成。因为出口到欧盟的童车必须出具《出口商品质量许可证》，采购合同中必须列明厂家要出具该证书。

已知童车的增值税为 17%，退税率为 9%，国内费用为包装费 1 元/箱。每个 20'集装箱费用如下：仓储费 500 元，国内运杂费 800 元，商检费 150 元，报关费 50 元，港口费用 400 元，业务费用 1200 元，其他费用 2100 元。保险：发票金额加成 10%，投保一切险 0.7%和战争险 0.3%。海洋运费：从上海到伦敦港一个 20'集装箱运费为 1350 美元。汇率为人民币对美元为 7.25:1；公司预期利润率为 10%。每个包装纸箱的尺码规格一样，毛重 15kg，净重 13kg，体积 100cm×80cm×30cm。张明先生需要计算每种型号童车的进货成本，然后填写下列采购合同（单证 9-9）。

单证 9-9

宁波远大进出口公司

采 购 合 同

编号：SH0731

供应商：

日期：______

请供应以下产品：

货　　号	品名、规格	单　　位	数　　量	单　　价	金　　额	备　　注
合　　计						

1．交货日期：　　年　　月　　日以前一次交清。
2．交货地点：
3．包装条件：
4．付款方式：交货后 1 个月凭增值税发票付款
5．不合格产品处理：　　　　　　　　　　　　另议
6．如因交货误期、规格不符、质量不符合要求造成本公司的损失，卖方负责赔偿责任。
7．如卖方未能按期交货，必须赔偿本公司因此蒙受的一切损失。
8．其他：

采购单位：（盖章）　　　　　　　　　　　　　　　供应商：（盖章）

任务三　履行合同和信用证的规定——租船订舱单据的制作与审核

业务导入

宁波远大进出口公司在备货的同时，为了按时履行合同的交货义务，应及时填写订舱委托书，并随附相关单据委托货运代理公司办理租船订舱，也可由公司自行办理。

工作任务一

列出租船订舱所需的单据清单

宁波远大进出口公司单证员方玲在制作租船订舱单据前，首先要弄清租船订舱的流程，列出办理租船订舱所需单据的清单（表 9-2），确保不要落下重要的单据。

表　9-2

单 据 名 称	单 据 份 数

工作任务二

制作商业发票

宁波远大进出口公司单证员方玲根据清单列表，依据落实的信用证及信用证分析结果单，制作商业发票（单证 9-10）。

制单补充信息：发票号码：NI 10888。制单时间：2010 年 8 月 1 日。包装标志：NY 010808/LONDON/NO.1-1400.

单证　9-10

<table>
<tr><td colspan="2">ISSUER</td><td colspan="3">COMMERCIAL INVOICE</td></tr>
<tr><td colspan="2">TO</td><td colspan="2">NO.</td><td>DATE</td></tr>
<tr><td colspan="2"></td><td colspan="2"></td><td></td></tr>
<tr><td colspan="2">TRANSPORT DETAILS</td><td colspan="2">S/C NO.</td><td>L/C NO.</td></tr>
<tr><td colspan="2"></td><td colspan="2"></td><td></td></tr>
<tr><td colspan="2"></td><td colspan="3">TERMS OF PAYMENT</td></tr>
<tr><td>MARKS AND NUMBERS</td><td>NUMBER AND KIND OF PACKAGE DESCRIPTION OF GOODS</td><td>QUANTITY</td><td>UNIT PRICE</td><td>AMOUNT</td></tr>
<tr><td></td><td></td><td></td><td></td><td></td></tr>
</table>

（续）

SAY TOTAL:	Total:

工作任务三

制作货物明细单

宁波远大进出口公司单证员方玲根据清单列表，依据落实的信用证及信用证分析结果单及其相关信息制作货物明细单（单证 9-11）。

单证 9-11

出口货物明细单

开证银行			银行编号		标记唛头	
			外运编号			
经营单位（装船人）			合同号			
			许可证号			
			运输方式			
收货人			出口口岸			
			目的港			
			信用证号			
提单或承运收据	抬头人		金额			
			开证日期			
	通知人		收到日期			
			贸易性质		贸易国别	
			可否转运		可否分批	
	运费		装运期限		有效期限	

货物名规格及货号	件数及包装样式	数量或尺码	毛重	净重	价格（成交条件）	
					单价	总价

本公司注意事项		总体积		
		保险单	险别	
			保额	
			赔款地点	
外运外轮注意事项		船名		
		海关编号		
		放行日期		
		制单员		

工作任务四

制作装箱单

宁波远大进出口公司单证员方玲根据清单列表，依据落实的信用证及信用证分析结果单及其相关信息制作装箱单（单证 9-12）。

单证　9-12

Packing list

EXPORTER				INVOICE NO.		INVOICE DATE	
				FROM		TO	
				SHIPPED BY			
TO				SHIPPING MARK			
C/NOS	NO. AND KINDS OF PKGS	GOODS	QTY	G.W.	N.W.	MEAS.	
TOTAL PACKAGES IN WORDS							
				ISSUED BY : S			
				SIGNATURE			

工作任务五

制作出口订舱委托书

宁波远大进出口公司单证员方玲根据清单列表，制作出口订舱委托书（单证 9-13）委托金发国际货代公司办理租船订舱手续。

单证　9-13

金发海运货运委托书

经营单位（托运人）				金发编号		
提单项目要求	发货人： Shipper:					
	收货人： Consignee:					
	通知人： Notify Party:					
海洋运费（√） Sea freight	预付（　　）或（　　）到付 Prepaid or Collect		提单份数		提单寄送 地　　址	
起运港		目的港	可否转船		可否分批	
集装箱预配数	20×　　40×		装运期限		有效期限	
标记唛码	包装件数	中英文货号 Description of goods	毛重（公斤）	尺码（立方米）	成交条件（总价）	
			特种货物冷藏 货危险品	重件：每件重量		
				大件（长×宽×高）		
内装箱（CFS） 地址	宁波逸仙路 2960 号三号门 电话：6820682-215		特种集装箱：（　　　　）			
门对门装箱地址			物资备妥日期	年　月　日		
外币结算账号			物资进栈：自送（√）或金发派送（　　）			
声明事项			人民币结算单位账号			
			托运人签章			
			电话			
			传真			
			联系人			
			地址			
			制单日期：　年　月　日			

工作任务六

制作出口订舱委托书

宁波远大进出口公司单证员方玲根据清单列表，制作托运单（单证 9-14）。

单证 9-14

货代留底范本

SHIPPER		D/R NO.	
CONSIGNEE		货代留底	
NOTIFY PARTY			第八联
PRE-CARRIAGE BY	PLACE OF RECEIPT:		
OCEAN VESSEL VOY.NO.	PORT OF LOADING: NINGBO		

PORT OF DISCHARGE: HONGKONG	PLACE OF DELIVERY		FINAL DESTINATION FOR THE MERCHANT'S RETER-ENCE		
CONTAINER NO.	SEAL NO.	NO.& KIND OF PKGS OR CONTAINERS	DESCRIPTION OF GOODS	GROSS WEIGHT	MEASUREMENT
TOTAL NUMBER OF CONTAINERS OR PACKAGES (IN WORDS)		SAY ________ ONLY			

FREIGHT & CHARGE	项目	数量	费率（含转运费）	
	20'			
	40'			
	BAF			
	DDC			
	附加费			

EX. RATE	PREPAID AT	PAYABLE AT	PLACE OF ISSUE
	TOTAL PREPAID	NO. OF ORIGINAL B/L THREE	

Service Type on Receiving ( ) CY ( ) CFS ( ) DOOR	Service Type on Delivery ( ) CY ( ) CFS ( ) DOOR	Reefer Temperature Required	F	C
Type of Goods	( ) Ordinary（普通） ( ) Reefer（冷藏） ( ) Dangerous（危险） ( ) Auto（裸装车辆） ( ) Liquid（液体） ( ) live Animal（活动物） ( ) Bulk（裸装）	危险品	CLASS ： PROPERTY **IMDG code Pade** **UN No.**	

发货人或代理地址：			联系人：	电话：
可否转船	可否分批	装运期限	备注	集装场站名称
有效期		制单日		
海运费由： 支付				

任务四　履行合同和信用证的规定——投保单据的制作与审核

业务导入

合同和信用证规定成交贸易术语是 CIF，宁波远大进出口公司需按规定办理投保手续，单证员方玲必须制作投保单、保险单等相关单据向中保财产保险有限公司宁波市分公司进行投保。保险公司核准投保申请后，收取保险费，签发保险单。保险公司为出口货物投保。

工作任务一

列出投保所需的单据清单

宁波远大进出口公司单证员方玲在制作投保单据前，首先要弄清投保的流程，列出办理投保所需单据的清单（表 9-3），确保不要落下重要的单据。

表　9-3

投保所需单据列表（在已有的单据后面标“ √ ”）	
单 据 名 称	份　　数

工作任务二

制作投保单

宁波远大进出口公司单证员方玲根据清单列表，首先制作投保单（单证 9-15）。

制单补充资料：根据货代公司的托运情况，船只名称：ZHOUSHAN；船次：V18；装船日期：2010 年 8 月 17 日。

单证　9-15

中国人民财产保险 The People's Insurance (Property) Company of China, Ltd. NINGBO Branch

进出口货物运输保险投保单

Application Form for I/E Marine Cargo Transportation Insurance

<table>
<tr><td colspan="4">被保险人
Assured's Name</td></tr>
<tr><td>发票号码（出口用）或合同号码（进口用）
Invoice No. or Contract No.</td><td>包装数量
Quantity</td><td>保险货物项目
Description of Goods</td><td>保险金额
Amount Insured</td></tr>
<tr><td></td><td></td><td></td><td></td></tr>
<tr><td colspan="4">总保险金额：
Total Amount Insured:________________________
装载运输工具________________航次、航班或车号______开航日期______
Per Conveyance　　　　　　Voy. No.　　　　　Slg. Date
自__________至__________转运地__________赔款地__________
From　　　　To　　　　W/T at　　　　　　Claim Payable at

承保险别：</td></tr>
</table>

（续）

Condition & / or Special Coverage 投保人签章及公司名称、电话、地址： Applicant's Signature and Co.'s Name, Add. And Tel. No.	
备注： Remarks	投保日期： Date

保险公司填写：　　　报单号：　　　费率：　　　核保人：

工作任务三

制作保险单

宁波远大进出口公司单证员方玲根据清单列表，制作保险单（单证 9-16）。

单证 9-16

中保财产保险有限公司

The People's Insurance (Property) Company of China, Ltd.

发票号码 Invoice No.		保险单号码 Policy No.			
海洋货物运输保险单 **MARINE CARGO TRANSPORTATION INSURANCE POLICY**					
被保险人： Insured:					
中保财产保险有限公司（以下简称本公司）根据被保险人的要求，及其所缴付约定的保险费，按照本保险单承担险别和背面所载条款与下列特别条款承保下列货物运输保险，特签发本保险单。 This policy of Insurance witnesses that the People's Insurance (Property) Company of China, Ltd. (hereinafter called "The Company"), at the request of the Insured and in consideration of the agreed premium paid by the Insured, undertakes to insure the undermentioned goods in transportation subject to conditions of the Policy as per the Clauses printed overleaf and other special clauses attached hereon.					
保险货物项目 Descriptions of Goods		包装方式和数量 No. And Kind Of Packages;		保险金额 Amount Insured	
承保险别 Conditions			货物标记 Marks of Goods		
总保险金额： Total Amount Insured:					
保费 Premium		运输工具 Per conveyance S.S		开航日期 Slg. on or abt	
起运港 Form		目的港 To			
所保货物，如发生本保险单项下可能引起索赔的损失或损坏，应立即通知本公司下述代理人查勘。如有索赔，应向本公司提交保险单正本（本保险单共有　　份正本）及有关文件。如一份正本已用于索赔，其余正本则自动失效。 In the event of loss or damage which may result in acclaim under this Policy, immediate notice must be given to the Company's Agent as mentioned here under. Claims, if any, one of the Original Policy which has been issued in　　original (s) together with the relevant documents shall be surrendered to the Company. If one of the Original Policy has been accomplished, the others to be void.					
赔款偿付地点 Claim payable at					
日期 Date		在 at			

任务五　报检单据的制作与审核

业务导入

合同和信用证规定，该批货物必须有官方机构出具的品质检验证明。因此宁波远大进出口公司需按规定办理报检手续，单证员方玲必须制作报检委托书、报检单等相关单据委托货运代理或报关报检行，也可由公司自行办理报检。

工作任务一

列出报检所需单据清单

宁波远大进出口公司单证员方玲在制作报检单据前，首先要弄清报检的流程，列出办理报检所需单据的清单（表 9-4），确保不要落下重要的单据。

表　9-4

报检所需单据列表（在已有的单据后面标“√”）	
单 据 名 称	份　　数

工作任务二

缮制报检委托书

宁波远大进出口公司单证员方玲对照清单列表，首先制作报检委托书（单证 9-17），委托金发货代公司代办报检手续。

单证　9-17

报检委托书

__________ 出入境检验检疫局：

本委托人郑重声明，保证遵守出入境检验检疫法律、法规的规定。如有违法行为，自愿接受检验检疫机构的处罚并负法律责任。

本委托人委托受委托人向检验检疫机构提交“报检申请单”和各种随附单据。具体委托情况如下：

本单位将于________年________月间出口如下：

品　　名		HS 编码	
数（重）量		合同号	
信用证号		审批文件	
其他特殊要求			

特委托____________________（单位 / 注册登记号），代理本公司办理下列出入境检验检疫事宜：

□1．办理代理报检手续；

□2．代缴检验检疫费；

□3．负责与检验检疫机构联系和验货；

□4．领取检验检疫证书；

□5．其他与报检有关的相关事宜。

（续）

请贵局按有关法律法规规定予以办理。 委托人（公章）：　　　　受委托人（公章）： 年　月　日　　　　年　月　日 本委托书有效期至　　年　月　日

工作任务三

方玲缮制报检单

宁波远大进出口公司单证员方玲对照清单列表，制作报检单（单证 9-18）。已知报检单位的登记号为 68467890。

制单补充资料：HS 码 9501.0000，报检单位的登记号为 68467890。

单证　9-18

出境货物报检单

报检单位（加盖公章）：　　　　*编号 ______________

报检单位登记号：　　　联系人：　　　电话：　　　报检日期：　　年　　月　　日

发货人	（中文）
	（外文）
收货人	（中文）
	（外文）

货物名称（中/外文）	H.S.编码	产地	数/重量	货物总值	包装种类及件数

运输工具名称号码			贸易方式		货物存放地点		
合同号			信用证号			用途	
发货日期		输往国家（地区）		许可证/审批号			
启运地		到达口岸		生产单位注册号			
集装箱规格、数量及号码							

合同、信用证订立的检验检疫条款或特殊要求	标记及号码	随附单据（划“√”或补填）	
		□合同 □信用证 □发票 □换证凭单 □装箱单	□厂检单 □包装性能结果单 □许可/审批文件 □

需要证单名称（划“√”或补填）		*检验检疫费
□品质证书 □重量证书 □数量证书 □兽医卫生证书 □健康证书 □卫生证书	□动物卫生证书 □植物检疫证书 □熏蒸/消毒证书 □出境货物换证凭单 □通关单	总金额 （人民币元）
		计费人
		收费人

报检人郑重声明：	领取证单
本人被授权报验。 上列填写内容正确属实，货物无伪造或冒用他人的厂名、标志、认证标志，并承担货物质量责任。 签名：__________	日期
	签名

注：带*号的由检验检疫机构填写。

任务六　报关单据的制作与审核

业务导入

按照出口业务流程，宁波远大进出口公司需按规定办理报关手续，单证员方玲必须制作报关单委托书、报关单并随付相关单据委托货运代理或报关报检行，也可由公司自行办理报关。

工作任务一

列出报关所需单据清单

报关所需单据比较多，有主要单证、基本单证、特殊单证和备用单证，单证员在制作、准备报关单据时，首先列出该批货物出口所需单据清单（表 9-5），以免报关时落下重要的单据没有备妥。

表　9-5

报关所需单据列表（在已有的单据后面标“√”）

单 据 名 称	份　　数

工作任务二

缮制报关委托书

对照报关单据清单列表，单证员方玲首先制作报关委托书（单证 9-19），委托金发货运代理公司代办报关手续。

单证　9-19

委托报关协议

为明确委托报关具体事项和各自责任，双方经平等协商签订协议如下：

委托方		被委托方		
主要货物名称		*报关单编码	No.	
HS 编码		收到单证日期	年　月　日	
货物总价		收到单证情况	合同□	发票□
进出口日期			装箱清单□	提（运）单□
提单号			加工贸易手册□	许可证件□
贸易方式			其他	
原产地/货源地		报关收费	人民币：　　元	
其他要求： 背面所列通用条款是本协议不可分割的一部分，对本协议的签署构成了对背面通用条款的同意。		承诺说明： 背面所列通用条款是本协议不可分割的一部分，对本协议的签署构成了对背面通用条款的同意。		
委托方业务签章： 经办人签章： 联系电话：　　年　月　日		被委托方业务签章： 经办报关员签章： 联系电话：　　年　月　日		

（白联，海关留存；黄联，被委托方留存；红联，委托方留存）中国报关协会监制

工作任务三

缮制报关单

对照报关单据清单列表，单证员方玲制作主要单证——报关单（单证 9-20）。

货物拟从北仑口岸出运。方玲查阅北仑海关关区代码为 3104；经营单位的代码是 330293734；核销单编号为 831459552；该批货物投保的保险费率为 3‰，保险费=保险金额×保险费率=80730×1.1×3‰=USD266.4，1 个 20 英尺集装箱自重 2 275 公斤；该批货物的法定计量单位为辆/千克。

单证 9-20

中华人民共和国出口货物报关单

预录入编号：　　　　　　　　　　　　　　海关编号：

进口口岸		备案号	出口日期	申报日期
经营单位		运输方式	运输工具名称	提运单号
发货单位		贸易方式	征免性质	结汇方式
许可证号	运抵（国地区）		指运港	境内货源地
批准文号	成交方式	运费	保费	杂费
合同协议号	件数	包装种类	毛重（公斤）	净重（公斤）
集装箱号	随附单据			生产厂家
标记唛码及备注				

项号	商品编号	商品名称规格型号	数量及单位	最终目的地国/地区	单价	总价	币制	征免

税费征收情况	
录入员　　　　录入单位　　　　兹声明以上申报无讹并承担法律责任	海关单批注及放行日期（签章）
	审单审价
报关员　　　　　　　　申报单位（签章）	
	征税　　　　统计
单位地址	
邮编　　　　电话　　　　填制日期	查验　　　　放行

工作任务四

办理原产地证书

对照报关单据清单列表，单证员方玲申领报关所需的特殊单证之一：原产地证书（单证 9-21）。

回答下列问题：

一、问题：一般原产地证书和普惠制原产地证书的分别由什么机构签发？

二、问题：原产地证书的申领程序是怎样的？

三、填写普惠制产地证明书申请书。

单证　9-21

普惠制产地证明书申请书

申请单位（加盖公章）：　　　　　　　　证书号：__________

申请人郑重申明：　　　　　　　　　　注册号：88559966

本人被正式授权代表本企业办理和签署本申请书。

本申请书及普惠制产地证明书格式 A 所列内容正确无误，如发现弄虚作假，冒充格式 A 所列货物，擅改证书，自愿接受签发机构的处罚并承担法律责任。现将有关情况申报如下：

生产单位		生产单位联系人电话	
商品名称（中英文）		HS 税目号（以六位数码计）	
商品 FOB 总值（以美元计）		发票号	

最终销售国		证书种类“√”	加急证书	普通证书
货物拟出运日期				

贸易方式和企业性质（请在适用处划“√”）							
正常贸易 C	来/进料加工 L	补偿贸易 B	中外合资 H	中外合作 Z	外商独资 D	零售 Y	展卖 M

包装数量或毛重或其他数量	

原产地标准：

本项商品系在中国生产，完全符合该给惠国给惠方案规定，其原产地情况符合以下第（　　）条：

（1）“P”（完全国产，未使用任何进口原材料）；

（2）“W”其 H S 税目号为__________（含进口成分）；

（3）“F”（对加拿大出口产品，其进口成分不超过产品出厂价值的 40%）。

本批产品系：1. 直接运输从______上海______到______伦敦______；

2. 转口运输从__________中转国（地区）__________到__________；

申请人说明　　　　　　　　　　领证人（签名）

电话：

日期：

现提交中国出口商业发票副本一份，普惠制产地证明书格式 A（FORM A）一正二副，以及其他附件一份，请予审核签证。

注：凡有进口成分的商品，必须要求提交《含进口成分受惠商品成本明细单》。

商检局联系记录

四、缮制下列普惠制产地证书。

单证 9-22

ORIGINAL

1. Goods consigned from (Exporter's business name, address, country)	Reference No.
	GENERALIZED SYSTEM OF PREFERENCES CERTIFICATE OF ORIGIN (Combined declaration and certificate)
2. Goods consigned to (Consignee's name, address, country)	FORM A
	Issued in THE PEOPLE'S REPUBLIC OF CHINA (country) See Notes overleaf
3. Means of transport and route (as far as known)	4. For official use

5. Item number	6. Marks and numbers of packages	7. Number and kind of packages; description of goods	8. Origin criterion (see Notes overleaf)	9. Gross weight or other quantity	10. Number and date of invoices

11. Certification It is hereby certified, on the basis of control carried out, that the declaration by the exporter is correct.	12. Declaration by the exporter The undersigned hereby declares that the above details and statements are correct, that all the goods were produced in CHINA (country) and that they comply with the origin requirements specified for those goods in the Generalized System of Preferences for goods exported to
-- Place and date, signature and stamp of certifying authority	-- Place and date, signature and stamp of authorized signatory

五、能力拓展：假设该信用证要求提供一般原产地证书，请缮制一般原产地证书。

单证 9-23

ORIGINAL

<table>
<tr><td colspan="2">1. Exporter</td><td colspan="3">Certificate No.</td></tr>
<tr><td colspan="2"></td><td colspan="3" rowspan="3">CERTIFICATE OF ORIGIN
OF
THE PEOPLE'S REPUBLIC OF CHINA</td></tr>
<tr><td colspan="2">2. Consignee</td></tr>
<tr><td colspan="2"></td></tr>
<tr><td colspan="2">3. Means of transport and route</td><td colspan="3">5. For certifying authority use only</td></tr>
<tr><td colspan="2"></td><td colspan="3" rowspan="3"></td></tr>
<tr><td colspan="2">4. Country / region of destination</td></tr>
<tr><td colspan="2"></td></tr>
<tr><td>6. Marks and numbers</td><td>7. Number and kind of packages; description of goods</td><td>8. HSCode</td><td>9. Quantity</td><td>10. Number and date of invoices</td></tr>
<tr><td></td><td></td><td></td><td></td><td></td></tr>
<tr><td colspan="2">11. Declaration by the exporter
The undersigned hereby declares that the above details and statements are correct, that all the goods were produced in China and that they comply with the Rules of Origin of the People's Republic of China.</td><td colspan="3">12. Certification
It is hereby certified that the declaration by the exporter is correct.</td></tr>
<tr><td colspan="2"></td><td colspan="3"></td></tr>
<tr><td colspan="2">--
Place and date, signature and stamp of authorized signatory</td><td colspan="3">--
Place and date, signature and stamp of certifying authority</td></tr>
<tr><td colspan="2"></td><td colspan="3"></td></tr>
</table>

工作任务四

申领并缮制外汇核销单

对照报关单据清单列表，单证员方玲制作报关所需的特殊单证之二：外汇核销单。出口单位编码：809854328。

回答下列问题：

1．问题：向什么机构申领取外汇核销单？

2．问题：简述报关阶段核销单申领和使用的程序，可绘图表示。

3．缮制出口收汇核销单。

单证 9-24

出口收汇核销单 存根 （苏）编号：
出口单位：
单位编码：
出口币种总价：
收汇方式：
预计收款日期：
报关日期：
备注：
此单报关有效期截止到

（出口单位盖章）

出口收汇核销单 监制章 （苏）编号：				
出口单位：				
单位编码：				
银行签注栏	类别	币种金额	日期	盖章
海关签注栏：				
外汇局签注栏 年 月 日（盖章）				

（出口单位盖章）

出口收汇核销单 监制章 （苏）编号：		
出口单位：		
单位编码：		
货物名称	数量	币种总价
报关单编号：		
外汇局签注栏 年 月 日（盖章）		

任务七　装运单据的制作与审核

业务导入

货物通关后，就要装船出运，宁波远大进出口公司的单证员必须提前准备好装运阶段所需的单据，交给货代，以便及时装船出运。要用传真发出装运通知，及时告知货运情况。

工作任务一

列出装运阶段所涉单据清单

为了不耽误装船，提前备好装运所需单据，单证员方玲首先列出装运阶段所涉单据清单。

表　9-6

装运阶段所需货物的清单（在已有的单据后面标“√”）	
单 据 名 称	份　　数

工作任务二

制作提单

单证员方玲对照清单装运阶段所需货物的清单，首先制作提单（单证 9-25）。

单证　9-25

海 运 提 单

Shipper	B/L NO.
Consignee	PIL **PACIFIC INTERNATIONAL LINES (PTE) LTD.** (Incorporated in Singapore) **COMBINED TRANSPORT BILL OF LADING** Received in apparent good order and condition except as otherwise noted the total number of container or other packages or units enumerated below for transportation from the place of receipt to the place of delivery subject to the terms hereof. One of the signed Bills of Lading must be surrendered duly endorsed in exchange for the goods or delivery order. On presentation of this document (duly) endorsed to the Carrier by or on behalf of the Holder, the rights and liabilities arising in accordance with the terms hereof shall (without prejudice to any rule of common law or statute rendering them binding on the Merchant) become binding in all respects between the Carrier and the Holder as though the contract evidenced hereby had been made between them. **SEE TERMS ON ORIGINAL B/L**
Notify Party	

Vessel and Voyage Number	Port of Loading	Port of Discharge
Place of Receipt	Place of Delivery	Number of Original B/L

PARTICULARS AS DECLARED BY SHIPPER – CARRIER NOT RESPONSIBLE

ContainerNos/Seal Nos.Marks and/Numbers	No. of Container / Packages / Description of Goods	GrossWeight((kilos)	Measurement (cumetres)

FREIGHT & CHARGES	Number of Containers/Packages (in words)
	Shipped on Board Date:
	Place and Date of Issue:
	In witness whereof this number of Original Bills of Lading stated above all of the tenor and date one of which being accomplished the others to stand void. for **PACIFIC INTERNATIONAL LINES (PTE) LTD.** as Carrier

工作任务三

制作装运通知

货物装船出运，船公司签发已装船提单后，方玲对照清单制作装运通知（单证 9-26），及时告知货运情况。

单证 9-26

SHIPPING ADVICE

DATE

DEAR SIR,

WE ARE PLEASED TO INFORM YOUR ESTEEMED COMPANY THAT THE FOLLOWING MENTIONED GOODS WILL BE SHIPPED OUT ON THE JAN.18, 2009，FULL DETAILS ARESHOWN AS FOLLOWS:

1. INVOICE NO.:
2. BILL OF LADING NO.:
3. OCEAN VESSEL:
4. PORT OF LADING:
5. DATE OF SHIPPMENT:
6. PORT OF DESTINATION:
7. DESCRIPTION OF GOODS:
8. MARKS AND NUMBER ON B/L:
9. ETD:
10. ETA:

....
Authorized Signature

任务八　结汇单据的制作与审核

业务导入

货物装船出运，宁波远大进出口公司单证员方玲取得已装船提单并发装运通知后，及时整理并制作相关结汇单据，到议付银行——中国银行宁波分行办理结汇手续。

工作任务一

列出结汇所需单据清单

为了能及时向银行及时准确无误地交单，单证员方玲再次对照已修改的信用证并参照信用证分析结果单，列出结汇所需单据清单。

表　9-7

结汇所需单据清单（在已有的单据后面标“√”）	
单 据 名 称	份　　数

工作任务二

制作汇票

为了能及时向银行及时准确无误地交单，单证员方玲再次对照已修改的信用证并参照信用证分析结果单，制作下列两种不同格式的汇票（单证 9-27、单证 9-28）。

单证　9-27

汇票格式一

BILL OF EXCHANGE

1

凭

Drawn under ……………………………………………………

信用证　　　　　第　　　　　号

L/C　No……………………………………

日期

Dated ……………………………………

按息付款

Payable　with　interest　@......……………...%　per　annum

号码　　　　汇 票 金 额　　　　　　　　　中　　国，　宁波　　年　　月　　日

No. :………………Exchange　for　　　　　　　　Ningbo,　China.……………………

见票　　　　　　　　　　　　　　　　　日　后（本　汇　票　之　副　本　未 付）

At……..……………………Sight of this　FIRST　of Exchange (Second of exchange being unpaid)

pay to the order of ……………………………………………………………或其指定人

付金额

The sum of

To……………………..　　　　　　　　　　　　For and on behalf of

(Signature)

单证 9-28

汇票格式二

BILL OF EXCHANGE

1

No.____________________

For____________________ ____________________

(amount in figure) (place and date of issue)

At______________ sight of this FIRST Bill of Exchange(SECOND being unpaid)

pay to______________________________ or order the sum of

____

(amount in words)

Value received for______________ of ____________________

(quantity) (name of commodity)

Drawn under____________________

L/C No. ______________ dated____________________

To:______________

For and on behalf of

____

(Signature)

工作任务三

缮制受益人证明

对照结汇清单列表，单证员方玲根据信用证要求制作受益人证明书（单证 9-29）。

单证 9-29

____

____

BENEFICIARY'S CERTIFICATE

DATE

INVOICE NO.：

TO:____________________

RE:

Dir sir :

…………………………………………………

Authorized Signature

工作任务四

审核全套结汇单据

对照结汇清单列表，单证员方玲汇集所有的结汇单据，按照纵横审单法，对全套结汇单据进行审核，确保准确无误交单结汇。

回答下列问题：

1．简述单证审核的基本方法。

2．简述单据审核的要点。

3．列出出单中比较常见问题。

4．本套单据审核结果单

任务九　出口收汇核销与退税

业务导入

自1991年起，我国为加强出口收汇管理，实施了出口收汇核销制度，由国家职能部门对出口企业的出口货物进行了逐笔“跟单”核销的管理。初次办理出口收汇核销前，出口企业必须在本地外汇管理局办理核销备案登记，领取有编号的纸质核销单，并进行填制，并随附报关与议付单据进行报关议付。银行结汇后，在出口收汇核销结水单或收账通知上注明核销单号交出口企业。出口企业持经海关签章的收汇核销专用联、结水单或收账通知及报关单到外汇管理局办理核销。核销完毕后，将核销单（出口退税专用联）、报关单（退税联）、商业发票、增值税发票、出口专用缴税书等文件连同“外贸企业出口货物退税汇总申报审批表”交税务局办理退税。

工作任务一

准备出口收汇核销单据

初次办理出口收汇核销前，出口企业必须在本地外汇管理局办理核销备案登记，提供单位介绍信、申请书、外经贸部门批准经营进出口业务批件、企业法人营业执照、组织机构代码证、海关注册登记证明书等材料。核销备案登记后，领取有编号的纸质核销单，并进行填制，在领单90天内随附报关单据向海关报关。海关核准无误后，在核销单“海关签注栏”处加盖“验讫章”，退还出口企业。出口企业在汇票和发票上注明核销单编号，持全套结汇单据向银行办理议付。银行结汇后，在出口收汇核销结水单或收账通知上注明核销单号交出口企业。出口企业持海关签章的收汇核销专用联、结水单或收账通知及报关单到外汇管理局办理核销。即期支付应在出口报关之日起100天内办理出口收汇核销手续，远期支付应当在合同规定收汇日起 10 天内办理出口收汇核销手续。外汇管理局在核销单上加盖“已核销”章后，将核销单和报关单（出口退税专用）给出口企业。

宁波远大进出口公司方达先生填制核销单进行议付，得知本批货款已到账户上，及时到银行领取中国银行进账单的收账通知联和出口收汇核销专用回单联，在规定的时间内凭两票三单（外销发票、增值税发票、报关单、核销单、收汇水单）办理出口收汇核销。

回答下列问题：

1. 简述出口核销程序分哪几个阶段？

2. 列出办理外汇核销所需单据清单。

表 9-8

办理外汇核销所需单据（在已有的单据后面标“√”）	
单 据 名 称	份　数

3. 整理下列单据。

（1）中国银行开立结汇水单

单证 9-30

中国银行宁波分行进账单（回单）

2007 年 8 月 10 日　　　　第　060611　号

<table>
<tr><td rowspan="3">出票人</td><td>全称</td><td colspan="4">MANDARS IMPORTS CO., LTD.</td><td rowspan="3">收款人</td><td>全称</td><td colspan="10">宁波远大进出口贸易公司</td></tr>
<tr><td>账号</td><td colspan="4">FB44667755</td><td>账号</td><td colspan="10">THY6684321337</td></tr>
<tr><td>开户银行</td><td colspan="4">LONDON BANK</td><td>开户银行</td><td colspan="10">中国银行宁波分行</td></tr>
<tr><td colspan="6" rowspan="2">美元：
USD 126000.00</td><td>千</td><td>百</td><td>十</td><td>万</td><td>千</td><td>百</td><td>十</td><td>元</td><td>角</td><td>分</td></tr>
<tr><td></td><td></td><td>1</td><td>2</td><td>6</td><td>0</td><td>0</td><td>0</td><td>0</td><td>0</td></tr>
<tr><td colspan="2">票据种类</td><td colspan="4">BP XT173</td><td colspan="10">申报号码：</td></tr>
<tr><td colspan="2">票据张数</td><td colspan="4">核销单号：325623454</td><td colspan="10">No.0606775588</td></tr>
<tr><td colspan="6">中国银行国际
结算专用章</td><td colspan="10">出口收汇
核销专用章</td></tr>
</table>

（2）整理前面填写的核销单

单证 9-31

出口收汇核销单
存根
（沪）编号：325623454

出口单位：
单位编码：
出口币种总价：
收汇方式：
约计收款日期：
报关日期：
备注：
此单报关有效截止到

出口单位盖章

出口收汇核销单
（沪）编号：325623454

出口单位：			
单位编码：			
银行签注栏	类别	币种金额	盖章
海关签注栏：			
该票货物已于　　结关			
外汇局签注栏： 年　月　日（盖章）			

出口单位盖章

海关盖章

出口收汇核销单
出口退税　用
（沪）编号：325623454

出口单位：		
单位编码：		
货物名称	数量	币种总价
报关单编号：		
外汇局签注栏： 年　月　日（盖章）		

（3）其他单据略。

工作任务二

准备出口退税单据

外汇核销后，宁波远大进出口要到国税局办理出口退税，单证员方玲要配合公司财务做好单据的准备工作。

回答下列问题：

1．简述出口退税的程序。

2．绘制外贸企业出口退税申报流程图。

3．列明申报出口退税所需单证清单、理单并审单。

4．列明单证员主要向财务提交的单据清单。

项目十

T/T 结汇单据的制作与审核

知识目标

了解我国有关对外汇款的规定；熟悉电汇业务流程，掌握《贸易进口付汇核销单》（代申报单）、购汇申请书、对外电汇付款申请书的填写规范。

能力目标

能掌握合同条款的有关规定；填写购买外汇申请书；能正确填写对外汇款申请书。

任务分解

- 任务一：填写《贸易进口付汇核销单》（代申报单）
- 任务二：填写购买外汇申请书
- 任务三：缮制对外电汇付款申请书

任务一　填写《贸易进口付汇核销单》（代申报单）

任务导入

宁波中兴公司与日本 MADAYA TRADE CO., LTD.公司签订了一份购货合同，合同规定用前 T/T 支付，单证员李枚凭合同书与有关证明材料向中国光大银行宁波分行申领并填写《贸易进口付汇核销单》（代申报单）。

完成上述任务的步骤如下

第一步：弄清贸易项下汇款所需的单据清单

贸易项下汇款所需资料如下：

（1）《中国光大银行宁波分行汇出汇款申请书》；

（2）《中国光大银行宁波分行购买外汇申请书》（购汇支付提供）；

（3）《贸易进口付汇核销单（代申报单）》；

（4）货物进口合同；

（5）海关报关单（预付货款时不需提供）；

（6）银行要求提供的其他资料。

第二步：申领《贸易进口付汇核销单》(代申报单)

申领机构：进口付汇核销单（代申报单）一般向付汇银行购买1式3联。

使用：（1）付汇时交给银行审核；

（2）报关结束后，凭进口付汇核销单和报关单到外管局做进口核销。

所谓的代申报单是到付汇银行处做预付货款前的网上申报，然后打印出来，为正式的进口付汇核销单，与电汇申请书一起付汇。

第三步：填写《贸易进口付汇核销单》(代申报单)

训练任务

依据10-1外销合，宁波中兴公司单证员李枚填写进口付汇核销单（代申报单），向中国光大银行宁波分行做预付货款前的网上申报。补充资料：单位代码00001183-8，人民币账号10473968756488，外汇账号62234801066968。

单证 10-1

MADAYA TRADE CO., LTD
300 -310 SKURAMAJI OSAKA JAPAN
SALES CONFIRMATION

TEL: (0574)74099535 **S/C No.: MDY060988**
FAX: (0574) 74099536 **DATE: 2010-09-10**

To Messrs: ZHONGXING TOY IMPORT & EXPORT TRADE CORPORATION
530 ZHONGSHAN ROAD NINGBO CHINA

Dear Sirs,

We hereby confirm having sold to you the following goods on terms and conditions as specified below:

SHIPPING MARK	NAME OF COMMODITY AND SPECIFICATIONS，PACKING	QUANTITY	UNIT PRICE	TOTAL AMOUNT
M.D.Y MDY060988 OSAKA C/NO. 1-60	PLUSH TOY ART NO.88 ART NO.44 PACKED IN ONE CARTON OF 100PCS EACH	 3000PCS 3 000PCS TTL：6 000PCS	CFR OSAKA USD 0.33 USD 0.33	 USD 990.00 USD 990.00 TTL：USD1 980.00

LOADING PORT: OSAKA PORT
DESTINATION: BEILUN PORT
TIME OF SHIPMENT: LATEST DATE OF SHIPMENT NOV. 31，2010
PARTIAL SHIPMENT: PROHIBITED
TRANSSHIPMENT: PROHIBITED
INSURANCE: BY THE BUYER
TERMS OF PAYMENT: T/T IN ADVANCE

THE BUYER：李枚 THE SELLERS: HEROSIMA

NINGBO ZHONGXING
IMPORT & EXPORT

MADAYA
TRADE CO.

单证 10-2

贸易进口付汇核销单（代申报单）

根据《贸易进口付汇核销暂行办法》（1997 年 1 月 7 日发布），特制发本核销单。

请按规定填写。　　　　　　　　　　　　　　　　制表机关：国家外汇管理局

单位名称：　　　　　　　　　单位编码：　　　　　　　　核销单编号：No.

付汇银行名称		所在地分局	
进口合同号		进口发票号	
商品类别	玩具	进口批件号	
对外付汇币种：______ 对外付汇总额：______ 其中：购汇金额：______ 现汇金额：______ 其他方式金额______			交易编码
付汇性质	□正常付汇 □不在名录 □90 天以上信用证 □90 天以上托收 □异地付汇 □90 天以上到货 □转口贸易□		
结算方式	信用证 □90 天以内 □90 天以上 承兑日期 □ / □ / □ 付汇日期□ / □ / □ 期限□天		
	托收 □90 天以内 □90 天以上 承兑日期 □ / □ / □ 付汇日期□ / □ / □ 期限□天		
	汇款 □预付货款 □货到付汇（凭报关单付汇） 报关单号______ 报关日期______ 报关币种______ 金额______		
付汇日期： / / 外汇账号： 人民币账号：			
应到货日期： / / 收款人国别：日本 折美元金额：			
外汇指定银行审核无误后填写此栏			
银行业务编号：申报号码			
营业员签章： 业务公章： 审核日期： / /			

进口单位（签章）

年　月　日

注：核销单编号为 8 位顺序号，由各印制本核销单的外汇局自行编制。

训练要求：

（1）学生独立填写上述进口核销单，若有疑问可查阅下列贸易进口付汇核销单（代申报单）填写规范。

（2）填写完毕，小组交流讨论后，将结果上传到天空教室。

第四步：教师点评，核对答案

填写完毕，教师随机选择一个或多个小组某一同学的作业进行集中点评，核对答案。

知识链接

贸易进口付汇核销单（代申报单）填写规范

“贸易进口付汇核销单（代申报单）”（以下简称进口核销单）是指由国家外汇管理局

监制、保管和发放，进口单位和银行填写，银行凭此为进口单位办理贸易进口项下的进口付汇和核销的凭证。每份进口核销单只能凭此办理一笔付汇手续。

根据《国际收支统计申报办法实施细则》，进口核销单既用于贸易项下进口付汇核销，又用于国际收支申报统计。

在填写进口核销单时，应注意各项内容与付汇情况是否一致。

（1）印单局代码：为印制本核销单的六位外汇局代码。

（2）核销单编号：由各印制本核销单的外汇局自行编制。

（3）单位代码：应根据国家技术监督局颁发的组织机构代码填写。

（4）所在地外汇局名称：即指付汇单位所在地外汇局名称。

（5）付汇银行名称：通常为进口地银行。

（6）收汇人国别：即指该笔对外付款的实际收款人常驻国家，即出口国家。

（7）交易编码：应根据本笔对外付汇交易的性质对应国家外汇管理局国际收支交易编码表（表 10-1）填写。

表　10-1

交易编码	付汇交易性质	交易编码	付汇交易性质
0101	一般贸易	0109	来料加工装配进口的设备
0102	国家间、国际组织无偿援助和赠送的物资	0111	租赁贸易
0103	华侨、港澳台同胞、外籍华人捐赠物资	0112	免税外汇商品
0104	补偿贸易	0113	出料加工贸易
0105	来料加工装配贸易	0114	易货贸易
0106	进料加工装配贸易	0115	外商投资企业进口供加工内销的料件
0107	寄售代销贸易	0116	其他
0108	边境小额贸易	0201	预付货款

（8）交易附言：这是付款人对该笔对外付款用途的描述，可不填。

对外付汇币种：报关单币种，应按币种的英文缩写填写，如 USD。

对外付汇总额、购汇金额、现汇金额、其他方式金额：汇款中报关单“金额”一栏，应用阿拉伯数字填写。

（9）人民币账号、外汇账号：应根据如下规定填报，如所付款项是从现汇账户中支出，则在“外汇账号”栏填写该现汇账户的账号；如所付款项是从银行购得的外汇，则在“人民币账号”栏填写其用于购汇的人民币账户的账号。

（10）付汇性质：应选择适当的付汇性质打“√”。其中，“正常付汇”是指除不在名录、90 天以上信用证、90 天以上托收、异地付汇、90 天以上到货、转口贸易、境外工程使用物资、真实性审查以外，无须办理进口付汇备案业务的付款业务；“90 天以上信用证”及“90 天以上托收”均是指付汇日期距承兑日期在 90 天以上的对外付汇业务；除“正常付汇”之外的各付汇性质在标注“√”时，均须对应填写备案表编号。

（11）结算方式：应选择适当的结算方式打“√”。其中：90 天以内信用证、90 天以内托收的付汇日期距该笔付汇的承兑日期均小于 90 天且含 90 天；90 天以上信用证、90 天以上托收的付汇日期距该笔付汇的承兑日期均大于 90 天；结算方式为“货到付汇”时，应同时填写对应“报关单号”、“报关日期”、“报关单币种”、“金额”。

（12）申报号码：共 22 位。第 1 至第 6 位为地区标识码，第 7 至第 10 位为银行标识码，第 11 和第 12 位为金融机构顺序号，第 13 至第 18 位为该笔贸易进口付汇的付汇日期或该笔对外付汇的申报日期，最后 4 位为银行营业部门的当日业务流水码。

（13）其他各栏：均应按栏目提示对应填写。

自我能力测评

能力形成性评价表

评价指标	分值	实际得分
能列出贸易项下汇款所需单据清单	20 分	
能看懂外贸合同，准确翻译合同条款	30 分	
能根据外贸合同准确填写贸易进口付汇核销单（代申报单）	50 分	

任务二　填写购买外汇申请书

任务导入

宁波中兴公司单证员李枚申领了《贸易进口付汇核销单》后，根据贸易项下汇款所需的单据清单，填写《交通银行宁波分行购买外汇申请书》，向交通银行宁波分行购汇以支付货款。

完成上述任务的步骤如下

第一步：弄清并备齐 T/T 结算方式下购汇应提交的商业单据和有效凭证

银行售汇应审核的单据和有效凭证就是购汇时应提交的单据和有效凭证。

（1）用货到付款方式结算的贸易进口的付汇。经办行应审核进口合同、进口付汇核销单、发票、正本进口货物报关单正本运输单据、进口付汇备案表。

（2）货到付款项下单笔报关单金额在等值 10 万美元以上的，每一笔均必须事先向海关核对进口货物报关单的真伪，由海关确认为真实的方可凭此办理付汇。银行与海关电脑联网后，10 万美元以下的，须通过查询电脑进行确认。报关单的核对，不得委托境内机构自行办理。

（3）用预付货款方式结算的贸易进口的付汇。在规定比例和金额以内的，经办行应审核进口合同、进口付汇核销单、形式发票、进口付汇备案表（如需）、经银行核押/签符的预付货款保函（3 万美元以下不需提供该付款保函）；超过规定比例和金额的，经办行凭外汇局核发的进口付汇备案表和付汇通知单及上述有效凭证和商业单据办理。经办行办理的不超过合同总金额的 15%但超过等值 30 万美元的预付货款付汇后，应当按月填制“大额预付货款，佣金备案登记表”，于每月初 10 个工作日内报外管局备案。

第二步：填写客户购汇申请书

训练任务

依据 10-1 外销合同，宁波中兴公司单证员李枚填写下列购汇款申请书（单证 10-3，向中国光大银行宁波分行申请购汇。补充资料：李枚的电话号码为 0574-81808888；美元兑人民币汇率 1:6.97；外币资金划入银行名称：日本京都银行名古屋分行，外币资金划入银行账号 86978934613。

单证　10-3

中国光大银行买入外汇申请书

2010　年　9 月 25 日　　　　编号：

单位名称			
单位地址		联系人及电话	
本单位申请按市价买入外汇，金额为（大写）		（小写）	
折人民币金额		人民币资金扣划账号	
外币资金划入银行名称		外币资金划入银行账号	
收款单位名称			
购汇用途及商业单据名称	用途:贸易进口付汇　商业单据: 进口合同、进口付汇核销单、形式发票		
银行审批意见 经手人(签字) 审批单位(印章) 年　月　日		我单位同意本业务按照国家外汇管理局规定执行，如果我单位违反规定,将对由此给贵行造成的一切经济损失负赔偿责任。我单位保证所提供的有关资料、证明文件真实、完整、有效。由于本单位错误填写本申请书或其他原因，而造成不能购汇延误的，损失由我单位自行承担。 申请单位印鉴 年　月　日	

制单要求

（1）学生尝试独立填写客户购汇申请书，若有疑问可查阅下列客户购汇申请书填写规范。

（2）填写完毕，小组交流讨论后，将结果上传到天空教室。

第三步：教师点评学生制作的单据，核对答案

知识链接

客户购汇申请书填制要点

（1）进口付汇核销单号：填进口付汇核销单的编号。

（2）银行编号：售汇银行的编号。

（3）用汇金额：合同金额。

（4）应根据如下规定填报：如所付款项是从现汇账户中支出，则在“外汇账号”栏填写该现汇账户的账号；如所付款项是从银行购得的外汇，则在“人民币账号”栏填写其用于购汇的人民币账户的账号。

（5）用汇单位（人）：购买外汇的企业。

（6）购汇请凭以下有效文件：在需要的文件前面“()”里打“√”。

（7）折合美元：按照购买日汇率折算的美元金额。

自我能力测评

能力形成性评价表

评价指标	分　值	实际得分
能列出T/T结算方式下购汇应提交的商业单据和有效凭证	20分	
能掌握购汇申请书的填写规范	20分	
能根据外贸合同准确填写购汇申请书	60分	

任务三　缮制对外电汇付款申请书

任务导入

宁波中兴公司向银行购得外汇后，单证员李枚填写《对外电汇付款申请书》，向交通银行宁波分行办理电汇业务。

完成上述任务的步骤如下

第一步：弄清电汇业务流程

电汇业务流程图如图10-1所示：

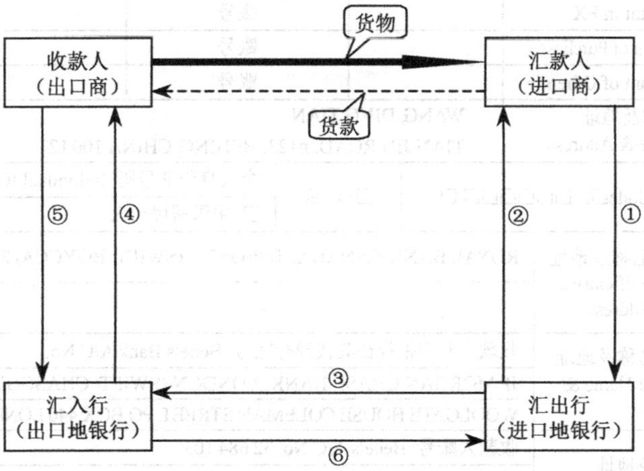

图 10-1

说明

① 进口商在合同规定的期限内， 填写境外汇款申请书，向银行（汇出行）申请电汇，交付汇款并支付手续费；

② 汇款人向汇出行取得汇款回执，作为款项已汇和日后核查的依据。如果汇款申请人提交的汇款申请不符合要求，汇出行将全部文件退还汇款人；

③ 汇出行按进口商指示，通过 SWIFT 方式把资金划给汇入行，电报通知汇入行或付款行向收款人付款；

④ 汇入行给出口商发出汇款通知书；

⑤ 出口商凭汇款通知书取款；

⑥ 汇入行转寄汇出行该款项的付讫收据，与汇出行进行结算。

第二步：缮制境外汇款申请书

制单步骤如下：

步骤一：导学，教师向学生展示已填制好的一份境外汇款申请书，提示填制要点，如图 10-2 所示。

境外汇款申请书

APPLICATION FOR FUNDS TRANSERS (OVERSEAS)

日期

致：中国银行 **Date** Jan. 10. 2007

To: BANK OF CHINA		☑电汇 T/T ☐ 票汇 D/D ☐ 信汇 M/T		发电等级 Priority☑ ☐电汇 Normal ☐电汇 Urgent
申请号码 BOP Reporting No.		☐☐☐☐☐☐ ☐☐☐☐ ☐☐ ☐☐☐☐☐☐ ☐☐☐☐		
20	银行业务编号 Bank Transc.Ref. No.		收电行/付款行 Receiver / Drawn on	
32A	汇款币种及金额 Currency & Interbank Settlement Amount	CAD 2,000,00	金额大写 Amount in Words	TWO THOUSAND CANADIAN DOLLARS

图 10-2（续）

其中	现汇金额 Amount in FX		账号		
	购买金额 Amount of Purchase		账号		
	其他金额 Amount of Others		账号		
50a	汇款人名称及地址 Remitter's Name & Address	WANG, DING TIAN TIAN JIN ROAD, #123, BEIJING, CHINA 100 123			
□ 对公组织机构代码 Unit Code□□□□□□□□ □		□ 对私	个人身份证号码 Individual IO NO. □ 中国居民个人　　□ 中国非居民个人		
54/56a	收款银行之代理行名称及地址 Curreipotdent of Benificiary's Bank Name & Address	ROYAL BANK CANADA. TORONTO (SWIFT: ROYCCAT2)			
57a	收款人开户银行名称及地址 Benificiary's Bank Name & Address	收款人开户银行在其代理行账号 Bene's Bank A/C No. JP MORGAN CHASE BANK. LONDON (SWIFT: CHASGB2L) WOOLGATE HOUSE COLEMAN STREET. PO BOX 440 LONDON. UNITEDK INGDOM			
59a	收款人名称及地址 Benificiary's Name & Address	收款人账号 Bene's A/C No. 32 684 103 FX SOLUTIONS LLC ONE ROUTE 17 SOUTH. SUITE 260. SADDLE RIVER. NJ 07458 UNITED STATES			
70	汇款附言 Reinittance Information	只限 140 个字位 Not Exceeding 140 Characters FX 123 456	71A	国内外费用承担 All Bank's Charges If Any are To Be Born By □ 汇款人 OUR □收款人 BEN □共同 SHA	
收款人常驻国家（地区）名称及代码 Resident Country/Region Name & Code				□□□	
请选择：□ 预付贷款 Advance Payin ert □ 货到付款 Payment Against Delivery □ 退货 Refund □其他 Others				最迟装运日期	
交易编码 BOP Transac. Code	□□□□□□ □□□□□□	相应币种及金额 Currency & Amount		交易附言 Transac. Remark	
是否为进口核销项下付款		□ 是 □ 否	合同号		发票号
外汇局批件/备案表号			报关单经营单位代码	□□□□□□□□□□	
报关单号		报关单币种及总金额		本次核注金额	
报关单号		报关单币种及总金额		本次核注金额	
银行专用栏 For Bank Use Only		申请人签章 Applicant's Signature		银行签章 Bank's Signature	
购汇汇率@ Rate		请按照贵行背页所列条款代办以上汇款并进行申报 Please Effect The Upwards Remittance, Subject To The Conditions Overleaf:			
等值人民币 RMB Equivalent					
手续费 Commission					
电报费 Cable Charges					
合计 Total Charges					
支付费用方式 In Payment of the Remittance	□ 现金 by Cash □ 支票 by Check □ 账户 form Account	申请人姓名 WANG, DING TIAN Name of Applicant 电话 Phone No. 011-86-10-12 345 678		核准人签字 Authorized Person 日期 Date	
核印 Sig. Ver		经办 Maker		复核 Checker	

图 10-2

注：图中加阴影的部分表示由银行填写。

步骤二：巩固训练，学生尝试独立填写下列境外汇款申请书（单证 10-4）。

训练任务

依据 10-1 外销合同，宁波中兴公司单证员李枚填写下列境外汇款申请书（单证 10-4），向中国光大银行宁波分行申请电汇货款。

单证 10-4

APPLICATION FOR FUNDS TRANSFERS (OVERSEAS)

致：
To: 日期
Date

□电汇 T/T□票汇 D/D□信汇 M/T	发报等级 Priority	□电汇 Normal□电汇 Urgent	
申报号码 BOP Reporting NO.	□□□□□□ □□□□ □□ □□□□□□ □□□□		
20.银行业务编码 Bank Transaction Ref. No.		收电行/付款行 Receiver/Drawn on	
32A.汇款币种及金额 Bank &Inter-bank Settlement Amount		金额大写 Amount in Words	
其中 现汇金额 Amount FX		账号 Account No.	
其中 购汇金额 Amount of Purchase		账号 Account No.	
其中 其他金额 Amount of Others		账号 Account No.	
50a.汇款人名称及地址 Remitter's name & address			
□对公组织机构代码 Unit Code□□□□□□□□□		□对私	□对个人身份证号码 Individual ID No. □中国居民个人 Resident Individual □中国非居民个人 Non-Resident Individual
54/56a.收款银行之代理行名称及地址 Correspondent of Beneficiary's Bank Name &Address			
57a.收款人开户银行名称及地址 Beneficiary's Name &Address		收款人开户银行在其代理行账号 Beneficiary's Bank Account No.	
59a.收款人名称及地址 Beneficiary's Name &Address		收款人账号 Beneficiary's Account No.	
汇款附言 Remittance Information（略）	只限 140 个字符 Not Exceeding 140 Characters	71A.国内费用承担 All Bank's Charges If Any Are to be Bone By □汇款人 OUR□收款人 BEN□共同 SHA	
收款人常住国家（地区）名称及代码（略）Beneficiary's Resident Country/Region Name &Code（略）			
请选择：□预付货款 Advance Payment□货到付款 Payment against Delivery□退货 Refund□其他 Others			
交易编码（略）BOP Transaction Code	□□□□□□ □□□□□□	相应币种及金额（略）Currency &Amount	交易附言（略）Transaction Remark
是否为进口核销项下付款	□是 □否	合同号	发票号（略）
外汇局批件/备案表号（略）		报关单经营单位代码（略）	□□□□□□□□□□
报关单号（略）		报关币种及金额（略）	本次核注金额（略）
银行专用栏 For Bank Only	申请人签章 Applicant's Signature	银行签章 Bank's Signature	

（续）

购汇汇率 Rate@（略）		请按照贵行背页所列条款代办以上汇款并进行申报 Please effect the upwards remittance subject to the conditions overleaf	核准人签字（略） Authorized Person 日期（略） Date
等值人民币 RMB Equivalent（略）			
手续费 Commission（略）			
电报费 Cable Charges（略）			
合计 Total charges（略）		申请人姓名 Name of Applicant	
支付费用方式（略）	□ 现金 by Cash □ 支票 by Check □ 账户 from Account	电话 Phone No.	
核印 Sig.ver（略）		经办 Maker（略）	复核 Checker（略）

训练指导：学生可以根据刚才老师的引导，示范，先尝试填写一份境外汇款申请书，若有疑问，可查阅下列境外汇款申请书的填制要领；也可以先看境外汇款申请书的填制要领，再去填制境外汇款申请书。

步骤三：填写完毕，小组交流讨论后，将结果上传到天空教室。

步骤四：老师点评学生制作的单据，核对答案。

知识链接

《境外汇款申请书》填制说明

（1）凡采用电汇、票汇或信汇方式对境外付款的机构或个人（统称“汇款人”），须逐笔填写境外汇款申请书。

（2）日期：指汇款人填写此申请书的日期。

（3）申报号码：此栏由银行填写。

（4）银行业务编号：此栏由银行填写。

（5）收电行/付款行：此栏由银行填写。

（6）汇款币种及金额：指汇款人申请汇出的实际付款币种和金额。

（7）现汇金额：指汇款人申请汇出的实际付款金额中，直接从外汇账户（包括外汇保证金账户）中支付的金额或汇款人将从银行购买的外汇存入外汇账户后对境外支付的金额。

（8）购汇金额：指汇款人申请汇出的实际付款金额中，向银行买外汇直接对境外支付的金额。

（9）其他金额：指汇款人除购汇和现汇以外对境外支付的金额，包括跨境人民币交易，以及记账贸易下交易等金额。

（10）账号：指银行对境外付款及扣款的账号，包括人民币账号、现汇账号、现钞账号、保证金账号、银行账号等。如从多个同类账户扣款，填写金额大的扣款账号。

（11）汇款人名称及地址：指汇款人预留银行印鉴或国家质量监督检验检疫总局颁发的组织机构代码证或国家外汇管理局及其分支局（以下简称“外管局”）签发的特殊机构代码编码通知书上的名称及地址。

（12）组织机构代码：按国家质量监督检验检疫局颁发的组织机构代码或外管局签发的特殊机构代码通知书上的单位组织机构代码或特殊机构代码填写。

（13）个人身份证件号：此栏针对因私业务，因公业务不填。

（14）中国居民个人/中国非居民个人：此栏针对因私业务，因公业务不填。

（15）收款银行之代理行名称及地址：为中转银行的名称，所在国家、城市及其在清算系统中的识别代码。这项信息一般由收款人提供，如若没有，可以不填。

（16）收款人开户银行名称及地址：为收款人开户银行名称，所在国家、城市及其在清算系统中的识别代码。

（17）收款人开户银行在其代理行的账号：为收款银行在其中转银行的账号。这项信息一般由收款人提供，如若没有，也可以不填。

（18）收款人名称及地址：指收款人全称及其所在国家、城市，另外还需要填写收款人账号 Bene's A/C NO.。

（19）汇款附言：由汇款人填写所汇款项的必要说明，可用英文填写且不超过 140 字符。

（20）国内外费用承担：指由汇款人确定办理境外汇款时发生的国内外费用由何方承担，并在所选项前的□中打"√"。OUR 指汇款行的费用和其他银行的费用都由汇款人承担。该项一般在境内汇款中不应该使用。BEN 指汇款行的费用和其他银行的费用都由收款人承担。SHA 指汇款行的费用应由汇款人承担，但除此以外的其他银行的费用都由收款人承担。

（21）收款人常驻国际（地区）名称及地址：指该笔境外汇款的实际收款人常驻的国家或地区。名称应用中文填写，代码根据"国家（地区）"名称代码表填写。

（22）交易编码：应根据本笔对境外付款交易性质对应的"国际收支交易编码表（支出）"填写。如果本笔付款为多种交易性质，则在第一行填写最大金额交易的国际收支交易编码，第二行填写次大金额交易的国际收支交易编码；如果本笔付款涉及进口付汇核销项下交易，则核销项下交易视同最大金额交易处理；如果本笔付款为退款，则应填写本笔付款对应原涉及收入的国际收支交易编码。

（23）相应币种及金额：应根据填报的交易编码填写，如本笔对境外付款为多种交易性质，则在第一行填写最大金额交易的相应的币种和金额，第二行填写其余币种及金额。两栏合计数应等于汇款币种及金额；如本笔付款涉及进口付款核销项下交易，则核销项下交易视同最大金额交易处理。

（24）交易附言：应对本笔对境外付款交易性质进行详细描述。如果本笔付款为多种交易性质，则应对相应的对境外付款交易性质分别进行详细描述；如果本笔付款为退款，则应填写本笔付款对应原涉外收入的申报号码。

（25）外管局批件/备案表号：指外管局签发的，银行凭以对外付款的各种批件或进口付汇备案表号。

（26）报关单经营单位代码：指由海关颁发给企业的"自理报关单位注册登记证明书"上的代码。

（27）报告单号：指海关报关单上的编码，应与海关报告数据库中提示的编码一致。若有多张报关单，表格不够填写，可附附页。

（28）最迟装运日期：指货物的实际装运日期。境外工程物资和转口贸易项下的支付中，最迟装运日期应为收汇日期，书写格式为 YYMMDD。

（29）购汇汇率（银行专用栏）：指对境外汇款金额中，以人民币购汇部分的汇率。

第三步：向银行递交下列贸易项下汇款所需资料，办理电汇业务

（1）《交通银行宁波分行汇出汇款申请书》；
（2）《交通银行宁波分行购买外汇申请书》（购汇支付提供）；
（3）《贸易进口付汇核销单（代申报单）》；
（4）货物进口合同；
（5）海关报关单（预付货款时不需提供）；
（6）银行要求提供的其他资料。

自我能力测评

能力形成性评价表

评价指标	分值	实际得分
能绘制电汇业务流程图	20分	
能准确填写境外汇款申请书填写	60分	
能向银行递交列贸易项下汇款所需全套资料	20分	

参 考 文 献

[1] 童宏祥. 新编国际商务单证实务[M]. 上海：上海财经大学出版社，2006.

[2] 王莉，陈琳，等. 进出口业务单证操作手册[M]. 广州：广东经济出版社，2006.

[3] 余世明. 国际商务单证实务[M]. 广州：暨南大学出版社，2008.

[4] 报关员全国统一考试教材[M]. 北京：中国海关出版社，2010.

[5] 广银芳. 外贸单证制作实务[M]. 北京：清华大学出版社，2007.

[6] 鲁鸿雁. 外贸单证实务[M]. 北京：中国财政经济出版社，2008.

[7] 胡越明. 外贸单证业务[M]. 杭州. 浙江工商大学出版社，2010.

[8] 李京. 国际贸易单证[M]. 北京理工大学出版社，2008.